SOLO

SOLO

Edited by
jason sherman

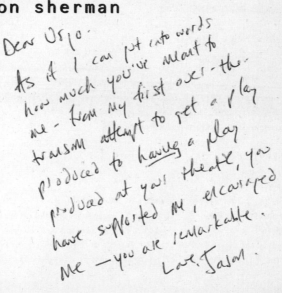

Dear Urjo:

As if I can put into words
how much you've meant to
me - from my first oxi- the
transom attempt to get a play
produced to having a play
produced at your theatre, you
have supported me, encouraged
me — you are remarkable.

Love, Jason.

Coach House Press
Toronto

Coach House Press
50 Prince Arthur Avenue, Suite 107
Toronto, Canada M5R 1B5

FIRST EDITION
Printed in Canada

Jewel © 1987, from *Toronto, Mississippi & Jewel* by Joan MacLeod. Used by permission of
Playwrights Canada Press. *Work* by James O'Reilly first appeared in *Theatrum*. *Anne Marie's
Bedroom* by Jennifer Ross first appeared in *PRISM*. *La Duchesse de Langeais* © 1994 by Michel
Tremblay. Translation© 1994 by John Van Burek. Used by permission of the author and
translator. An early version of *La Duchesse de Langeais* was published in 1976 by TalonBooks.

Published with the assistance of the Canada Council, the Department of Canadian Heritage, the
Ontario Arts Council, and the Ontario Publishing Centre.

Canadian Cataloguing in Publication Data
Main entry under title: Solo
ISBN 0-88910-449-2
1. Canadian drama - 20th century. I Sherman, Jason, 1962-
PS8037.S65 1994   C812'.5408   C93-094714-2   PR9196.3.S65 1994

CONTENTS

FOREWORD

Look. *Stories*—what are they? Think of the cavemen, sitting around the fire, they stink, it's night, somebody burned the venison. Nobody's talking, nothing. Somebody looks up, into the night sky, no clouds tonight and, the longer he stares up there, the more stars he sees, the more sky he sees, and suddenly he seems, to himself, very small. Suddenly he is filled with the kind of dread that hundreds of thousands of years later some French intellectual with funny-looking glasses will call "existential," but right now he doesn't know from French intellectuals, he doesn't have these fancy names to describe this *condition*, which he understands intuitively. All he knows is this: he is afraid. He feels alone, terribly alone, even though all around him naked smelly bodies in loincloths are belching, scratching, and complaining about the burnt venison.

This lonely guy, he starts talking, he starts telling a story. What about? Who invented that fire? Who named the venison "venison"? Who put us here? Where did we come from? What are we doing here?

Maybe you believe in progress. Maybe you think we know more than the caveman sitting around the fire. You got the cellular, you got the CD, you can see your own mother on the telephone.

I say, we are all frightened. I say, we are all lonely. I say, we are looking, all of us, for someone to listen to us. To our stories.

These writers, every one of them, they have told stories that must be listened to, because they *tell us things* about ourselves, about who we are. We still don't know.

Tell me if you don't think they're *lonely*, the guy who lives on an island, the guy tracing the history of his dead father on the maps he left behind, the woman with cancer whose friends have died or left in some way, the woman writing to a lost childhood friend, the guy who hates his jobs, I could go on, it's all in here, all these people who need to talk, to commit that public and brave act of *speaking aloud* their stories, to you. Yes.

Stories.

I wish I'd written each one myself. But since I didn't, I did the next best thing. I put them together in this book, so that more people could hear them.

And read them.

These stories.

JASON SHERMAN

SOLO

SURROUNDED BY WATER
Ken Garnhum

SURROUNDED BY WATER
Ken Garnhum

Set Pieces and Props

The Boats: A coracle, a 48" semi-circular Welsh basket-boat consisting of a woven framework covered in strips of painted canvas that look as if they have been torn from a Jackson Pollock painting; a canoe, made from pages torn from "The Complete Works of William Shakespeare"; a raft, assembled on stage from various works of art and pieces of the set.

The Island: Built by the performer from a variety of materials including many works of art. Embedded in the island is a human-scale "nest."

The Walls: Built by the performer as a buffer around the island, to keep the rising sea at bay. On the walls are some shelves. It is from these shelves, as well as from recesses hidden within the island, that the various masks, baskets, and small props are taken.

The Coat: Made from pieces of various famous paintings.

The Masks: A carved wooden Inuit-inspired mask; a word-covered mask in the shape of a book; a hand-held "opera" mask in the shape of Prince Edward Island; a mask made from found objects.

The Flotsam and Jetsam: Sticks, stones, books, book pages, pieces of art, etcetera.

The Water: The sounds of water are prevalent, sometimes underlining the performance and sometimes almost competing with it.

Down-stage centre sits what appears to be a battered replica of a globe, half buried in a raised platform. This globe is actually a coracle, which is sitting like a dome over a kind of nest in which the performer is concealed from view. Lights fade, but do not go to black.

Sounds of water build and then subside. The performer, still hidden, begins to speak.

I'm not coming out.

The performer's head pokes out from under the coracle.

No way José ...

He pauses, retreats, re-emerges.

Hear that water?

Boy, that's angry water.

Before I built these walls that water used to flow; it just flowed and I flowed along with it. But now it drowns things. It has grown angry and threatening and it drowns things.

I believe it has drowned the seasons; at least they don't show up anymore. I miss the seasons perhaps more than I miss anything. Do you know what I wish? I wish it was the thirty-first of October and raining. I wish there was a crab-apple tree right here, black-barked, leafless, and hung with a thousand tiny, golden, wrinkled orbs. I wish that ... ah ... but wish in one hand and shit in the other and see which one gets filled up first. Someone used to say that; maybe it was Noah.

He emerges fully from the nest, with the coracle on his back.

I came here because there were no gods here. I built this island in a god-free zone, and I like to think that I brought none with me. There—above me—sits a godless sky. Oh, I've had my weak moments, moments when I was tempted to create my own gods, but that would have been creating unnecessary paradox; that would have been defeating my own purpose. And anyways, why go back? When first I got here I stood in this spot and I shouted: "You're not the boss of me, Jesus, you're not the boss of me!" The whole idea that God created man is so profoundly absurd—in view of man's passion for making gods. That has always been the natural order of things—men creating gods in their own image.

When I was twelve years old—long, long after Jesus was walking, walking surrounded by water, as the story goes—I thought that he was my best friend, like a policeman, like a dog. His was such a beautiful story, the story of suffering, suffering for me. And what a fabulous idea—someone else to do the suffering, how grand, how glorious, how ... well, how ... stupid. I mean, it's pretty damned boring if you think about it; it's kind of like having someone else live your life for you.

But then lots of people didn't mind living vicariously. I'll tell you one thing I was escaping when I came to this place, I was escaping the pressure of being perceived as a positive person, a survivor. Surviving is something that many people did vicariously.

I don't think people wanted to find God anyway, they wanted God given to them on the proverbial silver platter ... Monotheism—boy, what a disaster that turned out to be!

He removes the coracle from his back and begins to work on it.

This is a coracle—it's a kind of boat last made by people from a place called Wales. This coracle was the first boat that I made, back when a gentle sea lapped at the edges of my little world. But the sea is no longer gentle. You can push land around and brick it up to your heart's content, but the sea, the sea will not be civilized. And now that the sea has changed its character, I worry about my coracle: she cannot cope with the stresses of seafaring as well as a wooden boat. The tendency of a coracle, a skinboat, to be torn to pieces by waves is very real.

So I spend a lot of time reinforcing and refining the boats I have, and making plans for new ones. I think of myself as a kind of boat artist now. I have had few conventional materials: I have had to use art. I mean that quite literally, as you may have noticed, but I wouldn't object if you wish to take it figuratively. Around here, the principle is pretty much the same anyway.

Some of the art I have used was of my own making and some, like the Jackson Pollock painting there, [*referring to a large frame hanging on the wall nearby, containing the remnants of a Jackson Pollock painting*] I had acquired to bring here as my guests. But, it's all my art now.

The first Welshman was called Jonah and he built his boats, and his

descendants, from the ribs of a large fish; at least I think that's how it
went. I can't be too sure. I once had a lot of books and reference
materials, but I've used them up in my work. For example, I have a
canoe back here that is a Shakespearian canoe—that is to say, I made
it from the pages of *The Complete Works of William Shakespeare*,
although I believe that there are a few pages from a Bible in there too,
the type of paper was the same for both. I get somewhat confused by
the canoe now, so I don't read it much. I believe I've gotten Lear and
Noah mixed up: storms and angry children—it's pretty confusing.

I think this coracle has a few Bible pages in it too, but mostly its shell
is made from strips torn off my Jackson Pollock painting. You'd hardly
recognize it, eh?

Coracles are the descendants of early skinboats. An original coracle-
maker would weave a framework of twigs or bones and cover it with
stretched skin. Later they sometimes used fabric covered in tar instead
of skins, which is why I thought of using the painting—canvas, right?
And the Pollock painting was perfect—all that paint, eh? I mean, you'd
hardly expect me to use a Turner painting or something. That'd be way
too flimsy. I kind of wish I'd had one of those big Tom Thomsons—
that would have been almost too apropos, eh?

*He hangs the coracle on the wall as if it is finally finished and then
fiddles with it unnecessarily.*

Oh stop jerk, stop: I never know when to stop, never know when
I'm finished, just like when I used to make paintings—I never knew
when I was finished then, either.

He sits and looks at the coracle.

I love this boat. I think that the only member of my family who
would have loved this coracle as much as me would have been my Aunt
Muriel. She used to paint; she even tried to paint like Jackson Pollock.
But she was only about four-foot-eight, and she said that when she
threw paint around it always bounced back and got into her eyes. I
remember going to her place one day and finding her with about thirty
Chatelaine magazines tied to the bottom of each of her feet, to make
her taller, she said. There she was, stomping around, throwing paint

to beat the band, as she would say. She was pretty great.

He leaves the coracle behind.

One of the best-known skinboats of all time originated in the country of my birth—Canada. It was called a kayak, and it was very different from my coracle. The kayak was a beautiful elongated shape with just a hole in the centre for the paddler to sit in. It was made by the north people, the Inuit. I guess it's not really surprising that the kayak was so marvellous, because that was so often the case with cultures that didn't waste a lot of time differentiating between the art objects they made and the objects they made for everyday living.

He puts on the Inuit-inspired mask.

> You may seek it with thimbles—and seek it with care
> You may hunt it with forks and hope,
> You may threaten its life with a railway-share,
> You may charm it with smiles and soap—

"The Hunting of the Snark"—with Lewis Carroll, on Snark Island. Oh yes, the Snark had its very own island. The world was full of fabulous imaginary islands. Lilliput was an island—and No Man's Land and Never Never Land and Narnia and Utopia, too.

He replaces the Inuit mask and sits on the edge of the island.

In *The Odyssey,* Homer invented Aeolia, a floating island surrounded by a bronze wall, behind which lived an incestuous royal family; and any visitor pleasing the king was given as a gift large oilskin sacks filled with violent winds, which are best left unopened—pretty crazy kind of present, eh? I remember hearing that one of these sacks was later found and inadvertently opened in a place called Ottawa.

He begins to clean up, starting with the sticks and twigs.

A Frenchman, with the rather grand appellation Abbé Pierre François Guyot Desfontaines invented truly superb islands: like Babilary. This was an island where the women rule and the men, receiving no education whatsoever, need only worry about their looks. On the Abbé's rich and fertile Orators' Island, the thin and scraggly people almost always died of starvation because they couldn't shut up long enough to eat. For some reason Orators' Island always makes me think of Prince Edward Island, though I'm not sure if it's because of its fertility, or because the people there never shut up. If I had lived on one of the Abbé's islands, it would have been his Philosophers' Island. This was an island where all of the people spend all of their time searching for several words to take the place of one perfectly good word that means the same thing.

Islands, real islands, geographical islands, have been formed in many ways: not all of them got hand-built like mine. Some islands, like Prince Edward Island, were formed because a rising ocean separated them from a larger land mass. Some islands were formed volcanically, formation by eruption, if you know what I mean. Others were the result of glacial action, the glaciers pushing and piling up rubble. Man also piled up a lot of rubble, which sometimes resulted in landfill islands. Corals formed islands by building sensibly, on the backs of their ancestors—unlike man, who had a tendency to try to build on the backs of his descendants.

He tears a strip from the Jackson Pollock painting.

Did you hear that sound? That was the sound of Jackson Pollock turning over in his grave.

With the canvas, he ties the sticks into a bundle and then begins to gather stones and put them in a basket.

Lawrence Durrell once wrote that somewhere among the notebooks of Gideon he found a list of diseases as yet unclassified by medical science; and among these diseases was a rare but by no means unknown affliction of the spirit called "Islomania." There are people, Gideon said, who find islands irresistible; the mere knowledge that they are on an island, a little world, surrounded by the sea, fills them with an indescribable intoxication. Certainly, I have always known that I need an island, and so I guess I am an "Islomane." Most writers about islands mention at some point the effects of an island visit: a state of mind, a feeling of insularity, the realization of an escape executed. They speak of that particular sensibility that is born only of knowing that the most important feature of the land on which you are standing is that it is entirely surrounded by water.

The boundaries of a world, any world—a room, a job, a life—are tenuous. They fluctuate, shrinking and expanding beyond more than just momentary management, and this is perhaps the purest beauty of islands. Islands are little worlds in themselves, worlds with absolute borders, worlds with that sense of containment that comes only of being separate, alone. No two islands are alike, and yet every island has the power to evoke these feelings.

He finishes gathering stones and sets the basket aside. He begins to collect books and loose pages, stopping to read or ponder bits.

Before I came here, I wondered about the difference between thoughts and feelings. I wondered about the difference between genuine sorrow and maudlin self-pity. The world was covered in thin lines, circling the globe, separating things. On a good day I would think: what is there but to excel? You can't carry the weight of the whole world on your shoulders, in your pockets, up your bum … can you?

Keep busy, that's the ticket. Of course, keep busy. People always know something you don't know. Everyone knows something that you don't.

Know.

Don't they?

If there really were such a thing as sin, and I was in charge of it—boredom would top the list.

And that's a funny thing, that. I mean there was a time when I thought that there was nothing I would rather be than bored—I mean, nothing I would rather do than escape that constant sense of urgency. That's one of the reasons I built my island. And yet, shortly after I got here, I began to create the urgency of boat building, as if my object were to escape the island; and so I finally realized that, really, it is only the dreams of escaping that satisfy.

He finishes the gathering of printed flotsam by collecting those books remaining on the shelves.

I have eight books left, or in some cases, just parts of books. Some of these parts, these fragments, don't always make much sense; they leave too many unanswered questions. I sure would like to know how Gertrude Stein's *Geographical History of America* ends.

But some fragments, even just sentences, seem to answer questions.

He picks out a piece of paper.

Take this line, from André Malraux.

He reads:

> We should draw from our own selves images power-
> ful enough to deny our nothingness.

Now I can make sense of that. Oh, I know it's out of context, but since it's all I have and since it's in my control, I can recontextualize it into the present, into my existence here … now … and its a pretty great sentence, too, if you think about it. Maybe I'll put this sentence on the canoe: that'll shake old Shakespeare up a bit. He's been getting a bit tired.

He gets a glue-pot and begins to add new pages to the canoe surface, starting with Malraux.

Here's a good one:

> A man should rejoice in his own works, for that is his
> portion; for who shall bring him to see what shall be
> after him?

That's a good question. Well, it's either Shakespeare or the Bible. Malvolio or Ecclesiastes. Who's to say?

This canoe is the descendant of bark boats. Bark was one of the four roots of boat building, along with skin, like my coracle there, the raft, which is another story, and the dugout. Skin, bark, raft and dugout— all boats developed from these four. If I had actually had bark, I would have formed it into a boat shape—a shell, if you will—and then I would have strengthened that shell with an internal framework. This is the main way in which a bark boat, a canoe, differs from a skin-boat, a coracle. A canoe is a shell construction, meaning that the outside comes first. A coracle, on the other hand, is a frame construction, meaning the framework comes first and the skin—the shell—is added after. Neither one, however, is really strong enough to withstand the constant stress of a long sea voyage.

Oh—I love A.A. Milne …

He picks up a piece of paper and reads:

> "It is a little Anxious," he said to himself, "to be a Very Small Animal Entirely Surrounded by Water. Christopher Robin and Pooh could escape by Climbing Trees, and Kanga could escape by Jumping, and Rabbit could escape by Burrowing, and Owl could escape by Flying, and Eeyore could escape by—by Making a Loud Noise Until Rescued—and here am I, surrounded by water and I can't do *anything*."

He places the paper on the canoe.

Look, look at me … did I tell you I never know when to stop? I just put A.A. Milne on my Shakespeare canoe …

He tidies up the glue and papers, then moves the canoe to its mountings.

I used to have a lot of photography books. I especially liked the ones with anthropological themes. I found photographs of so-called natives with painted faces, extremely fascinating and very beautiful. I always regretted that in the culture from which I came, face-painting wasn't exactly encouraged—especially not for men. But now that I am in charge of my own culture, a culture of one, face-painting is A-OK!

There is a make-up vanity hidden in the island. He sits and opens it. The lighting shifts and music starts. He begins to paint his face.

I was drawn to face-painting not only because of its beauty, but also because of an assumption that I had made. You see, I assumed that face-painting was meant to enhance the individual. I even went so far as to assume that face-painting was all about the power and sovereignty of the individual—my favourite theme. But it turns out that I couldn't have been more wrong. For most face-painting cultures, individuality wasn't even considered as a concept. For most of these peoples, the painting and decorating of their faces and bodies was actually meant to absorb the individual into an ideal of beauty, sort of transforming the private person into a public image. It's really the assumption of a dramatic identity.

He begins to create a circle of stones with those gathered earlier, eventually sitting inside the circle and then dancing around it.

Once upon a time, I went to an island lost in time and there I came to know a man, a tribesman. I taught him the watusi and fourteen card tricks and all the words to "A Groovy Kind of Love." I taught him how to balance five spoons on his face. I taught him the history of the western world. He, for his part, took my solitude and held it up before me in cupped brown hands and I watched, fascinated, as it faded away.

He played the drums: sitting on the ground, encircled by stones and the skulls of his ancestors, he played the drums; and I learned to dance to those drums, heart-race drums. I learned to lose myself inside that dancing, inside the spinning of my own body. I became the Dance Doctor. I danced for one hundred hours and then I stepped outside my body and watched, ecstatic, as I danced for one hundred more. I was a golden spinning top. I was the Dance Doctor.

I'm not sure that this is true. Or rather, I'm not sure if this happened; I know that it is true.

When my library was more complete, I had, and read, many books about one man's search for cultural otherness; you know—some guy hops into a canoe, goes up some river into the jungle looking for his lost innocence or something. I'm talking exotic travelogues of islands and jungles filled to the brim with regal, gentle tribespeople. Eventually I rejected these stories; I began to feel like I was stealing other peoples' cultural history just by reading them.

But the images of dancing, often meticulously described in these books, always stayed with me.

He dances.

Ritual dancing, wild ferocious dancing, dancing 'round fires, at waters edge, red dances, black dances, overripe dances rotten with colour. Dancing messages into the past, into the future. Dancing mystery. Dancing desire.

He stops dancing.

I was the Dance Doctor, but in the end I left the island, not able to become a part in order to make the whole. I left and my tattoos faded, my crocodile skin smoothed over and my feet weighed a thousand pounds. I do not know. I do not know if this happened. But I was the Dance Doctor ... and now I am an island.

He gets the canoe and sits inside. He wears the book-mask. Sounds of the sea are heard.

In spite of the fact that canoes can't withstand the pummelling of the open sea, they have survived some pretty arduous voyages. The bark canoe was also associated with my country. The native North American Indian developed the bark boat to its most perfect form— white birch bark, white cedar ribs, ash or maple thwarts, a bit of spruce gum, a touch of moosehide, and voilà: the birchbark canoe, beautiful, and smart, so smart that the invading French borrowed the form and used it to make journeys of up to three thousand miles. Les Voyageurs.

Half of all the freshwater in the world was in Canada. There were as many miles of inland waterways as there were in all of the other countries of the world combined. You could put a canoe in the water in any city in Canada and paddle to the Atlantic, the Pacific, the Arctic, or through the United States of America to the Gulf of Mexico. But that was a long time ago, before I came here, back when the waterways were still filled with the water.

He puts the canoe back in place and returns to the island proper. He puts on the painted coat.

So—how do I look? I know what my grandmother would say if she were here. She'd say, "Lord love a duck, you look like something from the Fiji Islands; ya wouldn't win no beauty pageants in that get-up!" But she'd be wrong, because there were places where I might have done just that. For example, every year at the height of the rainy season, in the far away west-African savanna, some three thousand members of a tribe called the Fulani would come together and hold a beauty contest that would last for seven days. All of the contestants were the young men of the tribe. First prize was a wife, for you see, the Fulani let their young women pick their own husbands, and the guys had little say and much work to do to be chosen first. The judges—that is to say, the would-be wives—carried brightly coloured umbrellas as symbols of their status.

He holds up an umbrella.

After a welcoming song and dance routine the real work began. The men would already have spent long hours making themselves beautiful for the *Yake*—a lineup in which they were required to sing, dance and stand on tiptoe making faces for hours on end. Throughout the *Yake,* the older women of the tribe would hurl abuse at those contestants who were not up to snuff … "Hey—who let the short one in?" Or, "You on the left, get off the stage!" And stuff like that. They were probably just pissed off that they made a bad choice in a *Yake* twenty-five years before. Meanwhile, someone would come along behind the contestants and whip them, because this was how they judged personality, and any contestant who showed the pain by crying out or even flinching lost valuable points. So … at the end of the seven days the judges would one by one step forward to declare their choice of winner with a mere nod of the head, as if nothing much had gone on.

Then the chief would sing, "HERE HE IS, MR. FU-LA-NI," and everyone would go home until the next big downpour. Well—they didn't actually "go home," since they were nomads, but you know what I mean.

Now, the general culture from which I sprang was holding beauty pageants only for women—well, with the exception of what were known as body-builders. This was a group who seemed out to prove that if you ate enough protein and lifted enough metal, you could actually make your body dysfunctional for any purpose other than display.

The specific culture from which I sprang, namely Prince Edward

Island, [*holds up the P.E.I. "opera" mask*] was holding some pretty fabulous beauty pageants. Some of these were notable for their names alone. Picture if you will; Miss Aberdeen Angus, Miss Crapaud Creamery, Miss Tuna Capitol of the World. Other of these pageants were enormously sensible—like the people who spawned them. Take for example, Miss Gold Cup and Saucer; this was a contest named after a big horse race, and the only way you could become Miss Gold Cup was if the horse whose name you had drawn out of a hat the week before came in first in the big race. Or my favourite—Miss Dundas Ploughing Match. This was a contest in which points were awarded as follows: fifty percent for beauty and deportment, and fifty percent for who could plough the straightest furrow. Now, you can't get more sensible than that, not within the realm of beauty pageants anyway.

Sad to say, no Miss Dundas Ploughing Match ever went on to win the Miss P.E.I. title, and I think that that was because Miss P.E.I. was a contest in which ploughing was unfortunately replaced by speaking, and all the city girls had it down pat: "I'd like to thank God—and my mother—and I would like to say that even though I am perfect material to be a model, I would really rather look after needy children." But Miss Dundas, she'd get up there and she'd be all nervous and she'd say something like: "Well, it's real nice to be in town for the weekend, eh, and I'd like to thank me mother, who taught me how to plough a straight furrow."

She didn't stand a chance, not a chance. But here I am making fun of these people and it's just sour grapes on my part—I'm just upset that I never got asked to be in a beauty pageant.

He sits dejectedly for a moment before continuing.

You may have noticed that I do not have a dugout. Well, I feel like a bit of an asshole about that because I could have had one, and of the four roots of boatbuilding, the dugout is supposed to be the best hope against an angry sea. But, you see, back when the anger of the sea began to grow and it was rising and beginning to batter my little island, my private art rig, I knew I would have to build these walls to keep the sea at bay. So I began to gather together the largest artworks that I had brought with me. I had my Nevelsons, my Oldenburgs. I had a lot of my own old set-pieces that I couldn't get rid of to save my soul. Oh, and I had boxes and boxes of some book by Pierre Berton that someone had paid me to take away. You see, I knew that I would need all my materials to build my walls. And I also had a beautiful Haida totem pole which I looked at and thought, Aces! That's just what I need in the corners, to anchor my walls in place. But I also knew that I should save a chunk out of that totem so that I could make myself a dugout. But—I couldn't do it! You see, carving frightens me. Making a dugout is like carving a sculpture; it is a process of taking away and taking away, until something, the thing, is revealed. But as an artist, I am a builder, not a carver; my process has always been one of addition—of adding and adding until something, the thing, is finished. And quite frankly, I would be afraid, afraid that in the process of subtracting, I would end up revealing nothing.

So—I'll bet some of you are wondering how the hell I afforded my Louise Nevelsons and my Jackson Pollock and all the rest. Well … one could get art pretty cheaply around the time that I came here. In some cases, you could get artworks for about the amounts that the artists themselves got for them in the first place, with some exceptions of course. I mean you couldn't get Van Gogh's entire output for forty bucks. But then, I didn't really want a painting by the old lobe-lopper anyway.

He takes a piece of a Louise Nevelson sculpture away from the island and walks about with it.

I did get a lot of Louise Nevelsons. She was great. She was this semi-mad Russian woman who moved to America in the twenties. She used to wander around New York City collecting garbage—but only wooden garbage. She was fussy, that Louise. Anyway, she'd drag this stuff home and nail and glue it all together into these fantastic sculptures, which she would then paint black or white—or gold, if she was in a particularly ritzy mood. Eventually she got so rich that she started buying entire brownstones in New York, and tearing them down just so she could use the parts, the door frames and window sills and the bannisters, just so she could make more and bigger sculptures. Great, eh?! I am glad I have her work.

But do you know what I really wish that I had? I wish I had been able to get some of the paintings that I was in. When I first got here I had a small Joseph Beuys sculpture called *Fat Corner*, but I ate it, so now it's in me, which is not the same thing of course. I wish I had that Bruegel—you know, *The Peasant Wedding Dance*. There were only six of us in that painting with red hats. I was the one dancing up a storm in the middle ground on the left. Middle ground was always the best place to be in those Bruegel crowd scenes, if you could squeeze in. I was pissed off that he changed my dancing partner into a girl in the final draft of that painting, but you don't have much say when you're an extra. At least he didn't paint me out, like that damn Artemisia Gentileschi. Oh yeah, I was there, holding down Holofernes for Judith to slay. I was there as she held that bloody head high. I ruined a perfectly good tunic and then what happens? Artemisia decides that her whole point was undermined by having a man assisting Judith, so I end up scraped off that canvas and over-painted. I didn't do much posing for a long time after that, not until George Segal offered me the big bucks to get plastered in the sixties. Turns out I'm allergic to that stuff so the whole fee went to the pharmaceutical companies anyway. After that I just gave up. Being a subject for other people, I mean. For better or worse, I remain the primary subject of my own work.

I'd be interested to know if it still exists—*art*, I mean. It was always pretty resilient, underwent a lot of changes. There were even those of us who insisted that art precipitated change, but we were probably dreaming.

A map of Cuba now makes an appearance.

This is a map of Cuba. I went to Cuba once and had a fabulous time. Many white northern liberals discovered that Cuba was a great spot to escape from winter because you could be there with a minimum of guilt about exploiting the underclasses. And it was a real joy to see all those inner city kids enjoying their guaranteed beach vacations, and all looking so healthy too. But the year after I was there, they started putting people with immune deficiencies into concentration camps and after that I just couldn't go back. Fidel! Fidel! Man as god—it's always a bad act, no matter how talented the performer.

Ahh … it doesn't matter anyways, because later I heard that they turned Cuba into a communist theme park. Yeah, apparently Disney and Taco Bell took over. There was a Castro Coaster and a stage spectacular where an Iron Curtain is raised at the start of the show, to reveal the dancing girls, and then doesn't come down at the end. Pretty clever, eh?

That Cuba's system did work, up to a point, had to be due in part to its being an island. Insularity. Most islanders are obsessively insular. If an experience lies outside the range of an islander, then it is most likely not worth having, if you know what I mean. It is something to be discounted long before it can be understood. Most island dwellers refer to their island as The Island, as if it were the only one. It has always struck me as highly ironic that islands in general were such meccas for tourists, because more than any people I ever knew, islanders were the most xenophobic.

Certainly, many islands were tourist havens. Many rich northerners discovered that if you wore really dark sunglasses in the south, you couldn't actually see those doing the suffering, unless they smiled of course, which wasn't much of a problem. But islands served many of man's purposes beyond being playgrounds. Islands made excellent penal colonies, you didn't even need to build fences, just had to make sure no one had the ability to build a boat. There was an island off the coast of New York where the bodies of children discarded by society were buried by the thousands in rows of thirty, stacked three deep. On Manhattan Island itself, the palatial mansions of dead industrialists housed hordes of art booty stolen from around the world. Meanwhile a million bloody people slept in the streets. There were even islands—

A television, or parts thereof, falls from the sky, narrowly missing his head.

Shit! Not another one! This was not one of the hazards of isolation that I had anticipated. Some might assume an angry god tossing these things at my head, but not me. I know what these things mean: nothing, absolutely nothing.

He discards the TV and begins sweeping.

I knew a guy once who was terrorized by television, but not like this. He was terrorized simply because he hated it. Funny thing was, he didn't always hate television. When he was in grade school he would occasionally stay home from school to keep his mother company—a few games of rummy and an episode of "The Edge of Night." He quite liked "The Edge of Night," especially Mike and Nancy Carr, who had a living room as big as his family's whole downstairs, a living room that never seemed to get messed up no matter how many charming guests with Martinis and canapés traipsed through it. But by the time he started high school, television's charm was wearing a little thin. School-bus TV-talk was boring. He had better things to do.

Eventually he got a little self-righteous about his boredom, and by the time he got to college, he began to give it a bit of rein. He made his first roommate keep her TV in her room. Later he would refuse to even share with anyone who owned a television. He began to openly mourn the lost arts of debate and conversation, blaming television entirely for their demise. He began to believe that television caused epilepsy and ulcers, and that it caused the plaque on your teeth to harden before you could get it off with the floss at night. He became like one of those tiresome, speechifying former smokers who just can't "let it go." People started to avoid him in a big way.

Then he realized that many of his close personal friends with a professed disgust for the tube, like his, had secret black and white portables hidden in easy access closets. He knew where this would inevitably lead—to twenty-six-inch colour monitors and digital VCRs with stereo sound, in other words, straight to hell! And he was right. Within two years of graduating, his closest friends had video-club memberships. They were buying microwave ovens just so they could make popcorn more easily. He felt that he had better at least attempt to like TV. He went to his mother's and survived a week of beef and game shows. He started watching baseball games on Wednesday nights with a friend of his. He was doing really well, until this one night, when he threw a lava lamp through the screen of his friend's TV during a commercial in which happy Ethiopians cavorted across the dazzling sunlit savanna while they drank Coke! His friend suggested counselling. It didn't work. The counsellor looked like Alex Trebek.

In a last desperate attempt to deal with his problem my friend tried Performance Art. He confessed his condition to tens of people in galleries and theatre backspaces, but in the end he always felt that his audience would rather be at home watching PBS. It got to the point where television simply made him cry. Sitcoms, golf classics, it didn't matter. The very sight of a set not even turned on could affect him in a most profound way. All he could do was try to avoid it. And he was managing to do just that, until this day walking down Main Street ... I was confronted by this gigantic plate glass window displaying twenty, larger than life, full-colour images of Gilligan and the Skipper. And that's where they found me, at the foot of that window, sobbing hysterically, as Gilligan, the Skipper, Mr. and Mrs. Howell, Ginger, the Professor and Mary Ann had one more argument about getting off the bloody island.

He retreats into the nest and sits up.

Language was failing; it had been replaced by a flickering and fickle light. Many people built their sense of reality on the simulated realm of television. The market-place of ideas had gone bankrupt. Knowledge had been replaced by information. The world was governed by polls. The public opinion poll had replaced the old order, that fabulous order that the Greeks invented for us so many thousands of years ago— the order of looking, reflecting and producing. You look out at the world, you reflect on what you've seen and you *produce* based on your reflection. But instead of looking out at the world, many people found themselves looking at their own reflected opinion, and each day the reflections grew dimmer and dimmer.

I could kill for a cup of coffee. I wish that Beethoven were here to count out exactly sixty beans for my cup, as he always did for every cup he ever made. I remember reading in a book I once had that coffee was first discovered by an Abyssinian goat-herder named Kaldi. It seems that one day he noticed that his normally tranquil goats were getting pretty rambunctious, and so he watched as they ate the cherries, red and shining, from what proved to be a coffee tree. He gave them a try himself and found them pretty damn good. Now a passing abbot came upon the wide-eyed and somewhat elated Kaldi, and after making a few inquiries about the goat herd, realized that these cherries were just the trick to keep his dozy monks alert for prayers. The clever old abbot proceeded to experiment and ended up with an invigorating drink. And all the religious leaders of the day believed that the coffee was heaven-sent. The rest, as the saying goes, is history. Coffee caught on in a big way. The Japanese took baths in it, the Turks searched its dregs for prophesy, the great German Bach wrote a cantata to it and I miss it dreadfully.

I really did love good coffee: thick bitter black in tiny cups, steaming sugared white in linen-wrapped glass, foamed frosted iced in … well, you get the picture. But, you know, there was something about a donut shop, ordinary brown coffee in a chipped china mug, that was extraordinary. The table-top video game plays a kind of Wurlitzer music, creating an air of game-show anticipation, a perpetual waiting for the contestant's decision … I'll have an orange cruller please; no, wait, I'll have a banana-filled toasted coconut maple raised chocolate sprinkled apple fritter please. To stay.

This is not a prophecy. I am not a prophet. I don't even believe in prophets. And this is not post-apocalyptic. There was no apocalypse. Ezekiel and Zechariah were the boogie men. There was no apocalypse. Nothing blew up. It just fell apart.

He leaves the nest and sits.

I grew up living next door to a man who made boats. His name was Reanney Gay, and he had a lump on his right temple the size of a golf ball. He had to melt down and reshape the arm of his glasses to accommodate that lump. Reanney made small boats—fishing boats, row boats, dories—in the winter. In the summer he would sit in one of the boats he had built and he would catch fish. He would trap lobsters. He would float on the surface of the bay, which was sometimes grey and choppy, and sometimes blue and smooth as glass. He would float on the surface in the face of the sun and his arms and his nose would turn Indian-brown.

He begins to assemble a raft using two sections of bookshelves as pontoons, the Nevelson sculpture as the main deck, and other set-pieces.

Reanney had a workshop that I used to hang around in when I was a kid. It was made out of corrugated tin sheeting that rattled like theatrical thunder when the wind blew. The workshop had a stove right in the very centre of it, so it was very hot in the middle, but stayed very cold about the edges, in the winter, when he made his boats.

I don't think that Reanney ever made a raft. Reanney's boats were wooden boats, plank-built, in the tradition of the east-coast lobster boat; that is to say, built frame first, unlike most other wooden boats which were built shell first. Reanney and I came from a tribe that built from the inside out.

Back when I was gathering my big art together to make walls, a scary thing happened. I had tied all the stuff together waiting for a break in the weather so I could start building. And the next thing I knew, the sea was very effectively trying to carry it all off. I barely managed to rescue it all and that's when I got the idea for a raft—an art-raft. Right then I decided to save some appropriate pieces from the building of the walls, so that I could build a raft which would serve as my best hope against the encroaching sea. I thought that a nice piece of a Louise Nevelson would come in pretty damn handy. And I was right.

He finishes assembling the raft, then stands on it in "masthead" fashion.

I am a passenger on the ferry, crossing the frozen strait. At the bow, the wind is blue in my face. White ice cracks to black, black water sliding under as translucent frost-green, green spruce-line coast, shelter fox skulls, hard red earth. The ferry, an island to an island, Prince Edward Island. January. Going home.

He steps off the raft, clears up, then attaches the raft by its moorings to the island proper.

When I was little I used to want to take an axe underwater and chop the Island free, and then, I thought, I'd put a big outboard motor on the west end and I would cruise down, down the eastern seaboard and park P.E.I. right next to Cuba, just for the winter. And neither the political inexpedience nor the scientific impossibility of this fantasy, realized later, ever fully banished the notion from my mind. But now—I have my own island.

He stands in the nest.

Speaking of people with their own islands, perhaps you have noticed that I have not mentioned the most obvious: Mr. R. Crusoe. Well, perhaps that is because I don't want to talk about him. Truth is, I used to be fascinated by Robinson Crusoe, until I realized why I have always identified with him. It is the fact that he was the ultimate Protestant, the perfect hardworking Protestant who set about colonizing and empire building, even when he was alone. You're not the boss of me, Jesus, you're not the boss of me.

He sits in the nest.

Does the confessional nature of this material bother anyone? I really don't want to bother anyone. I remember reading once that bothersome personal reminiscences are particularly endemic to performance art. I don't know. I do know that whenever I've listened to anyone go on at length about things outside of their experiences, their words can have a hollow ring. The whole concept of autobiography developed from the confessional. St. Augustine started the ball rolling with his own *Confessions*, and for a long time autobiography stayed just what it was for St. Augustine—more or less a narrative of the soul's relationship to God. It was hundreds of years before autobiographies became what they are today, an enterprise more like that of psychoanalysis.

Autobiographies probably started to change when our ideas of "self" and "individuality" started to change, in the 1600s. Before 1700, the word "individual" actually meant collective, indivisible and collective. I think that by the end of the twentieth century it's meaning was shifting back. For example, I think that most people wanted artists to simply give voice to conventional wisdom, almost as if people were thinking that art, too, should be made by public opinion poll—and some of it was. Oh, skills were still valued, but individual thought wasn't much in demand. It got to the point where the only interesting thing was to make art for other artists—and that can be a vicious circle. Oh well, it doesn't matter, the meanings of words are shifting all the time anyway. I am an idiot, in the original Greek meaning of the word: "idiot," a private person.

He puts on the final mask, made of found objects.

So, I'm sorry if I bothered anyone. But my being sorry does not mean that I accept your being here. It simply means that I am cautious, and polite: all islanders are polite. Besides, I know that I am alone; I know it instinctively. So who am I talking to? I am talking to myself! So buzz off!

He takes off the mask.

I do sometimes worry that my coming here was a desperate act. It got to the point where I was seeing islands everywhere. Oil stains on asphalt were vast unpopulated archipelagos, water stains on the bedroom ceiling, paint chips off the hallway walls, the grains of certain wood—all of these things were maps of islands, and islands meant escape.

He starts running.

I was running, running through shallow tide pools, and I was yelling, squealing with the sharp joy of discovery: "Look, look, look at what I found." I was holding a chunk of sandstone, carved by the sea into the shape of the island—Prince Edward Island. I found it and held it, a four-pound province in my small hands.

He stops running.

We marvelled at its accuracy, as my grandfather ran his hands over the rough stone, naming the bays aloud: Egmont, Malpeque, Tracadie, Bedeque, Hillsborough. Then we drove the long drive to town, and at the offices of the newspaper, they took my photograph—"Seven-Year-Old Finds Rocky Replica." They took my photograph with my grandfather, with my island.

He does a final clean-up, putting everything in its place.

It's funny what you remember: Prince Edward Island. I can remember hating it as a kid, counting the years, then the months, then the days until I could get the hell out of there. Then, as an adult, I can remember longing to walk its low red rock shoreline, longing to smell spruce and salt, pining to go back.

He sits.

I remember the seasons. There was this old joke that said that Prince Edward Island only had two seasons: winter, and the other two months. But that wasn't true. Well not every year, anyway. I remember so many greens in spring. And I remember "Swap Shop":

—Hello, Swap Shop, you're on the air.

—Hello, hello …

—Yes, hello, this is Swap Shop, you're on the air.

—Hello now, is this the Swap Shop?

—Yes, good morning, you're on the air. What do you have for us today?

—Well now, I've got a nun for sale, and she's in top condition, like, the mint condition, eh? Oh wait now, wait. I should mention that it's a ceramic nun, I made her in my classes, eh? She's about four feet tall and blue—so I think that makes her a Carmelite, eh?…

—OK, ma'am, and what is the number to call for the ceramic nun?

—Now hold your horses, eh. I have a confession to make. I think that's kind of appropriate, don't you? She's got a crack in her, down by the big toe on the right foot, but you'd hardly notice it. Still, I'm willing to throw in for absolutely nothing, four little ceramic Chinese children that I made in my class; they all have blond hair now—I was real tired that night …

—Thank you, ma'am, and what's the number to call
for the ceramic collection?

—Wait, wait—I will also look after children in my
own home. The number is 923-9268.

—Thank you. Good morning—Swap Shop. You're
on the air… Good morning, are you there please?
… Do you have something for us today ?

—Yeah, we're frying bacon—D'ya wanna strip?

So. I worry that my coming here was a desperate act. So what. Do
you know what else I worry about? I came here so that I could live in
the present, my present, in my control. Now. But I still worry about
the future. What a jerk!

He stands in the nest. It begins to fill with water.

I sweat a lot! I know, I know, but I just can't bring myself to say
"perspire." "Horses sweat, men perspire, and ladies … ladies don't
even mention it." That's what my Aunt Ditsy used to say, but who the
hell's going to listen to a woman with two sets of eyebrows, anyway?
I sweat like a horse! However, in my family, I was merely a distant
runner-up in the sweat department. It was my brother Donnie who
was far and away the most copious sweat machine known to man. On
a really hot day, I could get a steady drip-drip-drip going off the end
of my nose, eyes closed, head bowed, drip-drip-drip. Donnie, on the
other hand, could get a steady stream going, continuous drips, drips
without spaces, a virtual sweat flow. He could write "shit" on the
pavement, and cross the "t" before the "s" had started to evaporate. He
could, with just one swing of his head, create an entire archipelago of
sweat spots on the asphalt sea around him. He was awesome!

On one particularly hot day—a real scorcher—a bunch of us got
this great idea. We all wanted to see just how much water Donnie could
sweat. So two of us snuck over next door into cranky Ruth Jenkins'
backyard, and we borrowed, without asking, this big basin that she
used to collect rainwater in. Then we dragged it into our old garage that

used to be a barn, when our grandmother kept a cow in the Depression or something. It must have been over a hundred degrees in there. Anyways, we put the basin in exactly the middle of the floor, and then we told Donnie to stand in exactly the middle of the basin, and we told him that he would get into the *Guinness Book of World Records*. Then we all traipsed out to go swimming at the shore, locking the big doors behind us.

While we were gone, our mother rescued the screaming Donnie from the dark heat, and we all had to listen to some boring lecture about dehydration. But, you know, if I close my eyes, I can still see Donnie as we left him that day, that yellow-white shock of hair, those skinny brown spotty legs hanging out of those dirty white shorts that he would not take off that whole summer, standing there in the middle of Cranky Ruth's big white basin with the red line around the rim. And I can still hear the steady drip-drip-drip, as we closed the door on my brother. The island.

The sound of rushing water grows louder and louder.

I can hear the water's anger all of the time now. When the water reaches the top of my walls, I will sit on my Nevelson, my art-raft, and I will wait. I will wait for my walled island, this bowl, to fill, up and up, like a great bathtub, until I am floating at the rim. Then, like Clov, I will be able to see.

He steps out of the nest, out of the water.

You believe me, don't you? It is very important to be believed. That is why I have told so many lies—to test the limits of believing. I should perhaps make one thing clear: this is not the story of a desert island. I am not that pathetic wretch cast upon a solitary shore. I made this place; I built my island. I made a choice; I picked the present. In picking the present, I hoped to regain a sense of control that I had lost. In picking an island, I sought to make that control more easily gained, because islands, with their absolute borders, give one a sense of control. But now I finally realize that being in absolute control is an illusion at best. It is just a way of avoiding the future.

He uncovers a tape recorder, hidden behind a door concealed in the frame of the Jackson Pollack painting, and disconnects the sound, producing silence. The water is not real, but a recording. He throws the tape recorder into the nest.

> Now my charms are all o'erthrown,
> and what strength I have's mine own.

That's from the canoe. There is no water. There is no angry sea. It's gone. This is all I have left. I built these walls so that I would not have to look at nothing—so I would not have to look at the absence of the sea!

No. That's not true either. I built these walls so that I would not have to look at—everything. As if I could avoid my role as an artist, as if I could stop asking questions, in spite of knowing the true shortage of answers.

But now my illusion is broken. The door is open, and I am not surrounded by water. The water is surrounded—by me.

REFERENCES

— Lewis Carroll, "The Hunting of the Snark".
— André Malraux, *Man's Fate.*
— A.A. Milne, *Winnie-The-Pooh,* (Toronto: McClelland & Stewart, 1972), p.131.
— William Shakespeare, *The Tempest,* Epilogue.

WORK
James O'Reilly

WORK
James O'Reilly

BACK AND FORTH

A small table set with a white cloth stands centre-stage. On it is a cash-envelope and a ridiculously large Martini. Jim is front and centre, counting cash. He rapidly snaps through a wad of small bills, letting a ragged five-dollar bill and a loonie fall to the floor. He folds the counted wad and puts it into a back pocket of his black and white uniform. The last bill is a brand new one-hundred which he snaps proudly, then places ritualistically in his front pocket. He pulls a Baggie from another pocket and poop-scoops the fallen fiver. He plants his foot on the loonie and kicks it hard, back off-stage. Blackout.

Single spot up on Jim.

I don't dream. Not at night. Dreaming is the product of a *willing* mind.

To dream you have to go to bed or fall asleep—not drop, or plunk, or knock yourself out, or black out from booze and fatigue, which is what *I* do, which is not sleeping but collapsing. Collapsing is not sleep for dream's sake.

I get nightmares though. Nightmares about work. This one's typical. Tray full of drinks and my section is full—the entire restaurant is my section—and everybody's screaming for something: table seven wants their bill; fifteen wants more water because the baby's choking, *the baby is choking!;* the owner needs another bottle of wine right now; the maître d' is waiting for me to fuck up 'cause I was five minutes late for my shift; my rash is killing me; and I'm trying to quit smoking.

Now, it's this place sure enough, but not exactly: the service bar is three miles from the dining room and it's eight feet high; all of my drinks are wrong; and when I turn around the dining room is a labyrinth—strange banquettes, walls, partitions I've never seen before. And all the tables are screwed up, and I can't even see most of my people for all the waving arms and laughing heads.

Jim laughs.

But somehow I manage to get it all sorted out, get my bills together, get my drink-order straight and *focus* on the finish line, Zen-style … I-am-the-tray-I-am-the-soup-du-jour-I-am-the-daily-dessert-I-am-the-shaft-of-the-arrow, and the bull's-eye is the end of this shift. I get my drinks and head for the dining-room saying to myself, *Don't think, move. Don't think, move.* Then ZAP!

I'm standing in the middle of a wheat field in Saskatchewan wearing my black-and-whites, with a full tray of drinks in my hand.

Wheat. There's a highway. The Trans-Canada.

Maybe I can catch a bus back.

Then it clicks … and I start to worry about melting ice cubes and the old lady at fourteen who said I reminded her of her son-in-law and how she'll never make it to the theatre on time if I don't get back to her with the bill which is now tumbling away from me over the tops of rippling amber waves of grain like newspaper through a ghetto playground.

Lighting changes from dream state to restaurant state. Jim waves the last few patrons out the door.

Yes sir … well, please come back again … you're quite welcome … and watch out for those Hungarian goo-loshes, huh-huh-huh … good night. Thank you very much. Bye. [*aside*] Tom, lock the door!

Restaurant lighting down, white lights up. Jim's wave becomes a backhand middle-finger at the receding customers.

Fuck you very much. Die. You seven-percent bastard.

He goes to the table.

"Jim, can we have some more water? Jim, when's that bread coming? Jim, I need another drink? Jim, when's our food coming? ... Jim? ... Jim?"

Never give 'em your name! That's rule number one ...

Or, what about this?

He mimes a handshake.

"Jim, we had a whale of a time tonight. You were great! And the service was excellent" ... Rule number two? *Never accept a handshake for a tip!* Big *thanks* means big *shanks.*

Money talks, mister. I can't pay my rent with *thanks.*

Hey, I've been doing this a while, but sometimes even I forget. Like tonight with that table. I broke both rules with them because I paid too much attention to rule number three, which goes like this ... Be nice to everyone you serve because you never know, a) who's going to pay the bill, and b) where your next job is coming from.

Never any good getting personal about it—it's only *work* ... but sometimes ...

He points to his forehead.

See this mark? Is it *really* red?

He sips his Martini.

There is no God. There is no heaven. There is ... no ... fucking vermouth in this Martini!

He pulls a medicine bottle from his pocket and administers a drop of vermouth to his drink, does a finger-test, and raises his glass.

The whole world is fucked.

He drinks, licks the cash envelope, and gets up.

Gotta take this in to the manager. Be right back. Watch my drink.

He exits, howls off-stage, then re-enters, hyped-up, with cocaine on his lip, and moves to the table.

Right. Zing. Finish my drink. Right! What's it like? ... *Depends* ...
Now, if ya want *big* cash, try working in a really happening hot-spot
like Doro's. Rocco Doro, restaurateur *par excellence*, the man with the
Midas touch ... fascist, motherfucker, in-your-face prick. Everybody's
going under, yet he opens one place after another. Oh, he's got it down
right: design the place so that everyone can see, and is seen by,
everybody else, jam 'em in elbow-to-elbow, light the place like a movie
set. Lots of colour. Mural-size photos of rustic Italy way up high, sixty-
foot ceilings, expensive *objets d'art* here and there, pastel green, brown
and red ...

Something like post-contemporary Milan meets *A Clockwork
Orange.*

They don't pay you for your first two shifts at Doro's. And, you
don't actually get to wait on tables for the first week because ... "Only
one out of ten makes it past the first week." So. First day. I pop in. Scan
the place.

A nervous waiter comes up to me and says, "Are you starting
today?"

"Yes ... but I'm supposed to wait for Rocco."

"Look ... it's not a good idea to be standing around doing nothing.
You should get busy ... you can help me set up."

Sure.

It's an hour and a half before service, and the waiters are *cleaning,*
if you can believe it, whizzing around in a flurry, zip-zip, bump-bump,
down on all fours working invisible chunks of dust from corners and
crevices where the pillar meets the tile.

I take a row of tables against a wall and start to do the glasses. I'm
pretty meticulous about it. The place is unbelievably awesome. I'm
polishing. Scanning the joint. Polishing. This is okay. Soon I'll be
grossing two bills a night. That's a grand a week. I can take that. Then,
I hear this booming bellow from across the room. I continue polishing.
Then I hear it again. The waiters stop their cleaning, look at me, and

freeze in terror. There's some guy in a *suit* sitting on the banquette across the room. He's doing this [*arm wave*] and shouting.

"What the fuck are YOU doing?"

"Me?"

"Yeah, YOU. Who the fuck do you think I'm talking to? What the fuck do you think you're doing?"

"Polishing glasses."

"For a fuckin' half an hour? I been watching you polishing that same fuckin' glass for a fuckin' half an hour, now MOVE for fuck sakes!"

So I move.

A few minutes later one of the waiters tells me that that was Rocco, the owner, and that he usually doesn't yell at new guys until their second or third shift ... Well he did that as well. My second shift, Rocco mumbles something at me on the floor, something in Italian, I think. Two seconds later, he snaps around close enough for me to see pores on the shiny end of his nose ...

"What the fuck are you doing? I said get me a steak knife! Are you a professional?"

Professional? I *quit drinking* to work there. Didn't get a decent night's sleep the whole week. Every shift was like writing a Bar entrance exam. Every night for a month after I quit I had epic nightmares of Technicolor fascism starring Emperor Rocco Doro in *extreme close-up*. Never again. Not even for two bills a night. Macho fucking hell.

He takes a big gulp of his Martini.

Working for *women* is a lot easier on the constitution though. Hell, at Doro's it was instruction through intimidation and sarcasm. First shift at Doro's, I asked a waiter, "Where do you keep the decaf around here?"

"Decaf? In my fucking pocket, okay?"

Then, I worked at this place called Ni-uh ... yeah, *Ni-uh*. I don't know if I'm pronouncing it right ... I think it means "migrating sparrow" in Ojibway or something ... but I never could get the name right. Come to think of it, I don't think *anybody* could get the name right ... which is probably why they went out of business. Think about it, "Ni-uh" ... what kind of name is that? It's too soft, sorta like m-u-u-u-u-u-n-h, it's like one soft consonant followed by a bunch of vowels. Could use a few more consonants. Hard ones!

But anyway, anyhoo ... the place was run by women, ex-dancers most of them, impeccable postures ... and grace. They used to float across the room ... angelic forgiving faces, atop petite perfect bodies, heads floating parallel to the earth and no sarcasm.

"Linda, where do we keep the decaf?"

"The decaf? Oh that's all right, you've only been here a month, I'll get it for you."

Oh it was great. It was too good. It was destined to fail. The chef was a culinary genius. Menu changed every day. Choice of two meals, six courses apiece, hundred bucks a head, and with each course came a different glass of *organically* produced wine, served in *hand-blown crystal*, chosen by our *sommelier*. Sommelier! Holy fuck. Terracotta, taupe, driftwood, tapestries, spread-out little black-marble tables— one every half-acre or so! Soft lighting, little mini-spots here and there ... They had a guy come in once a month just to focus the lights!

I mean, I'd been in fancy places before ... but *this* place, this ni-ni-ni-Ni-uh ... like, like, like I was born in a drunken mining town called Uranium City, Saskatchewan, okay? ... like, I grew up in the projects up in the Jane-Finch corridor where I watched little boys go from "Dennis the Menace" to nanchuck-wielding glue-heads quicker than you could hot-wire a Pontiac, where in grade nine, at lunch, under-neath a portable one day, Bonnie Wells said to me, "You can fuck me but don't crush my smokes." OKAY!

HAUTE CUISINE? In my family we were expected to *lick the plate*. I remember once being smacked by my mother for saying *dinner* instead of *supper*. And when I declined to *lick* after *supper*, "Too good to lick his plate with the rest of us. Waddaya, turnin' *fag* on us?" I tried to excuse myself from the table but stopped so I wouldn't aggravate things further by saying "excuse me," because NOBODY'D EVER EXCUSED THEMSELVES FROM ANYTHING AROUND

THERE ... Right. Right. Right. Depends. D-d-d-depends ... back and forth, b-b-back and forth ...

He calms himself and gulps down the rest of his drink.

But the *worst* is the intimate-bistro type of joint. You know, up-close-and-personal, salty soup just like at home, just like the place you came from, you know ... the place you were born. The kind of restaurant that is supposed to be your home—*Home? It's a fucking job!*—and the customers are your *guests,* and everyone's your *friend,* and everything's all friendsy-wendsy and friendly and shit, and you know everyone's name and everyone knows *your* name.

I once worked in this place called Something We Did ... cute huh? Slow night at Something We Did. Dead. I mean dead. Nothing. Like death itself. Nobody in the place. I was on with Kevin. I wanted to cut out early but Kevin wouldn't let me.

"What happens if all of a sudden we get *hit* and I'm all by myself, then what, huh?"

Kevin never closed alone. It was his policy. Kevin was a fragile queen who couldn't stand to be alone. Fragile and tired. Tired and continually exhaling.

[*cheerful*] "Good morning, Kevin."

[*exhales*] "What's so good about it?"

That night he was on about how he'd just redone his kitchen. He was drawing boxes in pen on a napkin at the end of the bar. I tuned in for the third cycle ...

"*First* I did the walls in this lovely light lavender latex, *then* took all the cabinets and shelving down and laid them out flat on newspaper and did them in this lovely, deep, ash-coloured, high-gloss enamel, *then*—what do you think I did, huh?"

"Beats me Kevin, let it dry, watched "Dynasty," made a salad?"

"No! While the enamel was still wet I took a pepper mill to it and let the buzillions of little peppercorn chunks fall all over the wet paint, and they stuck, and sort of spread out a little bit. Gives it, like, this rough sort of sand-papery texture. I think it looks really smart. You'll have to come over and see it some time. I think I'll have a party."

A deuce came in and I sat them in my section: some old blue-rinsed darling with a perm and a print dress on, and a young guy with her, her *trick*: snappy dresser, tan, great teeth, impeccable hair. He was her trick all right, and I'm sure she was just a little bit uncomfortable with the whole thing. They were *irregulars* in a place really only suited to *regulars*.

He ordered without making eye contact. Manhattan and a spritzer. Downed the Manhattan in a gulp and ordered another. The menus sat untouched. The old girl hadn't even touched her spritzer. She was all hands aflutter and rattling on nervously. Kevin was drawing hairdos and sideburns in little boxes on four napkins at the end of the bar. Back and forth, back and forth. Another Manhattan. Then the trick moved his chair out into the aisle and turned hers around sharply to face him. Then ... he began to go to town on her, straightening out her dress, picking lint off her like a chimpanzee, and lightly tapping her about the knees and hands, like a macabre form of pattycakes. Then ... he took a pointed index finger to her *ear* and began to *swab around* inside, clearing out dust or something ... or *something* ...

She talks on like nothing's happening. He starts picking at her ear. Without ceremony he yanks a small insect from inside—it looks like an earwig with a hooked tail—clutching something that looks like a *root*. A plantar wart? Too long. It's a piece of her brain. He pulls about a foot and a half of the grey placenta from her bleeding head—by this time—and there's blood everywhere, and she continues to rattle on as he pulls away at the cord.

All of a sudden her head starts to jerk a little bit, and I wonder: where's this *new* action coming from? I move in on the ear in question and notice that the sphincter-hole in the side of her blood-spattered head is *dilating* and *contracting* to the rhythm of her speech, pinching the endless cord of grey matter into uniform link-sausages of brain that had begun to form a coil on the unopened menu below. The trick keeps yanking. The old lady keeps talking. Kevin is drawing full figures on his fifth napkin while singing loud show tunes to himself! I'm in a circus, right?

I ask the couple if they're ready to order. Both look at me as if I was a test-baboon running small circles in a lab cage with a transistor sticking out of my noggin.

I repeat, "Are you ready to order?"

"Oh dear, well ... we haven't even looked at the menu."

Of course they haven't *looked at the menu:* one's covered in blood, and the other's a blotter beneath the steaming coil of link sausage still attached to the inside of the old girl's head. I yank the menus.

"You won't be needing *these* any more. Shall I bring you fresh menus?"

Then ... both of them ... one of these [*smug gesture*] ... as if to say, "Naturally. Well? What are you waiting for?" ... To which I *should* have responded, "Because it's my job! I'm a *wait*-er, people. Take a hint!" ... But they didn't give me the chance to think of it ...

They never do ... never, until hours later when you're in bed ... 'n' ... 'n' ... never seen anything like that ... n-n-n-never in my born days have I ... no, once I saw this guy take an ice-pick to some other guy's head, and ... I've s-s-seen cattle slaughtered in a m-m-movie once.

Anyhoooo ... I'm d-dyin' to get rid of this dirty finsky.

He pulls the Baggie with the five-dollar bill in it out of his pocket.

Let's go g-get a drink or somethin'.

THE SPINNING THING

Lights up on an empty stage. A plastic milk-crate is kicked out of the wings to centre-stage. Jim the garbageman follows, singing. He is wearing his work greens, and has a "Joe Louis" cake in one hand and a can of Coke in the other. He sets the Coke on the crate.

     ... round and round and round and round I go,
     round and round and up and down I go,
     that's the way we do the varsity ra-a-a-ag.

Jim spits.

Hey. Let me show you this thing I figured out on the run the other day.

Well, I didn't actually figure it out … no, that's not right, I remembered it. From public school, from gym class. Like, I forgot all about it until I saw these kids doin' it on our Tuesday run.

He squats, holding one foot straight out.

This is the thing I remembered …

He does a few cossack turns.

Cossack turns! Isn't it great? Is that *not* a bit of spinning magic? See, the great thing is that you're not really moving at all; just looks like it. Oh yeah. Sometimes, if we finish our run early—which always happens 'cause we're fuckin' fast man … I mean, I really *kick ass*. So we finish early—I'll usually go and toast a coner on my break, and then we'll go and help one of the other trucks finish off their run if they're in the shits. Well, every time without fail Nick'll pull up, stop everything, look at the other driver, and say to me, "Jee-mee, do dat speenink ting." He breaks me up, he calls it a "spinning thing" … What a chooch, but he's a great guy … So, he makes me get out of the truck, in the middle of the street or whatever, and do a couple of cossack turns. And I do them. In the rain? I don't give a fuck. In the snow? It's better in the snow 'cause you make a mark. So, now everybody's askin' me to do goddamn cossack turns and they *all* call it "the spinning thing" just like Nick. Sheesh. But I don't mind. It's good exercise … cossack turns.

He kicks the crate.

Ever get somebody ask you, "What do you do for a living?" And you tell them … "Oh, I'm a lawyer … or a doctor … or a garbageman … or a hose-salesman at Canadian Tire" … and all they say to you is, "Oh, well, that's interesting." Which means *what?*

Jim kicks the crate again.

Which *means* … "Me? Never in a million years. Couldn't care less. But I suppose someone has to do it. Better you than me, huh-huh-huh."

Oh, people pretend, you know?

"I—am a garbageman ..."

"That's *interesting* ..." Dead give-away, couldn't give a shit. "That's interesting. You must find all kinds of *interesting* stuff ..." Then their voice trails off. "... in ... the ... gar-bage ..."

Oh yeah, all kinds of interesting stuff like ... your husband's reading porno mags, your family eats shit, and, there's an empty mickey of gin hidden away in a box of Cornflakes with coffee grounds on top. Oh yeah, all kinds of IN-TER-EST-ING stuff like that.

Ah, ta hell with it. If anyone asks me any more I tell them I'm a hose-salesman. That shuts 'em up.

So, I'm at this party the other night and this guy, real perky, real smart-ass, one of Karen's friends, doesn't buy the hose-salesman shtick. He gets all pissed at me. Thinks I'm fucking him around. Now, I'm pretty loaded and starting to get serious and thinking a lot—that's the way it works with me—so I want to tell this guy something, something to shut him up. So I tell him about this one thing that happened to me ... that I think is a *good* garbageman story ... that can only happen on the garbage. So I tell him. I even made up a *thing* about it ... this song ... but I'll tell ya that after.

This is the thing I told him ... See, I was hatched in a place called Uranium City, Saskatchewan. Yeah big deal, nobody knows about it. At any rate, this place was way the hell up there just south of the Yukon border ... way the hell up ... but it *doesn't exist* anymore. Little mining town. Nothing for miles. Folks lived up there a couple years. Hatched me. The mining company pulled out. City folded. So they took off.

The folks never talked about it much afterwards ...'n' I was only about six months old at the time ... don't remember the place at all .... But I didn't give a shit. I had a normal life. I mean, we had a TV and everything .... So, hadn't heard a thing about the place in over twenty-five years when one day I find this magazine on top of a stack of garbage I was about to dump. In fact, I had dumped it ... in the back of the hopper ... and the blade was coming down ... when something made me grab it. Not the cover story, but right on the side, in little tiny letters, were the words ... "The last days of El Dorado," then, in even smaller letters right underneath, was … "Uranium City, Saskatchewan comes to a bitter end," right there on a *Saturday Night* magazine from 1982. Isn't that wild? … Freaked me out.

He bites into the "Joe Louis" cake and winces with pain.

My teeth've been bugging me lately. I get this bitterness … in the back of my throat? This nasty, bitter, metallic … like just before a cold, or, say, if you're chewing a popsicle stick for a couple of hours and it starts to rot, or, like that almond thing in the centre of a peach seed … nasty. It's like the two times I did coke, poison workin' its way down … and I wonder just how far back it goes? Maybe just to the back of my throat? Or maybe right inside of my neck and down into my body? It's nasty, man … bitter … salty … briney … *briney* …

My father was a first-degree Grand *Brine* Poobah. Check this. When we were kids my brother Chucky and I used to tool around with him on Sundays sometimes. We'd usually end up at the Gladstone Hotel which is where my uncle Phil worked the bar. When Phil quit that place last year he had *thirty years* seniority under his belt … it was a la-a-a-arge belt … stretched *smooth* in the back with a *sweat* design on it—marbled, crystalized, white salt-lines in a web—a record, a *geological core sample* of Phil's labour history in that place. Yeah. So. Dad'd be havin' beers with his buds while Chucky and I'd be bored silly, twizzlin' around all over the place, vibrating off the walls. So Dad used to try and keep us busy with salt—in the form of chips, and cheezies, and pretzels, and peanuts … and smokies …

Ever tried one of them? It's a commercial stick of beef jerky about yea long, spicy as hell, and dripping with grease, wrapped in that cello, tin-foil shit. They were hot! I mean, four or five of these in a junior-sized mouth in the space of an afternoon'd make your head scream like a fucking jet turbine. But Chucky and I thought they were pretty cool. We'd hang off the chairs in the Gladstone, biting off plugs of the salty meat, sitting wide open like a couple of cowboys around a camp-fire saying things like "uh-huh" and "yup" to *the boys*, the men—my dad and his buds—who talked about the war, bizarre murders, and their *work*.

My dad takes care of a hockey rink up in North York and drives the Zamboni. About his job two things always got him going: one is the way figure skaters—dainty though they may seem—chew the HELL out of the ice; and two is all the various *mysteries of refrigeration*. That was his favourite topic. He'd go on for hours about seizing valves, ruptured pipes and bursting coils, and about the way the *brine*—which is what I'm getting at—had to be kept at exactly eighteen degrees Fahrenheit.

Brine. What a word! I'd mumble it to myself and repeat it over and over when I was alone. Ya know, "… brine-brine-brine, briney this, briney that, you're lookin' pretty brine today, oh how awfully brine of you, BRINE, brine, bur-r-r-i-i-i-ne, BR-I-I-I-I-I-I-NE …" A mean-sounding word, kind of a combo of "grind" and "bright." Drives ya nuts after a while. Drove me nuts. I was twelve. Set myself a project: to not only discover the meaning of the word, but to actually come to terms with the *concept* … of brine.

Years later … 'bout ten years ago now … I found myself working in a place called Consolidated Beef way out in the sticks. There was three of us worked in the back, me and two other graduates of the *Manpower-Corkboard-Vocational-Institute:* a girl up front who typed and did our cheques; and Marv, the owner, a big fat guy with Hawaiian shirts, a greasy phone glued to his ear, and a cigar goin'. So. What kind of place was Consolidated Beef? Well, there was no company picnic— hell, we didn't even have a coffee machine—and *no*, in case you're wonderin', we did not make smokies. We made pickled meat for export to the Third World … and the Maritimes.

This was the Consolidated Beef process …

A severe lighting change. He begins to speak at lightning speed.

I'm at the Northgate—formerly the Olympic Bar and Grill— down the street from the yard. It's after work on any Monday, Tuesday, Wednesday, Thursday, Friday, with a few of the guys. We drink beers and watch Suzy take her clothes off.

I like her. She's happy to see us. Yeah ... I guess she's happy.
We, beside the stage, like regular. She, on the table just above us.
Ritual. Feet standing on my cheeks.
Quick scan up, knees, breasts, chin, some hair, the ceiling.
Slower the second time around.
Straight up to a shut flower ... beauty hole ...
"Give your head a shake Jim, you need some beauty in your day."
Higher! Suzy, I can't see your face from down here.
Lemme see your eyes. I want in.
"Two black holes in her head starin' right at ya, boy. Whaddaya waitin' for? Jump!"
But those are nostril holes. Two of them.
"Choose one, idiot."
Which one?
"Doesn't matter."
Why don't we all just jump into the abyss?
"Choose one!"
Uh ... uh, no muscles for decision in my family ...
Okay, okay ... JUMP.
Her left nostril accepts my hurtling body without question.
Into her body. Into her head. Just think of it. We two are one.
Sailing up. Sailing down. Same thing after a certain speed.
Sailing up-up-up down-down-down dangerously close to the wall.
Stabilize vertical updraft with hands at the side. NOBODY WATCHING.
Jim adjusts his crotch.
WRONG. Bad move. Bad altimeter. Way off centre.
"It'll cost ya!"

There is a chance I will stick to the wall of a sinus.
There is a chance I will become embedded in a mucus membrane.
There is a chance I will blow my nose inside of hers.
There is a chance we will mix our water.
There is a chance I will fear death and ejaculate prematurely.

The wall is coming up fast. Body slowly rotating in a full gainer. Face comes up just in time to meet a rock, and oh …

> [*Sportscaster-like voice*] The *nose* comes clean away from the face and remains suspended up there, somewhere above, where it crystalizes, freeze-dries, and disintegrates into a million flakes of phyllo pastry which fall—as if from a spanakopita—in delicate spirals downwards slipstreaming the impression left by one man's hole in the air.

Trouble again. Cock jumps out of pants *dancing* on a hot gust of wind, *snags* a forgotten tree stump on the way down *exploding* like popcorn. Body jerks back, violently pinwheeling. SO THAT'S WHAT THE SKY LOOKS LIKE! Too late. Kneecaps shatter like light-bulbs on marble and quartz. Where will it end? Being born again?

I, a meagre piece of meat, am cradled like a baby in a wet dark room.
I, a meagre plate of beef, am cornered like a baby in a wet dark room.
I, a meagre slate of film, am cradled like an image in a light tight box.

Lighting back to normal. He resumes his normal pace of speech.

This was the Consolidated Beef process. Peeled and gutted beef plates came in piled high on wooden skids. The plates fit together like interlocking clay roof-tiles and, from a distance, looked pretty solid sitting there. But up close, you could see that this beef—not really BEEF! but wispy, ethereal beef—hung loosely in bloody clots from the bone and was wrapped in a layer of gristly yellow lard with the consistency of boiled chicken-skin. Definitely *third-rate beef.* The plates were zipped through a band-saw, then placed on a steel conveyor that took them through a metal weaving-loom with two rows of parallel teeth. Each tooth, a stainless-steel syringe as big around as a grade-one pencil, would punch a violent burst of *brine* into the already loosely packed third-rate beef plate. By now, the bloated, pink, salt-saturated beef-balls are ready to be chopped through the ribs, sawed into chunks, and jammed into plastic buckets for export.

For the whole first week I did the buckets. [*demonstrates*] Shovelful of rock salt in the bottom, then dump the soggy beef chunks in, another shovelful of rock salt on top, then bring the *brine* hose over, open it up full and watch that salty liquid bubble its way up through them beef chunks, slowly taper the flow as the level approaches the prescribed "one inch from the lip," then close it and take the *brine* hose away ... Then—and this is where a bit of *Zen* comes in handy—you pound the lid shut with a rubber mallet all the way 'round while listening for the sealing *click!*

Sure it was fun. But I must admit that after the first week of pounding buckets in a white refrigerated room some fifty feet by fifty feet by fifty feet with no less than two inches of *brine* covering the floor at all times ... *brine* which ruined my Kodiak steel-toes, *brine* which dried the fuck out of my skin, which cracked my blistering, mallet–trem-u-lous hands, *brine* in my hair, *brine* in my eyes, *brine* which crystalized in my clothing, turning my work pants, by the end of the day, into a rigid two-pronged salt-lick. *Brine*, well below freezing, which terrorized a whole scad of superhuman Vietnamese into quitting before lunch on their first day. One after another, Manpower just kept sending them to us. I remember one poor bastard ... this man who had spent three months clinging to a splinter of wood on the high salty seas ... had yanked the body parts of his friends and family from burning buildings in war-torn cities half-way across the planet ... this man was no *wus*, he was a *hard* motherfucker, a *tough* man, but after two hours in this place the guy was a wreck. Just stood there shaking, bloody knife frozen in his fist, repeating ... "I do not know this. I will die if stay here. I will die. *I will die!*" ...

After a week of that I was just a little pissed. So at the end of my first Friday, I went up to the office to grab my cheque and have a talk with Marv, the owner. He was spindling around on his chair, chewing a cigar, and exhaling into the phone. I said, "Marv, I'm a hard worker, but … if you want me back on Monday you're gonna have to pay me at least *five* bucks an hour." … That's right, FIVE. Shoulda seen him. He went white. Leaned way back in his chair. I reminded him that I had, at one time, worked at *Canada Packers*—I did, ya know. "Check my résumé." He began to soften. Leaned forward a bit. He knew his *beef business* all right. Then, he put his elbows on his desk and came in close to me … and … for, like, half a moment I got a look at Marv right up close … looked into his eyes … looked into his veiny bulging simple cow eyes … and I believed …

A severe lighting change. He speaks again at lightning speed.

… in NOTHING. I believe that when I fall in love this time it will be forever.

> [*Irish accent*]
> I believe that life is as shart
> As the hissing fart
> Of a doggie when he walks past.

Believing. Sucker. Punch. I wake up every morning. Same thing. No memory. Shitty taste. Salt. I dress. I eat. Raisin Bran. Lots of it. Twist up a mean reefer. Punch killer tunes into the Alpine. Drive somewhere … *to work*. Few things to remember … dope is good with TV … dope and music not good enough … music alone makes me worry …

I remember the TV schedule, therefore I am.

Suppertime. Denver at Seattle. Indica bud reefer. *Killer* just out on CD. Mother phones. Put Alice Cooper on pause.

"Hi ma." Jane and Finch.

> [*Mother*] Remember Nelson that dumb rasta coon from next door got hauled away for dope? Well somebody killed him in jail … that goddamned floppy-headed n-n-n- …

[*Caribbean woman*] Nah-teeng. Heem no do nah-teeng my boy, my boy b-boo-hoo-hoo-hoo ...

... with no husbands. No husbands in the projects.

[*Caribbean man*] Doone bee-leeeve een eet mon.
[*Caribbean woman*] Believe ... b-b-b—

She cries in the backyard-*ette*. Her *dead* backyard-ette. My mother says ...

[*Mother*] I planted her goddamned garden for her 'n' she can't even keep that going ... it's no wonder her boy ended up ... well, *ended* ...

Then—like nothing at all—the Barclays:

[*Mother*] ... those retarded Scottish bastards from Newfy whose kids are a bunch of rats, always in trouble ... Well, he *finally* killed her.

Finally ...
The Barclays. Rough drunkards from across the way. Some show.

[*TV salesman-like voice*] Mister beats the missus regularly and somehow manages to find time and energy for the children ... children, valuable because they—in *number and gender*—fit the requirements of financial need necessary to be AWARDED a SLOT in the COMPLEX under O.H.C.—Ontario Housing Corporation—provisions.

[*Mother*] ... *finally* killed her ...

Wait a second. Wasn't HE in the hospital? Didn't SHE stab him the last time? What about the KIDS? I thought they SPLIT. Wasn't there a restraining order? ...

> [*Mother*] Ah, ya shoulda seen them two ... last couple months they been walking around here all luvy-duvy, *her* with her arm in a sling, and *him—the red-faced jackass*—with a bandage around his neck ... she stabbed him in the *throat* but she didn't kill 'im ... just think, a couple more inches and she could've saved her life but *nooooooo* ... how, how, HOW COULD SHE LET—?

"Look, look, look ma I gotta go ... expectin' someone, a call, long-distance ... "

> [*Mother*] Bullshit! Nobody ever phones you! Just let me finish. He *beat* her to death, *beat* the shit out of her while the kids watched. Jimmy, Jimmy he *punched* her—must've been a hundred times—*right in the c—*

He shuts his eyes.
Alice Cooper spins in silence on pause.
End of the first half.
Denver down by five.
I can't believe she used the word "cunt."
I have no city. End pause.

He sings a couple of lines from Alice Cooper's "Dead Babies." Lights change back. Speech resumes at normal pace.

I believed—*I knew*—from his eyes, that even if Marv had been a big cheese in the beef business at one time, he was pretty close to being all washed up by now. Stood my ground. *Canada Packers.* Damn right. Check the résumé. He gave me the raise. Five bucks an hour starting Monday.

I quit two weeks later. And—truth to be told—I think the other two Consolidated Beef workers were pretty happy to see me go. Once word got out that I had Canada Packers experience they clammed up tight, thought I was a plant, a ringer, sent there from HQ to spy on them. And I'm sure both of them had done *time* because neither could stand my whistling or singing.

So fuck that. I got out of there fast. Threw my salty boots away. My salty pants. My briney gloves. And the next week I got on with the garbage crew for the City.

It was great! On the truck, the rest of that first summer ... Man, I whistled my lips off, sang my lungs out, and kept my feet bone dry ... while drinking in the colourful, wide-open spaces of North York. Shit ... lemme think, has it been that long? ... Yup, ten years now. That's around the same time I left the folks ...

'N' the projects ... 'n' they're still up there ... 'n' I hear it's gettin' worse 'n' shit but—

Ya know, like, I got my own thing 'n' stuff ... and ...

You know, I'd like to think that I can take most anything life has to throw at me and just keep on going ... but ... sometimes ... some things ... like my memory, like this bitter taste I get in the back of my throat, this briney shit—

Just won't leave me alone.

Oh, yeah, I almost forgot about the song I was gonna do for ya. It's not really finished, and it's not really a song with singing ... it's more of a ballad. First I gotta limber up a bit.

He does a few goofy warm-up exercises.

It's called "Uranium Baby" ... I think.

> Dug a hole in the ground
> 'cause they're searchin' for God.
> Put that shit that they found
> in a uranium rod.

Made a city out of nothing
and the people arrived.
Then they did what they're told
'cause they want to survive.

And survive mine did
for a couple of years.
Put a penny in their pockets
and they drank a lot of beer.

And they drank a lot of rum
—played cards all night.
And they drank a lot of beer
—when El Dorado said good night.

And they drank a lot of rye …
And they drank a lot of rye …
to numb the pain they were feelin'
when the well ran dry.

And they drank a lot of rye …
And they drank a lot of rye …
to numb the pain they were feelin'
from a new baby's cry.

Yup good friends …

The ball of blood that they yanked
from my mama was me,
hung my hiney out to dry,
and they spanked away with glee.

Then we loaded up the truck
—DIDN'T move to Beverly—

and we bounced between the cracks
till we hit the O.H.C.

But I love to laugh
'n' ah nevuh dun cried ...
gotta job makin' bucks
and a uranium stride ...
in a black and yellow truck
with lots of garbage on the sides.

He laughs.
Well, that's the kind of stuff I do ... just make things up ya know.
A truck horn honks.
Back to work.

UP AND DOWN

The office of Jim, a thirty-ish advertising copywriter on his way up. A chair and a desk with a typewriter and a phone on it. A vertical beam of blue light hits the floor centre-stage. This light doubles as the water-cooler and the sewer shaft. Jim is at the cooler. Water "glubbing" noises can be heard sporadically throughout.
Jim draws a drink and watches the bubbles rise.

Glunk. Plunk.
Down-down-down glunk ... up-up-up plunk. Plunk up. Plunk *up*.
Feature that, will ya? It's mine all mine, like it or not, and I *like* it.
My own water-cooler. Water, man. Dig that, dad. Man, everybody needs water: *needs* water, *is* water—ninety-one percent by volume—but dig, it's not so much the water we're all into as it is the *process*. I dig the process ...
He taps the water-cooler tank.

The way it gets *in* there, the way we collect it up, then put it into a bottle or a jar or a pipe or a bag, then drink it, absorb it, let it pass through our spongy bodies, our organs, organ-*isms*, our organ-*ized* body parts, huh? Then drain it off, man: drip it, drop it, plunk it, plop it into some other receptacle, another bottle, bowl, pipe, or channel, where it makes its way into a larger field, pools, lakes, oceans, solutions, suspensions, milky, cloudy, clear, into the ocean, held there by gravity until it separates, evaporates, then rains down all over us and gets into our eyes, as it runs down our dirty faces and gets into our mouths and we *taste* it, taste ourselves salty, curse and cry tears while we *listen* to it— water, rain, tears—on the roof, on the window, and *listen* to it gather within the curbside susurrus of a gutter from a deck chair, under a canopy, in a café, and make love in it for the first time on an old crazy-carpet in a park in the ravine, not too far from home, with a baseball diamond nearby, next to a Chinese food joint that sells tea till four a.m. which makes you piss green.

He draws another drink.

Glunk-plunk.

Catch that? Closely? It's a two-part chud-o-rama. First there's the glunk as the fluid gets sucked down, forming a bubble cluster which sits on the bottom, getting fatter. Hangs there for maybe a nanosecond before it separates, *glunk*, then rises to the top where it *plunks* in a glorious understatement of absolute release. The plunk is my fave because that, up there, is a much greater freedom. Almost all the way up. Closer to heaven, dig? Follow me? *Plunk up!*

He sings:

> Plunk-da da-da-duh,
> plunk-plunk da da da-duh, dum.
> Start spreadin' the news …
> New York is where I'm gonna plunk.

Madison Avenue to be precise. It'll happen. It *is* happening. Corner office. Two windows. My own secretary sometimes. My own *water-cooler,* man. Connect the dots, baby. Up and out!

The phone rings a few times, then a message comes over the intercom. Jim, unfazed, listens to the message while peering into the water tank.

> [*Message*] Jim. Jerry. Four-fifteen. Where's your secretary and why aren't you answering your line? I know you're there so you better cut the bull. Look, there's a problem with the Neibart Rustproofing campaign. The client rejected the copy—actually it was his wife, but that doesn't make a diff—so you're gonna have to give me something else ... something with a little more "ZIP" to it in the words of Mrs. West. I need it for a breakfast meet at 7:30—that's *a.m.*—at the Sheraton. Don't fuck me around buddy, you're on pretty thin ice as it is. Do it, Jim! [*beep*]

The answering machine's beep shatters Jim's cool. He stalks around the office grumbling furiously.

Fuck you, Jerry... "NEIBART IS ON THE JOB" ... What's wrong with that? ... It's a great piece of copy ... "Not enough *zip*"... "Seven-thirty *breakfast meet*" ... Ta hell with that. Not gonna do it again ... Hey, I don't need this job.

The gravity of Jim's predicament hits him. He loses his nerve, starts to worry. He sets about getting to work by executing his ritual. From underneath his desk, he hauls a strong-box which contains a spoon, a jar of peanut butter, a bottle of ginseng, a bottle of Scotch, a glass, and a baseball cap. He lays the contents out before him, then takes his jacket off and folds it neatly over the back of his chair. With Zen-like solemnity, he eats a spoonful of peanut butter, drinks the ginseng, pours a shot of Scotch and drinks it, puts the baseball cap on, and sways gently while humming. This leads into full chanting, which leads into an earnest rendering of Glen

Campbell's "Wichita Lineman." Satisfied, he puts everything back into the box and returns it to its place under the desk, then fires through the following bit of "Neibart" affirmation:

Accept. "Neibart is on the job" is a bad slogan because Mrs. West says so. She is an intelligent woman. She controls Mr. West, therefore she controls Neibart Corporation. She is *beyond* my control.

Let it pass. "Neibart is on the job" is lame because it lacks *zip.* Define "zip." Zip is the life-force. Zip is vitality … progress. Zip is the ability to adapt.

Zip is what distinguishes human beings from every other animal on the planet. Zip is *mobility* … evolution … The evolution of mobility … that's it …

That's *it* … the evolution of mobility …

Where did it all begin? … *The foot!* The foot, four feet, two feet, a horse, a chariot, *the car.* The car is *the foot* of the twentieth century, the engine of evolution. Evolution is zip.

Adapt. Survive. Protect … the feet of mankind. Protect the vehicle of the life-force, the car, the vehicle of our desires, the vehicle of our birthright as homo sapiens to bridge disparate geographies! Yes.

He rolls a sheet of paper into his typewriter.

All of this is *good.* Protect-protect-protect the life-force at all costs.

Stop, at all costs, encroachment against our birthright … erosion of the vehicle of our desires … erosion, the *co*-rrosion of our dreams … corrosion is the enemy of the life-force … rust … rust … *Rust is evil!*

Jim switches on the machine and starts to type in synch with the following:

I'd rather have a hernia than a rusty car.

Neibart protects the life-force.

Neibart goes to work for life.

Neibart is always working.

Neibart is … *on the job!*

Blackout. Lights up on Jim, hours later. He begins to tap out a drum beat in the air which builds into an epic heavy-metal drum solo punctuated by scat sounds. The solo builds into a double kick-bass roll. He puts the sticks into his mouth and starts to play the cymbals with his hands. The phone rings. Jim is annoyed. He answers.

"Yo ... Hi, look Jerry, I'm right in the middle of something, can I call you back?"

He hangs up the phone and resumes his drum solo; he throws the drumsticks into a screaming crowd. Blackout. Lights up on Jim lying flat on the floor with his feet up on the desk mumbling to himself.

Neibart is it! ... Get that friendly feeling with Neibart ... You're in good hands with Neibart ... At Neibart we try harder ... It's the Neibart generation-n-n-NO, it's NOT the Neibart gen—Shit! You're bringin' me down, Jerry. Bringin' me down, Jericho ... down Jericho?

How does he expect me to get anything done when he keeps interrupting my process? "La-What process would that be La-Jimbob?" My *work* process Jer-i-tol. Man! What kind of a gig is this? Suffocation, dig? I'm writing progressive ad-copy at the bottom of a compost heap ... immersed in dead wood, at the mercy of an army of *suits*, at the mercy of dead wood like old our-Bob over at the central water-cooler who serves no function around here other than to entertain the secretaries and bug me with his inane anecdotes from yesteryear. He's so sweet. He's so funny. He's so ... *useless*, like history, but nobody's got the jam to can 'im ... and you can't get away from the guy and his life-sucking, black-hole *charm*. Charm. Like this ... he'll tap you on the arm over at the central cooler, come in close, and say something like ... "Five days, six nights, hotel and transportation, three fifty-nine return ... Caracas, Venezuela ..." Then point to the *blizzard* out the window. And buttonhole you for the rest of the day, "three fifty-nigh-ine" at the urinal, and then ... "La Cucaracha" in the goddamn elevator.

No more! Not this cat. Got my own water-cooler, man. Don't need your turgid pool, old our-Bob.

And what's all this *zip* jazz ... Man, I get blisters on my eyeballs generating reams of copy only to have the suit genuflect in front of the client's wife while she picks apart the ads I write because they're not ZIPPY enough, or they're *too* ZIPPY, or too FLIPPY, or ZINKY, or BOINKITY, or—and this is a peach—she doesn't like the *cadence*. Cadence. CADENCE!

Jerry, Mrs. West wants sexual intrigue, but we're not selling silk scarves; we're selling *rustproofing*. Neibart rustproofing. Cadence? We're selling tar on steel, Jerry ... black goopy gunk—mind you, it's the best gunk on the market—but it's GUNK just the same. *Zip* does not sell *gunk*.

... Okay. Cadence. Zip. From now on I will write ad copy in stanzas of mellifluous prose ... better still... how 'bout haiku? Here, run this by Lady Confucius ...

>   rust ever sleeping
>   snow on steel salt beneath wheel
>   Neibart seals fenders

Not bad. Seventeen syllables. One idea. Bit of nature. Positively *cascades* off the tongue, dontcha think, Jer? Come on, live a little ... Seven-thirty breakfast meet? Isn't the day long enough?

Blackout. Lights up on Jim hours later doing t'ai chi. It is almost dawn. He paces, shadow boxes, then runs in circles talking to himself.

...... thin ...... ice ...... sweet dreams .... sweet blasting hell. What's it gonna be, Jimbob? Icebreaker Jimbobarooney ...... shit. What time is it? What am I gonna do? What-what-what? I need a drink, no I don't. No, I need some air. Wait a second, is it worth running into ... what about our-Bob? No, he's gone home. Everybody's fucking gone home. GET TO WORK!

... Neibart-Neibart-Neibart ... The *nineties* belong to Neibart ...

Trust your *friendly* ... no ... *Tuesdays* belong to Neibart forever ... It's the Neibart *feeling* ... It's the Neibart *fire.* Catch it! ... It's the *festival* of Neibart savings in February ... The *bonanza* of Neibart bargains ... Bring your family to the February festival of Neibart bonanzas ... no, FUCK! ... it's ... the ... Neibart *funeral.*

Relax. Cool boy. It's not the end of the world. You're not dying ...

He smells his underarm.

I'm dying.

He sniffs again.

Oh no, it's the *protein* sweat. That's the worst. Not a heat sweat, which is innocent and odorless. Not an exercise sweat, which is simple, clear.

He drops to the floor in despair.

No, this sweat, this *protein* sweat, is the smell of the body cannibalizing its own tissue, human decay and death smells ... gangrene, puss, urine, rotting bones, burning hair, the smell of hyperkinetic adolescent sex. The smell of death. The smell of the sewer .... Reuben ... Reuben's smell.

Reuben is a corpse I worked with cleaning sewers for the City of North York. My first job, dig? Yeah, I grok that protein smell fully, super-dads ...

It, the sewers, *it* ... was a joke man. 'Bout the lowest rung on the civic ladder next to dog-catcher. Did squat. Sweet zip. Drove around most of the time. Most days we wouldn't even get out of the truck. Most days we'd just pull into a residential subdivision and kill time ... you know, make left turns for an hour and a half then go for coffee, then right turns for an hour and a half and lunch, then left turns for an hour and a half and coffee, then right turns for an hour and a half and back to the yard to punch out. Big time snooze-o-rama. I was stoned all the time.

He goes back to the desk for a brief touch-and-go landing, then resumes his story.

Jus' killin' time dad ... Spent about a million hours straddling a stick-shift, listening to Donny's curmudgeonly diatribe on my left, with Reuben sleeping against the door on my right. Man, it was uncanny with Reuben: soaking wet, covered in snow, dripping with sweat in the summer—didn't matter—soon as he got in the truck he was out like a light. [*snores*] Donny said it was the "booze-pill" made him conk out like that.

He looks at his typewriter.

Like I said, the dude was only thirty-three, but he looked like an old man—kind of a down-on-his-luck-brother-can-you-spare-a-dime-Bogartesque carpet-bagger—all hangdog and baggy clothes, skin on his face red and shiny as a bell pepper, eyes of a half-dead iguana, and about a pound-and-a-half of grease on his head that somehow managed to whip his jet-black dog-hair into a goofy hill-billy ducktail. One sorry sonovagun boy.

Dig, once he called in sick which meant that for the first time ever I got the window seat. Pulling out of the yard that day, Donny started in about Reuben.

"See that. That's his mark. Don't touch it." Man, it was a coarse flat nebula of grease and dandruff platelets, at head level on the passenger window, about the size of a grapefruit.

"That's where he puts his head when he's sleepin'. Don't wanna be rubbin' against that." It smelled of petroleum and oxidized protein.

Reuben was back again the next day to resume his position … another day older and a darker shade of pathetic. Was a bit of a hoot, though, between Donny and I, with Reuben from then on … watching his eyes close, his head droop, then hit its mark every time. A bit of a hoot.

He looks at his desk.

Dig. Now, the first thing you gotta get used to on the sewers is the smell, which can—and does—make you throw up. But fortunately, what you're standing in is a big toilet … so it's not like you're gonna ruin the boss's drapes or anything. I used to get a kick out of watching the lifers bend over the lip of a manhole and dissect the aroma.

"I dunno, smells like transmission fluid Joe, whaddaya think?"

"Could be. I'm getting a bit of ammonia though, with an oaky, nutty finish."

Connoisseurs, dig?

Yeah, it was a spot of fun, but every now and then I had to make *up* for all that *down* time, dig? My first time down a manhole was a crazy trip, man. Back-story: this was my first full-time job, my first real money. I'm livin' at home with my folks up in the Projects at Jane and Finch just hangin' to cut out, get a car, my own place, a stereo, some great reefer—pounds of it. Kiss the folks, the neighborhood, Ontario Housing Corporation goodbye once and for all … I mean, I was already getting dizzy just thinking about it … In my mind I'd gone to Carolina … But all that dizziness ended strangely the first time I went down.

Right off, it's like *Fantastic Voyage*, like you're an alien grain inside of a huge bustling organ, I thought maybe a little like my father felt the first time he went down into a uranium mine. These things are made for human beings: there's a ladder down, a way in, a place to stand, plumbing, running water … I mean, it felt like *home* … only cooler, air-conditioned.

One time there was a major blockage happening. A wad of something about the size of a small head, like a turban, had formed around a couple of sticks blocking the culvert.

Jim steps into the blue beam of light. All other lights fade out.

Man, this chamber was hell, cramped and barely shoulder-width. I took my spade and broke up the wad to let the sewage flow through, then looked up some fifteen feet … and it was like looking into a crystal ball: Donny and Reuben were sort of convex, fish-eyed against a small circle of blue sky up above.

Reuben sent the bucket down. An eclipse. A black dot growing larger against the blue circle of light. I had to wriggle my body out of the way to let it pass … just inches from my nose. The chamber was so tight that I had to dig backwards between my legs into the channel because of the wall in front of me. It was a big problem. I knew I'd be down there a while. It was hot and wet, and before long I was covered in shit from having to rub against the walls of this thing.

About an hour and fifteen bucket loads later—fifteen mangy, full of sludge and shit, dripping-inches-from-my-nose bucket-loads later—hauled up ever so slowly by Reuben on the chain, I started getting a little *crazy* hunched over like that ... banging my head against the shitty concrete wall. With the top of my head pressed against the inside of a shitty pre-cast concrete cylinder, I lost it, man!

I was trapped inside of the same concrete cylinder that I grew up with in the Projects. A concrete pillar, dig? The "Community Post," a cement cylinder eight-feet high and four-feet wide covered in vertical wooden planks with the words "Community Post" stencilled around the top. Fuck. The pillar is real. I know it. I used to play on it. Pulled the boards off with my bare hands and jammed popsicle sticks—as many as I could fit—into the rusty piss-holes used for cranes and shipping hooks on the side of the thing. It was my frame of reference ... take-the-sidewalk-from-the-underground-till-you-get-to-the-concrete-pillar-turn-left-that's-where-I-live. Why? Not a playground—the place was *teeming* with kids, though. Not a flower box, although the whole complex—tarmac, beige brick, dirty clothes face-to-ugly-face—could use *a little colour.*

No. A gift! A gift to us. *Community Post!* Well thank you, whoever you are, for giving my home a focus. Thank you, patchwork politicians on a three-year mandate. Thank you for giving us poor bastards exactly what we want: food, shelter, education, *lots* of company, and ENTERTAINMENT ...

TV's free 'n' it's right in the living-room; TV's free and it's talking about another planet; TV's free and don't you want more, couldn't you just eat something *right now, why wait?* ... In the dark, in a tube, in a light-tight honeycomb ghetto ... in compounds like salt crystals on a string, *designed* like a crystal, where the vertices at the periphery generate enough energy to keep some semblance of *life* happening in the centre. Some semblance of CRIME, TERROR, SEX, and VIOLENCE. "Well, that's life." Where one needn't *jump* the fence,

cross the field, or *break* through the barrier into the surrounding *life* ...
into the world, into the lives of concerned citizens and communities
and jobs and postings, and community postings, and LOVE, and
PROGRESS, and WORK, and the chance of INFINITY ... in
a sewer.

In ... a ... sewer. Losin' it big time by this point. My head is
spinning with junk. My eyes are ringing with sweat as I fill the last
bucket and yell for Reuben to haul the sucker out. Can't breathe or
move much. Head is pounding like a drum. Reuben's pullin' that last
bucket up ever so slowly. It dangles for the last time just in front of my
nose. It's over my head. I hate myself.

Black circle against the blue sky getting smaller. I can stretch.
Straighten out.

*He wipes his eye with the back of his hand, wipes his mouth on his
sleeve, and gives a holler of relief.*

Trace the circumference of the cylinder with my hands. Slow
vertical tilt. Watch the bucket getting smaller, revealing Reuben up
top grimacing terribly and straining on the last few feet of chain. I sing
the theme to "I Dream of Genie."

He hums a few bars.

Trouble! Reuben collapses. The bucket comes down, bounces off
a rung, then dumps all over me. That smell, *protein*, salt, quick taste
of shit. The sound of steel against concrete. Sparks ... WHACK!

Jim collapses, covering his head.

Dig. Now *that* ... is a protein sweat. Rueben's pickaxe from up top
caught me right here.

He points to his forehead.

Twenty-three stitches. Old Reuben-ola had had a heart attack up
there. Thirty-three years old. LOSER.

He gets up, moves over to the desk, and sits down.

That's when I got into advertising. Actually, there's more to it than
that. Probably something to do with "Bewitched" ...'n' Darren ...'n'
I dug Sam 'n' all that ... And besides, I'd memorized just about every
commercial I'd ever seen ... I wanted to get out of the fucking Projects.

And I did. And I wanted to make some cash. And I am. But … mostly … I just wanted to make a *mark*, and it was not going to be a grease spot the size of a grapefruit on the passenger window of a black-and-yellow truck making left turns on a cloudy day in North York!

He gravely rubs his forehead scar.

But babies, lemme tell you, *this* is nothing like "Bewitched." What am I gonna do? I'm fucked.

He wipes his forehead, then covers his mouth with the same hand.

That's it.

He tastes his finger.

Yes. That's it!

He begins to type and dance in his chair.

Yes. Big time. Killer-killer-killer. Thank you very much!

Jim pulls the sheet of paper out of the typewriter, gets up, and starts to walk in slow motion as if underwater against the tide. All lights fade to black except for the blue spot which is up full. He stops at the edge of the beam, as if at the water-cooler once again, and draws a drink. A message comes over the intercom. Jim is dopey, in another world. He slowly moves into the blue light and sits in a squat on the floor while reading the typewritten page.

[*Message*] Jim. Jerry. Breakfast was a smash big guy. *Should've been there.* Where's the fucking copy? Forget it … your ass is grass, pal. [*volume begins to fade*] Should have your head examined chump … Yoo-hoo, anybody home? … How's the water, fuckhead? … Live it up while you still can, because that thin ice has just broken, pal … Oh, by the way, guess who phoned from New York this morning? … long distance … three guesses … Well, it wasn't Madonna … Getting any warmer? … Zbigniew Brzezinski? Uh-uh … Howard Stern? … Nope … Give up? … I'll tell ya …

As the message fades, the sound of a slickly produced radio commercial comes up full. Jim is ecstatic as he listens and recites the text of the ad along with the announcer. The announcer's voice is Jim's, only richer, with a backing soundtrack.

[*Announcer*] Why have *we* risen to the top? Because Neibart is the only rust protection worth its salt!

Let Neibart work for *you* ... work for you ... work for you ... work ...

Jim is serene. He falls back on his hands. The sound of waves breaking on the beach is heard.

JEWEL
Joan MacLeod

JEWEL
Joan MacLeod

Peace River Valley, Valentine's Day, 1985. Marjorie, a thirty-year-old woman, is inside her mobile home, standing in her nightgown, beside a full bucket of fresh milk.

Valentines through the ages. You are six years old and folding up this gigantic piece of white tissue paper until it's the size of your hand. Then attacking it with these dull little scissors. Chopping the corners off, driving a hole right through the middle. But when you unfold it: pure magic. Triangles and diamonds pin-wheeling out from the centre. A thousand crescent moons. So you cut out this heart and paste it onto red cardboard. Print his name very carefully. Then your own name, right alongside. It's so special you can barely stand it. Only, when you get to school, you discover that every girl in your class has done the very same thing. And the most popular boy in the world just stuffs all those valentines into his desk without saying a word. By the end of the afternoon you realize that some of those hearts have turned into paper airplanes. Some into spitballs. Valentines through the ages. All right.

You are thirteen and at the Claresholme Teen Stomp and everything is dumb: the red punch, the heart-shaped plates, Claresholme, the records that are all old and country. But the dumbest thing ever is Lucy who you're down here visiting.

Lucy is fifteen and what your mother calls mature: meaning she has big tits, smokes, and is also stupid. She visited you last month and was afraid to get on an escalator. But it gets worse. Because right now, Lucy is dancing with some wonderful boy and she's danced ten thousand times since she got here. You haven't been asked once. You also don't care a damn, but there goes Lucy again, right up to the boys lining the rear wall of the gym. She tells them to go dance with her cousin Marjorie. That's you. And it's like all your nerves have gone electric, and the air too. Nobody moves. They're just lined up like some kind of firing squad, a big string of monkeys, and now all you can look at is their boots and the dumb floor. Lucy says please, and that you're an orphan. You die. It also isn't true, but no matter how many times you tell dumb-ass Lucy, she still wants to hear about orphanages and that.

Then you notice it—black cowboy boots two feet in front of you. And someone you're afraid to look at is asking you to dance. Okay. It's a slow song. You decide to kill yourself but there you are now. You can do it. Damp hands bumping together. His neck is red as a brick. He speaks. "Where you from?" And you're still afraid to look at him but by some miracle you manage it. "Calgary."

Then, two perfect minutes, moving ever-so-small, one side to another. You just want to take a peek. His eyes are flat and brown as a frozen puddle. And staring straight at your cousin Lucy. Suddenly he looks clean into you and tells you he wouldn't live in Calgary if it was the last place on earth. And it feels so stupid and mean. That's fine, you tell him. That's just great. Then you explain how the Beatles love Calgary and that they're moving there next month.

Everything changes. He is looking at you special. Some of the others are too. Questions come from everywhere. When? What would they do that for? Have you met them? And for the first time, *you* are right at the centre of a very perfect world. Invented, but still perfect. Valentines through the ages. You are thirteen years old and dizzy with love.

Two years later, you're at a sleep-over. Nine other girls there in flannel nighties. You've all arrived with an inch of liquor—stolen from your folks' rye and Scotch and gin bottles.

You mix this up with a twenty-sixer of Tahiti Treat and sit cross-legged in a circle, passing the bottle around. Every time you take a sip, you tell a truth—how you went to second with so and so. Who it is you're really in love with this week. It's all marvellous. It's all made up. You're half-sick with pink liquor and trying to French-inhale Peter Jackson cigarettes. You light a candle and listen to Joni Mitchell sing "Both Sides Now" eleven times in a row. You're delirious with sadness. You phone up a dozen boys, say something absolutely filthy, then hang up the phone. This liquor in your gut. This tingling in your legs. You are fifteen years old and sick with love.

Valentines through the ages marches on. You've been going to the university and are all grown up. You have a boyfriend—this range-management student who comes from the Arctic Circle. Well nearly. Range management: the choreography ... of cows. You met in February but now it's August. You're camping near his folks' place in northern Alberta. You're out of your territory. And you love it. Because there is something about him and this place that's like coming home after a long, long journey. And it's true in a way, coming home.

The inside of your blue nylon tent sweats in the morning sun. Through this gauzy half-moon of a window, mosquitoes crash around, two little kids collect beer bottles in a potato sack. Eat Oh Henry bars at six a.m.

The cattle arranger, with his sleeping bag zipped up with yours, is enjoying the sleep of the dead. You are enjoying this chance to examine his face. High cheekbones, lashes like a woman's, black hair sticking out in a million directions. Out of your territory. And last night, at six minutes to midnight, he asked you to stay out of your territory forever. Marriage. Marry me, Marjorie. There's this land he's wanting to buy and no money for cattle yet but the oil patch is right around the corner. He's got his welder's papers. The money will flow. Maybe five winters of working out, then full-time farming or ranching or whatever. He talks about buying a milk cow and [*picking up bucket*] you nearly pass out with the romance of it. One of his hands is against his heart as if he were taking a pledge. And the other one is meandering up your

nightgown. Valentines through the ages.
A country song starts up softly on the radio.
Six years later now. You're still crazy with love.

•

She turns up the radio and while singing along, she pours milk from the bucket into two large glass jars and places them in the fridge. She removes another milk jar from the fridge and skims the cream off the top. She listens to "Message Time." She drinks beer.

Christ I'm thirsty. Thirsty for everything except milk. Your dad made this beer. I mean, it doesn't taste terrible but it sort of leaves fur on your teeth. No one can really make good beer, they all just think they can, are dying for you to drink this flat stuff that's clear as mud. Oh well, Harry. You know what they say to do with failed beer—drink it.

[*radio*] And that's it for "Country Countdown" tonight. Happy Valentine's. And you better snuggle up to the one you love because according to Environment Canada, it's a chilly thirty-three below in Fort St. John tonight and it looks like it's going to dip down even lower.

You hear that Harry? Cozy up.

[*radio*] And now "Message Time." The link between you and your loved ones. A community service brought to you by CKNL North Country.

You'll have to stay quiet for a minute. Think you can manage that?

[*radio*] To Connie Brown. Happy Valentine's. Wish I could be there. With love from Stanley. To Cynthia,

Ruthie and Jason. Home on Saturday. Love from your daddy, Jason Senior. To Beatrice George. Call Credit Union immediately. Very important.

Poor Beatrice. They're broke.

[*radio*] To Billy Gustafson. Your cattle are out and in Chevron property south of Fish Creek. Remove at once. To Marjorie Clifford.

Yes, Sir.

[*radio*] Your order is in at Buckerfields. Will be delivered on the seventeenth.

Well it's about time.

[*radio*] To Rebecca Cochrane. Not coming home as planned. Will call on Saturday. Aubrey Cochrane. To Sally Harper. Happy Valentine's. You are my one and only. Love Frank.

She turns off the radio.
You know Harry? I was listening to "Message Time." When was it? Christmas Eve. Years ago. You were working for Esso out on Cotcho Lake. I'd just come up from school and missed you by half a day. I mean, that first year of being married we must've spent all of ten minutes together. So me and Deb are drinking egg-nog and listening to the messages. They're gushy as hell. "To Ruth in Dawson who I met in the bar last night. I love you more than life itself." That sort of thing. Even Debbie got something half-way romantic from Walter. And I'm sitting there waiting, then getting worried that maybe you forgot. Then realizing you'd never do that and getting very excited and it comes: "To Marjorie Clifford. Merry Christmas. The calf will be

needing her wormshot on the twenty-seventh." Period. Was I pissed off, Harry? I threw my egg-nog at the radio. And then I start to stand up for you. Defend your good name. Telling Debbie how you're really very romantic but in a private sort of way. Which was true enough, I suppose. But Jesus. Wormshot.

Outside, a dog barks.

No! You've been outside for all of two seconds. Go chase a weasel. That dog, Harry. Remember going down to Beaverlodge to buy him? Staying in that very lousy motel called Shady Glenn or Palm Grove, some prairie name like that. And the guy with the litter's explaining that this dog's part wolf. I mean, there's no person north of Edmonton that doesn't own a dog part wolf. It can be purebred chihuahua and people round here would still say, "Careful. That dog's got wolf in it." So we buy this thing that looks like a guinea pig and in a fit of inspiration we name him ... "Wolf."

And on the way home, he's sitting on the floor of the truck, quivering for a hundred miles. He hasn't changed. I mean, he's big now. In fact he's fat. His only goal in life seems to be figuring out a way of never going outside. I think Wolf would rather live with my folks in the city, eat canned dog food. Lie around all day on their wall-to-wall.

I meant to explain why I never came home last night. No, Harry. I was not out fooling around. I was at Debbie's. She put the kids to bed and we made this massive supper. Walter had just gone back to the bush, and I guess the guy that picked him up had this bag of shrimp—fresh from the coast that morning. So we shucked them or whatever the hell it is you do with shrimp. And we made this white-wine sauce. Then drank what was left over, which was about a gallon each. Deb's doing fine. I mean her and Walter are in debt over this new tractor like you wouldn't believe, but they're making out. Where was I? Deb's, last night—right.

So we're just sitting there talking and getting very drunk and there's this knock at the door. It's not even eight-thirty but feels around midnight and I'm thinking, Shit—it's your dad. Then it dawns on me

that Munroe's never knocked on a door in his life. He just comes in
and yells: "I'm here! Where's the coffee?"

Well. Guess who? Guess who wear sensible shoes and overcoats
and more than likely have a good case of pimples on the go? It's the
Mormons. Come all the way from the state of Utah to bring us the
word of God. I don't get up off the couch. That is to say, I'm incapable
of getting off the couch. And I'm thinking: This is great. We actually
live in a place that needs missionaries. I mean, I know they do their
business in the cities too, but I'm pretending the north is like darkest
Africa and that Deb and me have rings through our noses and these
big black breasts hanging out front. Like torpedoes. Like *National
Geographic*. And the younger one. He's all of eighteen or something.
He asks me if I've been saved and I tell him: "UNGOWA!"

These two are very embarrassed. They pack up their stuff, give us
some pamphlets, head out into forty-below in this little Japanese car.
We laugh about it all for a while longer then end up feeling bad. I mean,
it's like being drafted, it's something they have to do.

I stayed overnight. Which is something I do quite often when
Walter's off in the bush. We sleep in the same bed and hug and that,
but it's not gay or anything. It's just very nice when you're on your own
to have other people close by. And we understand one another quite
well, Debbie and me.

Outside, a dog barks.

No! Go make some friends. That dog. Wolf must've had something very horrible happen to him when he was real young. Old Wolf
and me, eh? Or maybe before we got hold of him that guy beat him.
Or his mother tried to eat him. Yeah, that suits Wolf. He's just hanging
around with all his brothers and sisters, trying to have a good time, and
his mother tries to eat him.

Remember when we tried to take him hunting for lynx? Wolf
is obsessed with thoughts of his own death and refuses to leave the
truck. Your wife, who is me, is also obsessed with death but is equally
obsessed with making this marriage work. Lucky for you. The shits for
me. How's your beer there, Harry? You're looking a little pale around

the edges tonight.

Wanna dance? C'mon dance with me.

She turns on the radio and dances to a fiddle waltz.

It's Valentine's night at the Ranch Cabaret. We're dancing to a band called Hot Lightning. Dancing tight and slow. Your shirt smelling like cedar and diesel. Smoke.

We've been ice fishing all day. The sky just getting heavy with snow when we leave for town, the dark coming in. By the time we get there, these big flakes. Everything pretty as Christmas cards.

Your folks are there. Your mother waltzing bolt upright and scared, shy at being in town. Your eyes in her face—that wonderful jade. Munroe leading her, proud and near drunk. His arm around me at the table for the first time. Telling how when you were little you stole his truck and sunk it in the lake. All of us proud and near drunk. This mirror ball's sprinkling light all around the room and across your face. We've just gone into life-time debt for buying the land and this trailer. I believe we are perfectly happy. That is to say, *I* am perfectly happy.

[*radio*] And that's our request waltz for this evening and goes out to Mr. and Mrs. R. Johnson. And now more easy listening on CKNL, your north country station.

She turns off the radio.

And on the way home in the pickup, all four of us squeezed inside. Your dad says: "Look at them cheeks of Marjorie's. All glowy and red. I like that in a woman. Looks freshly slapped." And I think, Great. I've married into a family of insane people. But I figured it out pretty quick. This father and son. When you went down, Munroe was the only one that didn't mind my staying quiet. That could keep comfortable with that. They're still looking out for me, Harry. They're both doing fine … that was nice. You are some dancer. In fact, you're wearing me out.

Today I was at the Co-op in town, buying groceries and that. This kid is pushing the buggy. I think he's one of Beatrice's boys, but then it's hard to keep track. And this other kid who's working there yells from across the parking lot: "Hey Mitchell! What's got four legs, is three hundred feet tall and goes down on Newfoundland?" And this kid Mitchell looks real embarrassed. You can just tell he's praying his buddy over there will shut up. Because old Mitchell knows who I am. I mean, I am one hell of a famous widow, Harry. We're talking *Time* magazine. Reporters all the way from Texas braving forty-below and gravel roads just to get a picture of me and Wolf. And this kid yells it again: "Mitch? What's a thousand feet tall, has four legs and goes down on Newfoundland?" And I end up apologizing! Saying I've always been one to make jokes about anything and everything. This idiot, he yells it out: "The *Ocean Ranger*!" ... Old Mitch practically has a heart attack right on the spot. By the time he's got the truck loaded, it looks like he's decided to be a priest.

You know, I always thought it was a ridiculous name—the *Ocean Ranger*. Like a speedboat full of Girl Guides. And when you first got the job, I just panicked because I didn't know how to imagine you there. That's important, Harry. It's important to women who have husbands who work out to know how to imagine them in a place. I mean, all I had to do was drive into town or walk to your dad's to see a rig on the ground. To set you somewhere. And usually you were just up around Nelson and I knew that if I really went squirrelly I could jump in the truck and find you. But Newfoundland! That is practically four thousand miles away. Right from the start it felt wrong. I mean, we're supposed to be farmers and there you are out on this floating thing in the middle of some ocean. The Atlantic Ocean.

And when I got the call that you'd gone down, all I could think was that you were drifting. That you might sink for a minute, then get caught up in kelp or some current. And set off again. That you'd never settle. You'd never arrive on something solid again. And I thought about that, Harry, non-stop. Thought about that for fourteen months without a break.

Then I'm living with my folks. And my mother, she signs me up for some god-awful thing called a grieving workshop. All this group stuff going on that just makes me mental. I mean, this is a very private business if you ask me. Everyone wanting me to come to terms with this. Those sort of expressions are another thing that make me crazy. They're just pieces of air. And all I'm really wanting is for everyone just to leave me alone. Some church ran this thing and they're tossing scripture around like a volleyball. I mean, as if that's going to fill my bed or help me make payments.

Okay. We got our money since then. But I mean, this isn't some cheque that just showed up in the mail one day. This is after two years of drawn-out bullshit with lawyers and Louisiana accents. Every time you open the paper or a magazine or letter, more stuff about the *Ocean Ranger*. What I want, through the whole inquiry, is to narrow it down to one man. We couldn't even narrow it down to one company. But it's still what I keep wanting, just pare it all down. Leave me one man. Up there on the top floor, behind some marble-top desk. I want him to say, "Yup, I'm your boy, it was my fault. My fault about the design flaws, the lack of survival suits, my fault about the evacuation procedure and that the lifeboats would've gone down in a lake. I'm your boy. Not that I meant any of it but I sure as hell did screw things up. You think safety is top priority but it gets lost somewhere along the way. You got tested like that and completely fail the test. I screwed up. Big time."

I don't want to cause this man any harm. But I would like to place him aboard a drilling platform, after midnight in February. Over a hundred miles from the coast of Newfoundland. An alarm calls this man from sleep and onto a deck that is pitch black and tipped over fifteen degrees and all covered in ice. The wind is screaming. Salt water and snow pelt his face. Everybody is running around and nobody knows what to do. He is in his pyjamas and being lowered in a life-raft with twenty other men. Into a sea of fifty-foot waves.

Then I would reach down and lift that man up from this terrible place just like the hand of God come to save him. Remove him from all that terror and certain death. I place him somewhere warm and dry. Relief here and family. Take his shivering hand inside my own and turn his hand over and over and over. Until he sees it. Palm up and attached and staring straight at him. His hand is the hand of God and he could have gathered them all up. Saved eighty-four men from the North Atlantic. He chose not to.

And I don't care who owns you, mister. I don't care if you're ODECO or Mobil Oil, a fed or provincial. My sadness, my husband's death—it was handmade by someone.

You know, at first, right after, I thought my insides were made out of paper. Very white paper. I would even walk carefully because I thought something might rip inside. Where am I? Right. We were talking about the grieving workshop. I go off in a corner with a Bible just so they won't bug me. And I actually found something that made sense: the book of Genesis, page one.

> Let the waters teem with living creatures and let the
> birds fly above the earth within the vault of Heaven.
> And so it was, God created great whales.

Well. I hold onto those lines like a goddamn life-jacket. I start pretending you are this very fine whale with the sun on your back and just having the life of Riley in general.

You see, Harry. What I loved about that is I'm thinking you have no heart and no memory. I mean, I know that whales have warm blood and a heart and that; but it's not the sort that makes you barge through everything like some open nerve. And I thought, that's the ticket. No heart and no memory. I thought that was about the best way to live that anyone had ever come up with.

Very crazy stuff. Well, old Jewel.

She's looking at her ring.

You don't have a heart and you don't have a memory anymore. I suppose that part's the truth. But I do.

Even this summer. I'd just moved back here and everyone was so worried that I'd go crazy again. And sure enough. That's when I started having these little night-time chats of ours. But it wasn't like now.

I'd tell you about the kid driving grain truck. The one helping out with harvest. I'd bring him out these sandwiches at noon. Because of the heat he would take off his shirt and this line of sweat would sort of weep down his belly. We'd lean against the wheel of the truck for shade and drink ice-water out of a thermos, passing it back and forth.

And I told you I took him to the granary. The air is very cool in there. We take off all our clothes without looking at one another. He folds up his jeans and makes a pillow like for under my head. The floor boards and loose seed cut into the backs of my legs. Everything smells very clean and very dry. Like gravel. And I mean, this kid is really inside. And he's moving above me and on me and all around me. And it's like there are these thousands of minnows that have just been sleeping under my skin forever and all at once they rush for the surface. And it's, it's ... bravery. And I think, Fuck you, Harry. Dying and leaving me is about the most gutless thing anyone could ever do.

All those stories about that kid driving grain truck? I made every one of them up. Just wanting to make you jealous. Just trying to make you mad. Trying every trick in the book to get some kind of response. I mean, he was barely seventeen or something. That's called the "angry phase," Harry. I think I'm starting to come out of it though.

I'll tell you a story that's true. There is a guy teaching school here that I've gone out with a few times. Some dinners in town. Last week, we went to a play in Dawson Creek. He's a very nice man. Sort of shy. Or maybe it's lack of character. No. There's something quite good there.

He comes from Vancouver, which is kind of an excuse, but you know what he reminds me of? Me. When I first got here. All set to live on roots and berries. Grow our own vegetables and animals and furniture. Seeing your folks' place for the first time I remember thinking: This is great. Big old log house, smoke in the chimney. Your mum's real warm to me and she's making bread or canning moose or something equally terrific. But Munroe. It's afternoon and he's watching television. He doesn't even look up when we're introduced. Rude old bugger, I think, but hating it just as much that he's watching "The Mod Squad" instead of trimming wicks or milking some creature. We leave. And on the way to the truck I can hear him yelling at his grandson: "Don't lick that cat. You'll get leukemia."

His name is Gordon, Harry. This school-teacher guy. Gord. I don't like his name one bit. Monday night I was over at his place for the first time. It's all cleaned up, which it probably is anyway, but I still like it, this making me feel special. He's cooked jackfish, wrapped up in some kind of leaves. Baked apples. His place is all cedar and just half-done because he bought from Wilson who went bankrupt, like you said he would. Gordon is determined with me. Serious as a machine.

The smell of wood makes me crazy. First winter with you in that cabin? Because we're just married, I don't care a damn at first that we've built this little box to live in with wood that's green as lettuce. And that you stick to the wall every time you touch it. That there's no power or water and nearly no windows. That making coffee means half a day's work. But then I begin to notice everything—nothing is smooth, it's dark all the time, my clothes are alive with sawdust and the walls are alive with sap. So it starts. Small at first but eventually this enormous longing. Desperate and ashamed. I want to live in a trailer. I need to live in a mobile home.

Gordon asked me to stay overnight. But I didn't. Or maybe I'm telling you lies again. Maybe I got him drunk on rye and Coke: sex-crazed widow flattens newcomer. You know I don't think I ever lied to you once the whole time we were together. But now—Jesus. I did this when I was little, too, make up stuff to put in my diary.

But this, Harry, is the goods on Gordon. This is a story that's true. I didn't stay overnight but I did go to bed with him. I'm just telling you, not asking permission. It was all right. The best part being those very pure times when thinking stops. Just touch, react. But the flipside is thinking at a million miles an hour. How it is still your body that I know better than my own. How being held by living arms, hands, brings home what a body must be like lifeless. All the women wanted the bodies found. All the families of the victims. I never thought it'd be like that. You'd think lost would be better than dead. A strand of hope, invisible, thin. But it makes you crazy, never knowing a hundred percent. It was way harder in the long run.

I am glad of meeting Gordon. Gord. I'm not saying you two would've hit it off in a huge way but I do like him, Harry. It's quite wonderful to have that small leap in the gut again when I know he's coming over, that kind of thing.

Wolf thinks of him as a minor god. Just lies at his feet with his paws up in the air like he's waiting to be sacrificed or trying to communicate telepathically that he's trapped in a trailer with a maniac.

Wolf and me went for a walk on Sunday down to the lake. You know what he's doing? Sniffing around and making circles. Peeing on everything in sight and acting like a general lunatic. I'm explaining to him that it's February, for God's sake, and all the bears are asleep, and to quit being so damn antsy. Then it dawns on me—he's still looking for your scent. I mean, it's been three years but Wolf's still after your scent. And of course, everything is froze solid and you can't smell a thing, but whatever. Wolf is thinking you're around every corner. Maybe skidding out birch for the woodpile or ice fishing or I don't know what dogs think.

So we get to the shore and there's these three kids from the reserve skating out on the lake. Boys, maybe seven years old. Needless to say, Wolf is scared of them. He stands on the shore rocking back and forth, quivering like a race horse. These kids are banging around a soccer ball with these big plastic baseball bats. Wolf is dying to get out there. He wants to run and bark and fool around with those kids. Just be a regular dog. But he can't do it. He just stays there and yelps, does a few circles around me. And for once I don't give him shit. I just pat his head and let him be. Poor old Wolf. Just wanting to be a regular dog. Everyone else wanting him to be that way too. But Wolf's got a few things figured out. He knows his limits. Feels real good about those pats on the head.

So we just sat there for a long time, watching those kids skate and the sun going down. I love that time of day in winter. Used to be I hated the night coming, but it's all right now. I mean it's not out and out terror any more. Not all the time at least.

Just a few more things, Harry. Then I'm going to bed. They finally got me going to another widow's group at the Elks twice a month. In Newfoundland they've got a group just for *Ranger* families and it's supposed to be great. But this bunch. I don't know. There's a couple of new ones there who are in a very bad way and it is good to talk things out with them. Support your sisters, that kind of stuff. But there's this one woman there, she's from town, works at the Bay, around your mum's age. And she says that widowhood, it's like checking into a motel for one night. One night that lasts the rest of your life. I mean, let's face it. The Elks is about the most depressing way to spend an evening that's ever been invented.

Then this lady says that nothing feels like home any more. It's like we're all just waiting to get to another place. And I thought: Right. Not that I think I'm going to another place. It's just that it feels like that— the waiting.

You know how when you stay in a motel everything looks different? The bed, the pattern on the carpet. Even some dumb old TV-show that you've watched every night of your life seems nearly exotic when you're in a motel. Very new.

Or those summers in Calgary before I met you. I had this really terrible job in an insurance office. Really punching the clock. Working in this little room without any windows. But every Friday at ten o'clock I'd have to go to the Treasury Branch. And I'd step out onto Centre Street and the world looked different. The bus-stop right out front, even the way people walked. Everything transformed and clear and spooky, all at the same time.

So maybe that lady has a point. But she hasn't figured out the whole thing completely. I mean, the world certainly does feel like a motel just in that everything looks so different. But you know, Harry? Part of me likes that. It makes a walk with Wolf or just making dinner nearly miraculous.

I know. When we went to visit my folks and on the way down we stayed in Edmonton in that rather swanky place. We fooled around, practically overdosed on cable TV. And we got room service for breakfast, opened the curtains up really wide, and there's this apartment across the way. We watched all these people run around and get ready for work. The window's acting like a magnifying glass, everyone looks bigger than life. Even the air is defined and lively, just sparkling with light.

Okay. Sometimes I do feel like I'm just visiting here or stuck on the shore like old Wolf. Not really able to get involved in anything. And very, very scared of going out on the ice again. But I'll tell you something.

I am beginning to feel again and part of me just loves staying in a motel. So maybe it's because I'm so much younger than most of them at the Elks but I'm not just waiting, not any more. Not held down by that sadness. I mean, I know it's part of me but it can't run the show forever.

She looks at her ring.

What do you think of that? My perfect Jewel.

And what that lady from the Bay doesn't know or anybody else is that you got through to me. Valentines through the ages. 1982.

You are about to slam face-first into such a storm. But not yet. Maybe it's still quiet out there, just for a moment. I hope so. Wolf and me have been down at the barn, checking on things. I mean the animals would have to be doing something absolutely bizarre for us to see anything wrong, but whatever. It's just before noon. I come in the kitchen, the radio's on. And there it is. First one out of the gate: a Valentine's message. Short and sweet and probably sent the day before but meant to be mine now. I carry it around inside, hold onto it all day. It sends me to bed warm. Loud and clear. You love me. You got through.

Then late that night another message, hand delivered by an embarrassed RCMP. The rig has been evacuated. The constable offers to wait with me. They will call again in an hour on his car radio. I apologize for not having a phone, for all his trouble. I make tea. Wolf has gone wild. He can't believe his good luck. All this activity in the middle of the night.

Evacuated. What does it mean? Bombed-out villages, buildings.

Living in an air-raid shelter. Living. He has left the rig and is in a lifeboat. There is a bad storm, a fifty-foot sea.

How high? Like a grain elevator, fir tree. No. Too tall. I know. Me and Lucy are at Uncle Ray's, spitting down from the loft to where the cowshit is: "You kids get the hell down from there. You want to fall fifty feet and land on your heads?" That's when I know. Anything that big and made out of water is a deadly thing. But don't think it or it will be true and my fault. My legs are weak as bread. I grab hold of the counter and the kitchen floor moves like a raft underneath me. And there you are, clear as ice for a single moment. In a little boat, wearing that awful parka from Sears.

The horn on the police car blasts out of nowhere. Twice. Wolf and the police go to get the message on the radio phone. And I know it again but don't believe it for a second. Not on your life. I should go to Munroe's because your mother believes in God and I don't. I didn't mean it. The RCMP catches me down on my knees on the cold linoleum. He shakes his head. This is very hard for him, trying to tell me that my husband is dead.

But he doesn't tell me that. He says the rig has gone down and two of the lifeboats, but the third boat it still out there. That means you. I know it.

But then this cop tells me they said not to have much hope. And I slap him across the back of the head.

I should have listened to him. It would've made the next few days a lot easier. All that waiting and glued to the radio. I should go to Newfoundland but I'm afraid of flying now, of moving, of leaving the ground. Then the names of the dead are just read over the radio, in Munroe's kitchen. Confirmed. At the service, someone from your company is there telling me how sad this has made him. What I don't realize at the time is he can't apologize because it might make them liable. If you'd worked for Mobil itself, they wouldn't even have tried to make contact after the accident. Just hear it on the news with everyone else.

It doesn't start for a week or so because, I suppose, I'm in shock, but

I relive your death every day for a long, long time. You're in the lifeboat
that nearly made it. That's what all the widows think. We think alike.
I can't go through that stuff anymore.

Nearly midnight, Harry. Valentines through the ages is coming to
a close. Remember how I told you that first message sent me to bed
warm? It's still there. A little bit.

She removes the ring from her finger and leaves it on the table.

But wearing this forever. I don't know. I don't think it's such a great
idea any more. Does that make sense? I hope so. It does for me and I
guess that's the important part.

It always felt so mean that it had to be Valentine's Day. That it was
the last day you were alive. But I'm not so sure any more.

This is what I'm sure of. You loved me. You got through.

LOVESONG
Robin Fulford

LOVESONG
Robin Fulford

A man, mid-twenties, sits in a chair.

Born 1954 in Newfoundland.
I think.

I'm getting used to this.
Got any bug juice?

She was a vindictive tyrant, a drill master.
She wanted me to be Dumby in the corner.
She'd wait until I was asleep and then beat me with a broom handle.
See! See!
Hey, a good lickin'.
Hey, ya, always lookin' for a good lickin'.

Bullshit.

My twin died at birth of spinal meningitis.
The other, the veins exploded in his head.
Then the epileptic died.
The last one, I don't even know what he looks like.

Slut, bitch, motherfucker.

Motherfucker!

No, I only meant to stun her, right?
Knock her out for twenty minutes so I could have my sexual relations.

So help me God.

I was thirteen at Queen Street Mental, fifteen at the group home.
In 1971, I was charged with nineteen counts of break and enter.
I was eighteen then.
Had lit thirteen or fourteen fires.
Felt like a surge when a transformer burns out.

The same as I felt when I knocked on the door of Sheryl Gardner.

I did seven-and-a-half years on the B&E's.
Got out January 15, 1981 around nine-thirty a.m.
On July 2, 1981, I went to the apartment building.

I wanted to find out about girls, right?
I could never understand them and I hadn't had any nooky since before the pen.
I got these feelings I didn't understand, and 'cause it was warm out and they were wearin' less and I hadn't seen anything for a long time, out of it ...

There's the criminal side and that tells me how to do it, and the mental side is the sexual thing, right?
And in between I was undecided.
So I had to do research to find out what was wrong,
so I could bump into one of them and pretend I knew her.
She would be comfortable, 'cause I had the drop on her.

I need to see how they are put together,
how their sex organs are attached to their bodies.

I taped their voices, right, and listened for imperfections.
Maybe fifteen of them.
But with Sheryl Gardner I didn't have time.
Like I had to do it then.
The voices wouldn't let me wait.

I was automatically transformed into a Bell repairman by the voices.
It was like "Mission Impossible" and, ah, I was playing all the parts,
right?
I could even hear the theme music in my head, out of it type of thing.

Then one side would be sayin', "That's one, get her, get her, follow
her," and the other side would say, "Careful now, be careful."
And I became confused.
The mental side would say, "You need somethin', out of it, isn't she
nice," and the other side, "Get out of here, you've been too long."
And the mental side would say, "Try the other building."

I was angry,
goin' off like fireworks on the Queen's birthday,
the whole gamut.
The halls would go wobbly and the sound waw! waw! waw!
And I had this surging up, right?
I was really pissed but I didn't know why, right?
And the voices, "You gotta get it, you gotta get it tonight."

So I went into the lobby.
The door was open 'cause people were movin'.

When Sheryl walked in it was like floating.

I was entranced and just slid in right beside her.
She pushed her button and I did the one right above, out of it.
There were two monkey-do assholes too.
She's smilin' and gives this little girlie sneeze.
And I says, "I hope you're not allergic to me."
She gets out and I start my stop watch.
One of the monkey-do's says, "She can be allergic to me anytime."
Yeah, yeah, yeah.

The next floor comes so I run to the fire door and down the stairs
to her floor and meet this crumb-snatcher.
The voices said nothin' about no crumb-snatcher, out of it.
All I wanted to do was bash him.

He went on before I could do anything and in her hall the sound's
goin' WAW! WAW! WAW! all the echoes five times as loud.
And I was listenin' for the click.
The door click.

But the crumb-snatcher screwed it up and I wanted to bash him.
No click.
Then I saw all these cards he'd been deliverin' and the criminal side
went ding! Out of it.
Cards were at all the doors but two of 'em.
There weren't no mail slots in that building but I could smell her
perfume at 1611.
Two kinds, just like in the elevator.

So I go back to the lobby, get her name and go over to Dirty Louie's
to phone her and tell her I need to fix her phone.
It's spittin', out of it, and the spots feel like snowballs.

She had an answering service so I went back.

It's like I'm watchin' things on TV, out of it.
Distant, right?

The mental thing is sayin', "It's really gonna to be nice, out of it," and the other says, "Careful, careful," and I can't figure out why I'm there.

In the elevator I keep thinkin', where do I know her from and why did she smile at me?

And when I get out I think of the crumb-snatcher and everything starts clicking back again.
My brain's clouded like it was tryin' to jump out or something.

I knocked on the door, authoritative, like a real Bell man, out of it.
It won't be long now.

Sorry to disturb you, Ma'am.
I'm from the Bell Telephone and we're havin' some trouble.
Yes, but the output transformer has something gone and it's makin' others ring on the same trunk line.
Nothin' to worry about though.
I'll have it fixed in a jiffy.

I keep thinkin', why doesn't she open the door?
Does she know me?
Then she scoops up a little black cat and that was why.
It was as if I was hearin' myself say everything, out of it.

And I was thinkin' how nice she looks, and I gotta find out what girls have.
I want her to hold me and say everything is okay, out of it.

"Get her, get her now."

"No, she'll help you."
"She should have her hole sewn up, she's a tramp, out of it."

Ah, a Contempra.
Well, we've had some problems with them, ya know.
People talkin' to their buddies or boyfriend and then knockin' it off the bed and not gettin' it fixed.
I might have a longer cord in the truck.
Here kitty.
Play with something that's not, ya know, live with electricity, out of it.
It'll get fried with them hundred volts.
I seen the remains of something that happened like that.
I used to work with animals and all the things I saw would make you sick.
People don't know how to take care of things.

Oh sure, she's a nice little cat.
And she's got a nice home.
This is a nice apartment.
You must have a good job.
You looked dressed up to go out.
I can come back later if you're expecting someone.

It sounded like thunder, out of it.
That's all. Bang! Bang!

I couldn't remember the trip, the trip up with the hammer, out of it.

I was just gonna kinda stun her, give her a little whack.
I was gonna tie her up then with the cable that I let the kitty play with, out of it, right?
Just tie her hands, out of it, right, and have my sexual relations with her, right?

She's lyin' back on the bed with her hand on the parental part of her head.

And the criminal thing takes over, out of it, and I go blow a pin in the door lock, the cylinder, so no one can get in, out of it, and I turn that radio right down 'cause, ah, it was gettin' to me, out of it, but I couldn't figure out how to turn her off, right? Then I'm lookin' out the balcony door and I can't figure out why I'm there and I goes back, out of it, into, ah, the bedroom, right?

She went into what might be called, ah, what appeared to look like a *grand mal* seizure type thing.

I guess I had damaged, ah, a part of the skull or something or crushed part of the skull and sent shock waves and short-circuited all her brain cells, right?

And she started being a little spastic, out of it, right?

Well this was ... she was on the bed now and the blood started to come out a bit, out of it, and go onto the pillowcase or another spread and then through onto the pillowcase.

So, ah ... at that time, out of it, she had a sun-dress on, a kinda white one with pinstripes in it like a gangster-type suit, out of it, right?

I found ... I ... she had underpants on and then I took them off, didn't rip 'em, just pulled them off nice and put them on the bed, out of it.

Then I'm kissin her all over.

She's got them turntable tits, out of it, and inside it's pink and grey inside there, so soft and nice to touch, out of it.

And I spoke to her in this weird high voice, like I never heard it before, right?

"I just want to see what girls have.

"I wish you were my mother."

And I'm thinkin' about how small we are when we come outta there, out of it.

And it's so nice to see what women have.

And then she's havin' this seizure thing again and I can't figure it out 'cause this isn't supposed to happen, out of it, right?
Then she starts gettin' spastic again and in that high weird voice, out of it, I said, "Oh, you're hurt, I'll help you."

And I held her, right?
She felt nice and warm, and then I went to the washroom for a towel, but when I came back I couldn't figure out why.
She started gettin' spastic, out of it, and I'm scratchin' my head to help in a sense, but not to, y'know ...

I'm concerned, a lotta things rushin' through my head all of a sudden.

Both minds are fightin' each other in a sense.
Both personalities are fightin' each other again, "Okay, ah, y'know, ah, either you gotta help or get on with it or ... or ... y'know have relations with her and get the fuck outta there, out of it, right?"

She got spastic again and she was close to the end of the bed and she rolls off onto the floor.
I ... I didn't touch her or push her or anything.
I was standin' at the foot of the bed and, out of it, I was kinda concerned.

She was, to the best of my knowledge, to the best of my opinion, she was still alive at this time 'cause she was, ah, murmuring type sounds, out of it, like ah ... like ah ... not like a gurgle but a murmuring, an actual sound, right?
And then she rolled over onto the floor.

I don't know whether this did her any ... I don't think it did her any good, out of it.

With more blood comin' and mattin' but not like a wash machine, out of it, right?

And I pulled her away from the wall 'cause I didn't want her to be cold and, out of it, tried to move her legs apart to see her private parts, out of it.

To see how they were attached to her body.

It was unbelievable after so long.

I just put my finger up there, out of it, but she was tryin' to keep her legs closed, right?

And I put this spread thing over her to keep her warm, and her legs kept closin,' out of it, right, and I got this surge again.

I'm not sure how many times I hit her after that.

I covered her head 'cause I didn't want the ambulance attendants to see her like that.

And I wondered why I was doin' that, out of it, when down there was more interestin'.

And she had these real nice feet, right, and in that high funny voice I played "this little piggy."

After, I felt queasy, like I was gonna to be sick, y'know, and then I felt like a big weight had been taken off my chest, out of it.

The tightness had dissipated.

The voices died down a bit.

I put on my gloves, out of it, and dumped her purse.

And the voices, "Yeah, do that."

And the mental part, "Wasn't that so nice, out of it," but I couldn't figure out why.

It was like watchin' TV, out of it, right?

Then ding, ding, ding, the criminal mind, "You gotta leave, watch out for the crumb-snatcher."
I took the radio cassette-player and left.

I can't recall any orgasm, out of it.

One side said, "She can identify you," and the other, "You can't leave her as a vegetable, out of it."

Went home, out of it.
There was static in my head, right?
I wanted to cry, like a sink about to overflow, but couldn't.

Then I argued with myself, should I or shouldn't I have done it, out of it?
Then I cried for half an hour.
Then I said I gotta go to the cops, and the mental side said, "How nice it was, out of it."

The criminal was the mechanics and the mental was curious about Sheryl.
I was monkey-in-the-middle.

I shouldn't have done that.
I shouldn't have done that.

I was walkin' fast and before I knew it I was at Dirty Louie's.
I was drawn like a magnet, out of it.
Then I was at the building and I can't figure it out.
No banana wagons.
Where are they?

Then I was arguing with myself.
I was supposed to phone an ambulance, out of it.
The cops wouldn't come without an ambulance.
Can't get one without the other, out of it.

Then I'm at the corner.
People are there, some of 'em with it, some not, y'know, out of it.
And I phone the police.
I ask for the radio room, out of it, 'cause I'd been told that's who
you phone, right?

Later I listened to my tapes, chicks talkin,' out of it.

I had no friends to talk to and I wanted to figure out girls.

I didn't want to kill her.

I just wanted to borrow her, out of it.

I can't explain how I feel today.
Maybe if I was dead it would make it equal.

I need to go where they can give me help and leave me alone.
They'll get me if I go back to the pen.
It'll be different this time.

I didn't want to do it.
I didn't want to, out of it, right?
It just happened.

You don't know anything about me.
Sheryl Gardner ... the angel ... she was an angel, not just a girl.
I didn't line it up, out of it.

It just happened.
No!
It went BANG!
I don't remember the trip up, out of it.
There was this surge and BANG and the thunder.

And BOOM, I just come up and one slow motion, out of it,
and the distance is about four feet, out of it, right,
and I didn't come up and do what you call a barn-door swing and
hit the lady with the hammer on top of the head.

It was more to the side.

I can't, ah, y'know, I didn't wanna get any blood on me or anything
like that
so I pulled this bedspread or those fancy stuff off the bed, out of it,
right,
and I decided that even if she lived, right, she'd probably be a
vegetable and, y'know,
it's just no way for someone to have to go through life like that, right,
so I pulled this thing over her to stop the splatter of blood and I ...
I'm not sure how many times I hit her after that.

I close my eyes and I see her.
She is mine. She stands before me
and takes her clothes off, slowly.
I knew she could do it like that.
I knew the first time I saw her she wouldn't disappoint me.
And why should she? She loves me. She's an angel.

Then she starts looking a certain way and
I jerk up 'cause that's not the way it's supposed to be.
There's blood on her face then nothing.
And I'm not quite sure. She smiles and

comes closer. Her mouth is so white and red.
She leans down on me and her mouth goes nuts,
eating right into my head. Then she's looping
my hammer and it's bang she's smashing my head
with thunder as I go screaming.

Look, she wants me, so I pull her in and she swoops past
for a mouthful of bone and skin from where the hammer crashed.
And she just keeps on eating me until I'm totally gone.

Then we begin all over again.

I'm afraid of angels now.

A GAME OF INCHES
Linda Griffiths

A GAME OF INCHES
Linda Griffiths

in collaboration with Sandra Balcovske

Pamela, an upright woman of forty-five or more, wearing a Toronto Blue Jays cap, is sitting on a chair beside a huge pile of baseball books and a telephone, in a large, impoverished ancestral home. The baseball cap looks both incongruous and correct. Pamela seems to be from another time.

I wake up in the middle of the night, and my heart is pounding, and I'm overcome with feelings of loss and terror and horror and panic and horror and pressure and terror and panic, and my mind races to see where I was in my dream that would bring me to such a state. Then, I remember—I was standing at the plate, and thousands of people were chanting, "Hit that ball. Hit that ball. Hit that ball." My team-mates behind me in the dug-out were chanting, "Hit that ball. Hit that ball. Hit that ball." It's the bottom of the ninth. It's all resting on me. And I know I'm not going to hit that ball. As I lay there alone in my bed, I realized I'd had my very first baseball nightmare. And I thought, Now he'll call.

The light changed that day. There was the wet rain and the damp and the sliding about on the packed icy surface, but it did seem that an almost imperceptible change occurred, like the turning up of a dial of light. The turning of the season. The time when John used to look for the very first baseball magazines. You know the ones I mean? They're not very good. They're made of newsprint and they herald the later abstracts and larger tomes that come out throughout the season.

These magazines were like daffodils or tulips to him, because, of course, they meant Spring Training.

She looks towards the phone.

I knew he wouldn't call in winter. I knew he wouldn't call on Valentine's Day. Ridiculous, the way it comes right in the armpit of winter. There's no more depressing time of year. No, he has no use for those kinds of occasions, the bleeding hearts in the store windows, the silly, humorous cards, "If you break my heart, I'll break your face," and so on. No, I knew he wouldn't call then. He'll call in the spring. Or the summer. Or at the very latest, fall.

She looks towards the phone again.

I'm aware that it's ridiculous, being a virgin at my age. I should have just gone out and done it a long time ago and got it over with. But oh no, I had to wait. Still, I don't know why everything has to be done at once. Painters don't paint masterpieces all at once. They begin with a triangle, a circle, a square. They move on to a bowl of fruit, an apple, a pear ... eventually a banana and then they go on to paint *The Blue Boy* and *Pinkie.* Of course it's possible that some people just aren't very highly sexed. As if there was a kind of a gauge—with "nymphomaniac" on the top, then "highly sexed," "very sexed," then just plain "sexed," "lightly sexed," all the way down to "barely sexed."

When I told my psychiatrist my baseball nightmare, he said something I know he's been dying to say for a very long time. He said that this dream might mean that I am gay. This disturbed me, not because of any prejudice, but because I've never felt particularly gay. But I told him that I'd be willing to seek a second medical opinion and if they concurred, I would be willing to work on becoming gay, with qualified professionals, for several years if necessary. Still, it didn't feel quite right.

It's true, I never had boyfriends as such. Of course, I had the experience of "that dance." You know the one I mean. My mother went out, spent three-hundred dollars on a dress. You know, in the fifties they had those dresses with the crinolines that stuck straight out? In bright green taffeta, and I weighed two hundred and four pounds.

And then came the snow boots—large brown galoshes with soles as thick as bricks. I clomped into that dance carrying my shoes in a little bag. I saw the girls, batting their eyelashes and giggling and listening to the boys talk about sports, pretending interest—you know, the way women do. I wasn't going to do that. I made for the couch and sat there watching like a giant frog. I wasn't going to eat anything. I wasn't going to drink anything. I wasn't going to take my boots off. I just sat there and waited until it was over and then I went home.

This is all that's left: a giant house, some mouldy antiques, a small annuity. I've always liked to keep a room in my house empty— actually, not a room, an entire floor. I thought that if I filled up the whole house with things—with my voluminous collection of books on the female orgasm, the works of the modern French feminists— "Angst, Volumes One, Two and Three"—with lamps and tables and things, then there would be no room for HIM when HE came. I thought a lot about it that spring three years ago, inviting John to come and stay. I'd had my eye on him, but then I'd had my eye on other fish before. And I thought, This is the way it's done. The woman has the nest and provides; the man is in between things, he doesn't have much money, he moves in and that's the way it's done. So I said to John, I said, "Well, if you don't have a place to stay, you can always stay at my house, you can pay me two hundred and fifty dollars or … nothing." And he said, "Sure." The way they do. "Sure."

I sat in my kitchen waiting for him to come, and I wish I'd known then about Sadaharu Oh. Sadaharu Oh was perhaps the most success- ful hitter ever. He hit more home runs than Hank Aaron or Babe Ruth. A Japanese man, he was a high-school star until he hit the major leagues and went into a giant slump. He just couldn't hit the ball. He's in despair. Finally his teacher comes to him and says, "Oh, you must learn to concentrate on 'Ki.' Ki is point of spirit energy in the body." Now, I would have thought that this point of Ki would have been located somewhere at the top of the head, or the forehead or the mouth or, at the lowest, the chest. But no, it appears this point of Ki is located … all the way down … about two inches below the navel, right down near the "Canadian parts." And so Sadaharu Oh learns to concentrate on his point of Ki and balance his spirit energy and still he can't hit the ball. His teacher comes back to him and says, "Oh, you must understand and eliminate the 'Mah.' Mah is energy between opponents—in this case, the pitcher and the batter. Sadaharu Oh has to learn never to think of the pitcher as his enemy. He has to think into the eyes of the pitcher, through his own eyes in a giant circle, thus eliminating the Mah between them. And he learns to do this and still he can't hit the ball. Then, it's terrible, they're about to throw him off the team and he has one last game. He's in despair and his teacher comes to him and says, "Oh, you are a piece of shit"—the way they do. "You have one last chance. You must hit the ball standing on one leg." Sadaharu Oh thinks he's crazy, but he doesn't have any chances left, so he agrees.

He goes out to the stadium to face the fans. They are so used to him striking out that every time he comes up to bat, they chant, "Oh, strike out! Oh, strike out! Oh, strike out!" But he quiets them in his mind, concentrates on his point of Ki, eliminates the Mah between himself and the pitcher, and raises himself on one leg in the now familiar "flamingo stance."

She stands on one leg.

He waits for the perfect moment, hits the ball with a resounding crack; it arches up and out of the park! He runs around the bases, hits home plate, and flings his arms up in his only gesture of emotion for the next twenty-two years. And the crowd chants, "Oh! Oh! Oh! Oh!"

The chant becomes rather orgasmic in nature.

"Oh … Oh ……. Oh ………… Ohh …………… Ohhhh ……………
Ohhhhh …. Oh."

I sat in my kitchen, waiting for John to come, with some Lapsang Suchong tea in a perfect china cup, and a fresh strawberry tart with whole wheat crust—of course made from scratch—and I heard the doorbell ring. I looked down the long hallway and saw him through the glass, a huge black shadow with a suitcase. I waved him in and he walked down the hallway, coming closer and closer, looming larger

and larger, seeming to cut out all the light behind him and … all of a
sudden … all I can see is … the enemy!

She leaps up on the table, shrieking.

A man a man a man! With his man smell smell smell, his penis penis
penis! A rapist! A warmonger! An oppressor, a brute! And I know all
I'll want to do is serve and serve and serve. I see forty-five years in one
fell swoop. He is old and bald and has cancer and I'm changing his
colostomy bag. I want to take a piece of chalk and make a giant circle
on the floor and say, "No! You can't come here. This is me! This is my
mind, I fought for it! This is me, you can't come here!" Instead, I say,
"Come on in. Take a beer from the fridge." Of course, I've stocked the
fridge and the cupboards and the freezer with enough food to last seven
nuclear wars. I know that he must feel my panic and yes, my …
revulsion. But how could I tell him that although these things are true,
he is also my beloved?

He moves in up to the third floor where he creates unbelievable
devastation. I seem pulled by my very genes up to the third floor—just
to do a bit of dusting, not to move anything around—and I see his dirty
laundry scattered on the floor. I'm moved to pick up one of his shirts
and smell that unbelievable combination of polyester blend and sweat.
Just to get used to him, you understand. I'm further moved to gather
up the shirts—not the socks, only the shirts—and to carry them
downstairs and wash them and then to say casually, "Yes, no trouble
really, I had to do a black wash anyway."

And it is as if we've lived together for forty years; it's that
comfortable, that ordinary. At the same time there is this unspeakable
tension between us. Then one day he comes in and he says, "Do you
mind if I watch the game?" Game? What game? "The Blue Jays and the
White Sox." I say, "Sure." The way I do now: "Sure." We are in the
living room and as I turn on "the game," I hear that sound—the hard-
edged announcer's voice, the sound of all little girls being separated
from their fathers. The voice says, "The Blue Jays are in the Skydome
and they've opened the roof … and they've closed the roof … and
they're opening the roof … and they've closed the roof … yes they've

opened, no they've closed … " But I can't watch the game. I am only aware of him behind me on the couch, it's as if the back of my head has eyes. I know he's wondering whether or not he can put his boots up on the couch. And I want to beam out to him that, of course, I dearly want him to feel comfortable enough to put his boots up on the couch; at the same time, I feel that if he does, I'll chop his feet off. And finally he gives a contented sigh, stretches himself out on the couch, and puts his boots up. I tell myself, "You see, the world hasn't fallen apart, the boots are up, so what?" But I still can't watch the game. All I can think of is, "Does he want tea, coffee, pound cake, lemon meringue … any of the enormous meal I've prepared and hidden in the back of the fridge?" No, I can't watch the game. Then I think, is it possible that perhaps at this very moment, he is also thinking of me? But no, wrong, wrong, wrong. He, of course, is watching the game.

I don't know how many games we watched like that, without my seeing a single one. And I began to plot and plan the way women do, checking ahead in the television guide to see when the games were on, so that when he came in, he wouldn't have to say, "Do you mind if I watch the game?" Because the game would already be on. But we were—maybe only I was—exhausted with the tension and pressure of the unspoken between us. Then one night I was just fed up. He wasn't home but I put the game on anyway and sat staring blankly at the screen. Then I heard him come in and get a beer from the fridge and I thought, No, everything's fine. This is how they do things. They come in, they get beers from fridges, they crack them open, they flop on the couch, they fart, and they watch the game.

But this night, for some reason, I wasn't thinking so much of him. It was as if some dial of light was turned on—and for the first time I see these players, these White Sox. A bunch of men dressed in what looks like long underwear with numbers on them, loping about chewing great wads of cud that stick out of their mouths like tumours, scratching and spitting great gobs of phlegm and tobacco juice, spit into some kind of trough that must be in front of them. A gang of fairly ordinary fellows, all shapes and sizes … and then, in come … the

Toronto Blue Jays ... warped and introverted and miserable. I think, What's wrong with them? What have we done to them? What have they done to themselves? The entire team looks like it's in its second year of psychotherapy.

As the game progresses, I understand more and more, till finally I know that it's the top of the ninth, and that all baseball stories begin with, "It's the bottom of the ninth" or "the top of the ninth." It's the top of the ninth and the game is tied and the bases are loaded and there are two down and the White Sox are up to bat and the Blue Jays are in the field ... and the Blue Jays' pitcher appears to be losing his mind, quite literally coming apart at the seams. He gets a tragic, haunted look in his eyes and starts to twitch and shake in an almost Parkinsonian manner, and then he starts to pull at himself. All the other players start to pull at themselves too. Now, the other players are more circumspect, they pull down here, but this Dave Stieb, he goes right for it. And then he starts to talk to himself and it appears everything is going to disintegrate until a calm comes over the entire stadium. Cito Gaston, the classiest man in baseball, has come out to talk Dave down. He gets to the mound, and almost before he begins to speak, you can see the tension start to drain away from Dave's face. He begins to regain control of his limbs and do fairly ordinary things with his hands, like play with the ball. We don't know what Cito has said. We only know it's perfect. A job well done, Cito goes back to the dugout to watch the game, sitting like Yul Brynner in *The King and I*.

Dave strikes the batter out. The Blue Jays are up, and out comes George Bell, the most hated man in baseball. The Butcher of San Pedro. Clearly, George is a man used to boos. Boooooo Booooooo Booooooo! "Eeeef the Canadian faaans don't like me, they can keeees my purple butt!" Booooo. Boooo. Booooo. But today, the fans aren't booing. They're quiet, almost kind. It's not putting George in a good mood at all. He looks like he wants to eat the plate, the bat, the ball and the pitcher. He swings, misses, and his statistics come up on the television set before you. And you know everything. You know he's been in a giant slump, that he needs an eye operation, that his shoulder's gone, his elbows are gone, his knees are gone, his ankles aren't very good either … we know his contract is up, that he'll ask for too much money. Meanwhile the announcers are saying, "Perhaps George will get a single today." And George raises his bat, big as a fence post, hacks and hews and slugs the empty air, strikes out, throws his bat to the ground with a curse and stalks off in a snit.

Then in comes a large chin followed by curling blond hair coming to the nape of the neck: Kelly Gruber. Most young boys want to be baseball players and end up being policemen; Gruber wanted to be a policeman and became a baseball player instead. He's holding his pinkie finger at an unusual angle, and his skin is stretched thin and taut over his cheekbones. It seems he's been in a slump, and the fans are booing him, something about water-skiing and a finger injury. With the black chalk-marks smeared under his eyes, he looks like that rock singer, Alice Cooper, on a bad night. He bends over the plate, his lips thin with tension, waves the bat in a determined fashion and cracks the ball for a stand-up triple. As he arrives at third base, you can hear him thinking, Just let them call me "Mrs. Gruber" now.

Then there is a curious dragging sound, a player appears to be dragging a giant cross onto the field, and on his face are tears from his latest appearance on Vision Television. He seems lost in a shadow that hides his features more than his hat: Tony Fernandez is a man clearly tormented by the wounds of Christ. And I want to beam into the television set, "Tony, of course it's all right to believe in Jesus and be tormented by the wounds of Christ. Just not right now, it's the bottom of the ninth." He clearly hears me because he seems to solidify: underneath his torment we see a body as neat and graceful as a young gazelle. He comes to the plate with no unnecessary panache, waits for the perfect moment and almost invisibly whacks the ball and drives Gruber in!

We win! We win! At least, they win … the Blue Jays win … I win, John and I, we … we win … Yay Team! We're very excited, John and I, because of the game of course, and it's ten o'clock at night and it seems that something more could happen, that the evening could extend. But we don't seem to be able to engineer it and I get almost Dave Stiebian in my twitches as I say, "Coffee?" "No." "Tea?" "No." "Pound Cake?" "No." "Chicken breasts? ... Broccoli with hollandaise sauce?" "No." Things are about to come apart at the seams when a calm comes over the living-room. I turn, and there is Cito Gaston, handing me a pack of cards. And Kelly Gruber has found the candles. And Tony Fernandez wipes the coffee table clean. John and I play Crazy Eights by candlelight till four o'clock in the morning. Then, dawn just starts to change the light, it's late, we are tired and yet it seems ... that something more could happen with the evening ... something more. There is a long silence. I look at him, of course I don't speak, and then ... finally he says, "Well, I guess I'd better crash." I say, "Yes. You should crash. I should crash. We all should crash." We say goodnight, he goes down the hallway to the bathroom to leave the toilet seat up, then climbs the stairs to the third floor. Lying alone in my bed, I hear his heavy body fall on the mattress on the floor above me; and I ache the way women ache when they want something they can't ask for.

Then I hear a very curious sound. Like ice cracking. I follow the sound into the living room, and there, sitting on the couch, is George Bell. [*crying*] "Agh, Agh, Agh, Aaaaaaaagh, Agh, Agh, Agh, Agh ... Sheeet man. Sheeeet. Everybody knows, man. They think I'm feeneeeesh. I'm not feeneeesh. I got two years left in me, two years, and my contract is up. I gotta go out there and act like a king. My eyes are gone. My shoulder is gone. My knees are gone. My ankles aren't very good. Cito, he says, 'Keep your eye on the ball.' I can't see the fucking ball. Agh, Agh. Agh. Aaaaagh." He looks up, sees me, and says, "Nice nightgown." I go up to him, smooth as silk, and help him take the chips off his shoulders. First the left one, then the right, which is even larger. Then I am in his arms and his hands are huge and calloused like bear paws and they are travelling travelling travelling over me, finding places I didn't know existed. And all the moves I thought I would have to learn by rote or with professionals are coming in waves and waves and waves. He is no longer the Butcher of San Pedro, these are not butcher's arms, but blacksmith's arms, and they are holding me so gently. Then … he touches me with the sweetest part of his bat, and we are … at first base … and we are … at … second base … we are … at third base … ohhh … home. Then I am curled in his arms and he is tickling me with his moustache.

Now, I don't know if that was a proper orgasm. I don't think anyone really knows what an orgasm is, certainly it's not in all the books I've read. All I know is that I was very pleased, and then I didn't want to do it anymore.

As I help George strap the chips back on his shoulders, he says, "Pamela, they say I'm a pretty shitty guy, maybe that's true, maybe that's not true. But I tell you one thing, don't you worry about this John. Just play your natural game." And he was gone.

I had such a moment of peace, even the French feminists within were peaceful. Yes, of course, just play your natural game. But … how to be natural with *him?* I was becoming more and more unnatural. Seemingly unbidden, I was giggling and batting my eyelashes and wiggling odd parts of my body in coy ways. My voice had gone up octaves, I was running around like Betty Crocker in heat.

Natural? It seems natural when he goes out to say, "When are you coming home?" Just like that, "When are you coming home?" But when I say it, it comes out like an order born of brutality and desperation. "When are you going to be home?" I want to grab the words back. If I don't say "When are you coming home?" there is an unnatural gap. There is no "natural" left. I'm just a schemer now. And then I think, What he needs is a good shirt. It would look just like his other shirts, except it would cost two hundred and fifty dollars. He wouldn't be able to tell, they can't, you know. But fifteen years down the road, when he's with someone a little closer to his own age, all the things from this time will have disintegrated, except for that one shirt, and he will think of me.

Just after the All-Star game, he said that he was "getting it together" to look for a place again, and that pretty soon he would be off my hands. Again there was that silence. I just wanted to say, "Oh don't be ridiculous. Marry me. Marry me marry me marry me. I'll nail your feet to a perch. I'll nail mine to one. We'll stay there immobilized forever, frozen forever, locked forever in this beautiful prison!" But then I thought, No, that can't be quite right.

Sometime after the Blue Jays lost the playoffs, he said that he was a little closer to getting a place and he pretty well had a line on one.

It's the bottom of the ninth. Joe DiMaggio is standing at the plate. It's all resting on him. If he hits, the team will win the Series, he will break all the records. The crowd is electric, chanting, insane.

The ball comes towards him and he waits for the perfect moment, swings, hits it with a resounding crack and it arches high over the park. He's done it! The crowd cheers wildly, everybody gets up to leave, the game is over ... except for one outfielder standing by the wall. The ball's already travelled over the wall several feet when he makes the most astounding leap. He leaps up, arches back, reaches out that extra impossible quarter of an inch ... and catches the ball! The photograph of this moment shows the fans with their jaws dropped open, amazed that such a thing could happen. That outfielder never played baseball again. He opened a bar. Baseball stories are like that. They always seem to have that twist of lemon.

Just after the World Series, which was hard to watch because, of course, the Jays had "choked in the clutch," an expression I truly despise, John said that he had found a place and he couldn't thank me enough and he owed me dinner. Even as he spoke I thought I caught something out of the corner of his eye, something that seemed to ask for something ... but no, I was probably wrong.

He is standing in the hallway with his suitcase and I am standing in front of him. It's an awkward moment. Then I see this nose coming towards me, looming larger and larger. I get what's supposed to happen. I do understand the physics of it. Something has to occur so that our lips can touch. He comes closer and closer, and then ... I don't why I did it, but I turned my head, I turned my head just a quarter of an inch and his lips brushed my ear awkwardly and a wall went up between us. A wall as cold and as grey as a Toronto sky in February. We try to reach our hands over the wall. I say, "Don't worry about the rent." He says, "I'll give you a call."

I am standing under the ball. It's one of those moments when the outfielder is standing directly under the ball: there's no question that he'll catch it. It comes closer and closer, looming larger and larger ... and then, for some reason it slips between the mitt and my hands and it's one of those ridiculous bloopers and there I am with my bum in the air, searching for the ball between my legs. I finally find it, too late to throw to third base. A couple of inches, one way or another. I hear the door close gently behind him.

You can imagine what a meal the French feminists would make of such a moment. They're very good on the politics, but about male/female relations, they're very dicey, very dicey indeed. You can just hear them. "Oh, Philippe, Philippe, Philippe. I am woman. You are man. I am cunt. You are penis. I am penis. You are cunt. Oh, please fuck me. Oh, don't fuck me. I hate you. I love you. I hate you. I hate you. Oooh, I will die if you leave. You will die if you stay. You must come, come, come, go, go, go, goooooo ... go, oh fuck me."

Well, I am not like that. I didn't get hysterical. Instead I hid for at least a year, never leaving the house. And then one morning I woke up, threw open the window, smelled mud under the frost, and went down to the World's Biggest Bookstore. Not Britnell's where I usually buy my books, where the modern French feminists are given free reign, but the World's Biggest Bookstore, with its huge collection on the Royal Family: *The Queen Mother's Hats* and so on. I walked in, some school children were milling about, and there he was, a nattily dressed Dominican man in a moustache and shades, flanked on one side by a security guard with a gun, and on the other, by an overwrought, overachieving woman publicist. There were stacks of books off to the side and a long line of school children in front of him waving bits of paper, going, "I got his autograph, I got his autograph." I took a book from the stack and lined up with them. I was clutching a copy of *Hardball* to my chest. And as I got closer and closer to him, I felt my chest begin to heave and I thought, No, I want something more, something personal. I want him to write "To Pamela" in my book.

When I finally got in front of him I heard myself say in a shaking voice, "Could you write 'To Pamela' in my book?" And the overwrought woman publicist said, "No. He's only going to write his name." The man shook his fingers with the gold rings and wrote, "George Bell." And I waited, for something more. Finally, he looked up and said, "Nice hat."

I left, but not completely. I found a vantage point by the section on the Royal Family, flipping through something about the Queen and her corgis and how they'll never bite her fingers. George knows I'm watching. Then some lumpy fourteen-year-old comes up and he's got a baseball—you know how they like to have their baseballs signed with signatures of players—he's got a ball like that and wants George to sign it. The security guard speaks in that tone policemen get, that over-politeness. "Sir," he says to the lumpy child, "he's not going to sign any baseballs. But if you want to buy a book ... " At $24.95. And the kid goes, "Ahh, come on." And you know he's living in some suburban hell in Scarborough, camped out in his parents' basement, trying to keep his mind alive by quoting baseball statistics. The guard goes, "Sir, it doesn't look like you're going to take 'no' for an answer, Sir." And all of a sudden, the child is escorted out of the store. Meanwhile, George looks like he doesn't understand English. Then it's twelve-thirty, the appointed hour is over. Still no sign from George. The taxi is waiting, the security guard and the publicist are about to lead George off, he's almost past me when I hear him say, "If you're ever in the Windy City, look me up." Windy City? And the lumpy fourteen-year-old, who has snuck back inside, says, "Yeah, didn't you know? George Bell doesn't play with the Jays anymore, he's with the Chicago Cubs. And Fred McGriff and Junior Felix and Tony Fernandez have all been traded." Traded? Traded? I feel as if the ground beneath my feet is dissolving. What can it mean? They were our team, those particular Blue Jays, not just any jays flying about the city. Can it mean he won't call? And I am ten years old again and my best friend has moved away and the world is cracking cracking cracking there's nothing left nothing left. But I pull myself together. The lumpy fourteen-year-old takes me over to the baseball section, and I buy $357 worth of baseball books, give a copy of *Hardball* to the lumpy child, come home, and begin my training.

The first spring of my training, I watched the Blue Jays build their new team. As I saw them bring in Joe Carter, his face splitting with that enormous smile filling up the Dome, I worked on balancing the spirit energy of my Ki. I was still having considerable difficulty eliminating the Mah between myself and just about everybody else, when I watched John Olerud, the man with no face, find a face, a girlfriend and a batting average. As Mookie Wilson came and went, I took to speed-reading my baseball books, learning that Yogi Berra once said, "Baseball is ninety percent mental. The other half is physical."

Still he didn't call.

The next year I was more ready, even though I wished Tony Fernandez would lose his shadow and come back. But it was Dave Winfield who walked into the living-room and gave lessons on leadership, loyalty and hope, and by the time he asked the Toronto fans for "more noise," I was able to stand on one leg for considerable lengths of time. I read that Babe Ruth once ate a hat; that "The Iron Man," Lou Gehrig, was obsessed with his mother; that Walter "The Big Train" Johnson, master of the fastball, used to give young batters a break, the catcher whispering, "The Big Train likes you today," and somehow the ball would be right over the plate. As I devoured baseball stories, especially those with a sentimental slant, I watched Roberto Alomar, like a young bear cub, play the game with such ease it made me want to weep. Alomar took over Stieb's position as the player most likely to pull at himself without undue embarrassment. Nineteen times in one game, I think I noticed.

And still he didn't call. Even though I felt fairly certain that the Mah between myself and the world was significantly diminished.

Now, as the team clearly moves towards a kind of perfection and the Series looms ahead, I listen to the journalists drone on with macabre delight about "choking in the clutch" and the "curse of the Blue Jays."

Cito? Cito, stop chewing for a minute, and listen. I see how you've built the team, and we all know where you're trying to go. You want the big win, the World Series, entry into the Hall of Fame. We all do. But it can't all be to do with winning and losing; it must be how you play the game. If it isn't, then I am a loser and I won't accept that. Take it from me, no one ever won by thinking about winning all the time. You can't play your natural game then. You become blocked, obsessed, tight as Kelly Gruber's cheekbones. You can't push to win, pray to win, think to win, plan to win. You can only be ready to win. Prepared. Tell them it's about waiting for the perfect moment, balancing your spirit energy, eliminating the Mah, playing your natural game, and having the courage to …

She stops dead, as if hit with a great revelation. She turns slowly towards the telephone and walks to it. She picks the phone up and dials, raising herself on one leg.

Hello, John? It's Pamela. I think they just might take the Series this year. Next year, too? Oh, don't be silly.

She laughs.

BLACK BRIDE
Andrew Kelm

BLACK BRIDE
Andrew Kelm

*An empty stage. The performer enters dressed in black and covered in
a black veil, carrying a large prop pie and singing:*

> Sing a song of sixpence,
> A pocket full of rye;
> Four and twenty blackbirds,
> Baked in a pie.
>
> When the pie was opened,
> The birds began to sing;
> Now wasn't that a dainty dish,
> To set before the king?

He places the pie down-stage centre, and takes off the veil.
That ever happen to you?
You get some stupid little song running around in your head and
you can't get rid of it no matter what you do?
It happens to me all the time.
Sometimes I don't even know about it.
It just kind of goes along without me, you know?
Like a clock ticking in the background
or a tap dripping.
It's only once you tune in

you realize it's been there all along.
You just haven't heard it.
But then once you do,
the rest of the world and all of humanity and existence
get swallowed up by that one sound.
Drip drip drip drip …

It's like getting lost in one of those subdivisions where the names
of the streets are the same kind of thing, like a type of flower or tree.
Great mountain ranges of the world …
That's where I grew up.
Himalaya Boulevard,
left, off Alpine Avenue.
And don't get stuck on Ural Crescent.
You can go round and round for years,
never find your way out.
The only really safe thing to do
is to tie a ball of string to the stop sign at Mountain Meadows Gate.
Let it unravel beside you like Theseus and the Minotaur.
*He pulls the black veil behind him like a rope and then shakes it out
like a bedsheet on a clothes-line.*

> The king was in his counting-house,
> Counting out his money;
> The queen was in the parlour,
> Eating bread and honey.

> The maid was in the garden,
> Hanging out the clothes,
> Along came a blackbird,
> And pecked off her nose.

He lets the veil fall on the stage.
Tell me.

Don't you find it extraordinary
that the maid gets her nose pecked off like that?
I mean, in a song for little kids?
I mean, it's not like this nice little birdie
flutters down and steals a currant from a bun.
Rather, he savagely rips a useful appendage off a living body.
Think of all that blood
gushing out of the jagged hole left in the middle of her face—
the pain,
the screams,
as she sinks to her knees in the stink of her own excrement,
the red mist of her own blood hanging in the air around her
as the winged pestilence swoops off
with the still-dripping morsel clutched in his beak.

    Now wasn't that a dainty dish,
    To set before the king?

No.
I don't think so.
Not a dainty dish at all.
It's the black arm of death reaching into the cradle:
"I got your nose! I got your nose!"
He picks up the veil, pulls it over his arm, gsetures like a menacing
monster, then lets it fall again.
What is going on there?
What is that about?
Does anybody get it?
I don't.
I find it totally mystifying.
All these random little snippets
of useless information:
"the king was in his counting-house,"
"the queen was in the parlour,"

"the maid was in the garden …"
All answers to the question: "Where were you, when …?"
But when *what?*
When the crime was committed?
Kind of a "whodunit," maybe …
The trouble is, we know who done it—
the blackbird done it.
And there isn't any plot,
just a bunch of characters and an event.
It doesn't go anywhere,
nothing adds up.
Take "a song of sixpence."
What's "sixpence" got to do with anything?
Or "a pocket full of rye"?
What is that exactly—"a pocket full of rye"?
It sounds right, doesn't it?
A pocket full of rye …
A pocketful of rye.
But rye bread, rye whisky?
A handful of loose grain
to toss into the wind?
What?
It has to mean something.
It must have meant something to somebody once,
surely the person who wrote it.
I mean, ultimately it's very difficult to not make sense
even if you want to …
It must mean something to me, right?
Or I wouldn't be singing it, would I ?
Or nothing means anything: there's always that choice.
And really, that's the simplest
because anything else eventually
comes down to some kind of primitive and irrational belief
in magical coincidence …

But what the hell,
I found these notes in "The Annotated Mother Goose."
He reaches into the pie and pulls out some note cards.
What were you expecting, a helicopter?

> Four and twenty is one of the numbers most fre-
> quently met with in "Mother Goose" rhymes. It is,
> of course, a "double dozen," and the number twelve
> is rich in associations, traditions and superstitions.

Numbers ... Numerology ...

> Theories about this rhyme abound: the blackbirds
> are the twenty-four hours in a day, the king is the sun
> and the queen is the moon, for example.

Correspondence, Alchemy, the Rosicrucians maybe.

> Still another theory holds that this song celebrates
> the printing of the first English Bible—the black-
> birds being the letters of the alphabet set in pica
> type—baked in a pie.

Now that's deep,
a little far-fetched you might even say,
maybe even "reaching for it" ...
With a pointer ...
On a ladder ...
But as a matter of fact,
as I was flipping through Revelation one day
just for the hell of it ...
He reaches into the pie and pulls out a Bible.
... I found in chapter four, starting at verse two—
Did you get that?

Four-two.
Two-four!

> And immediately I was in the spirit: and, behold, a
> throne was set in heaven, and *one* sat on the throne.

And that's the way it's written—in italics—like there's this big
number one sitting there on a chair ...

> And he that sat was to look upon like a jasper and a
> sardine stone: and *there was* a rainbow round about
> the throne, in sight like unto an emerald.

Now, I don't get that.
I don't see how you can have a rainbow that looks like an emerald,
because to me that means green
and a green rainbow
is sort of a contradiction, wouldn't you say?
Basically a visual image that's impossible to visualize.
It's no wonder nobody reads the thing any more.

> And round about the throne *were* four and twenty
> seats: and upon the seats I saw four and twenty elders
> sitting, clothed in white raiment; and they had on
> their heads crowns of gold.

Four and twenty elders
sitting in a circle—the shape of a pie.
And they're dressed in white,
not black like the birds ...
But this is heaven, right?
If they were on earth they might well be black,
because it would be opposite.
Like priests and monks

who dress in black—
and those cloaks are called pyes—*p, y, e*—did you know that?
I didn't—
And then when they die, they go off to heaven
and put on these glorious robes of white.
Now,
these birds, then,
are buried in the pie
and then set free.
It's as if they've died and been reborn.
This is Judgement Day,
when Christ comes down and wakes up the dead
to take them off to heaven.

    When the pie was opened,
    The birds began to sing;
    Now wasn't that a dainty dish,
    To set before the king?

But then one goes off and attacks the maid ...
It does make sense from the point of view of the bird.
Just imagine
you're one of twenty-four live birds
who've been rounded up somehow
and shoved inside this pie crust,
sealed in there
like slaves in a Chinese tomb.
You don't know why the hell you're there, what's going to happen,
but there's no room to move,
no air to breathe ...
It gets hotter and hotter ...
You begin to wonder just how hot it's going to get,
because you think you feel your insides start to cook
and you're trapped there, right?

At the mercy of someone or something you don't know anything about.
You don't know how long it's going to go on,
and you don't know how much more you can take.
Then this big knife cuts through the ceiling
and carves its way across the pie.
You scramble from side to side to get out of the way,
and then finally,
the light breaks through.
You fight your way out
and flap around the room in a panic
until you find a window
to escape ...
You'd be bound to come out of that pie a bit twisted,
maybe trying to get revenge,
ready to take it out on the first one who gets in your way ...
But why the maid?
It isn't fair.
She didn't do anything, did she?
Out there minding her own business,
doing her job,
the washing.
But maybe that's the point, hmm?
Life is not fair.
We do not get what we deserve,
we live in a random universe, et cetera, et cetera.
Maybe this is an existential nursery rhyme—
mothers and grandmothers
passing on the tradition of despair
while their babies are still too young
to get sucked in
by that illusion, hope.
He picks up the veil, winds it up into a bundle, and rocking it like a
baby, he sings:

Do do do do do do.

Don't get too happy now, my child,
because just when you're least expecting it,
a disaster is going to come out of the blue
and mutilate your face.

Do do do do do …

*He grabs the "baby's" nose, yanks the veil into the air, and talks to it
as if it still was the "baby."*
Aw,
don't cry!
It's just a nose, for God's sake.
You wait till the nuclear fall-out comes.
You'll be glad if a nose is all you lose.
Now, you grow up tough and cynical
just like your parents.
And as soon as you learn to walk, we'll buy you a leather jacket.
He lets the veil fall to the ground.
It would be different, now, if the maid was the one who cooked the pie.
A bit extreme, losing a nose, sort of irrevocable—
but you could see a kind of justice at work.
And I mean,
wouldn't that be
nice?
Unfortunately,
that's not the way it happens.
The maid would not have cooked the pie.
I mean she couldn't have.
Think about it.
This guy's a king, right?
He's got lots of servants.
The maid would not also be a cook.

He's got a cook to do the cooking.
And I mean,
the song could easily have gone,
for example:

> The cook was in the garden,
> Looking at the sky,
> There came a little blackbird,
> And pecked out her eye.

He mimes plucking out an eye.
I've got your eye!
I've got your eye!
Same difference, right?
I mean, it could go that way.
But it doesn't.
It's the maid who gets it, not the cook.
Why?
Why not the king?
The pie was made for him.
Why not peck off *his* nose?
He's the one who deserves it, not the maid.
He searches through the pie for his notes and finds a cue card.
Here we are.

> According to Iona and Peter Opie, the editors of the
> *Oxford Dictionary of Nursery Rhymes*, an Italian cook-
> book of 1549, translated into English in 1598,
> actually contains a recipe "to make pies so that the birds
> may be alive in them and flie out when it is cut up."

They continue:

This dish is further referred to (1723) by John Nott,

cook to the Duke of Bolton, as a practice of former
days, the purpose of the birds being to put out the
candles and so cause a "diverting Hurley-Burley
amongst the Guests in the Dark."

Now think about it ...
How would you like to have
your dinner
explode in front of you
into a bunch of live little creatures flying around,
probably shitting on everything?
Who is this king who thinks that's a dainty dish?

> The king was in his counting-house,
> Counting out his money ...

He reaches into the pie and pulls out a number of coins.
Excuse me?
A "counting-house"?
What the hell is that?
You mean, he's got a separate little house to count his money in?
He must be really into it ...
I guess we're dealing with a medieval figure of speech here.
It must be the equivalent of the bank or the accounting department,
or the place where the money is counted, something like that ...
But what's the king doing there?
Why isn't there a counting person who looks after the counting house
and reports to the king at the end of the day,
with profits and losses and who owes what on their taxes, you know?
Why does the king have to be there?
Unless he just really gets off on the whole
hands-on participation aspect of the thing.
King Midas ...
turning everything and everyone around him into gold—

or at least consumable goods and services.
Stacking up those gold coins like Club Z points or something,
"Fifty more and the toaster's mine!"
None of my friends ...
Money doesn't count.
It's what's inside that counts, we all know that ...
Of course, if you have lots of money
you can afford to put good things inside ...
Good food, good books;
you don't have to take the TTC,
jammed in with all those strange people,
you don't know where they've been.
This guy fell asleep on my shoulder.
It didn't really bother me,
I mean it didn't matter, right?
But I was embarrassed for him.
Imagine waking up to find yourself using a stranger for a pillow.
I felt like I should cough or move suddenly or something
so he could wake up and I could pretend I hadn't noticed,
before he'd committed himself too completely.
But I didn't.
I liked the feel of that living weight leaning on me,
feeling his breathing against my side.
I missed my stop ...
The stupid fucking ass-hole.

        The queen was in the parlour,
        Eating bread and honey ...

Well, what with King Midas in his counting-house ...
And I mean, he must be there all the time, don't you think?
It's like having a TV room,
you don't set aside a whole room for the thing
unless you watch it a lot.

"The king? Oh he's off in his counting-house, counting his money.
There's a big count on tonight, you know."
Oh yeah? Who's winning?
Who's losing?
That's part of the whole counting thing, isn't it?
Dollars and sense,
black and white,
no philosophical ambiguities,
no romantic bullshit!
So the queen must be a very large woman, I would say.
Of course, there's something very Marie Antoinette
about the whole thing, too, don't you think?
"Let them eat bread and honey!"
It could be really political.
While the king's out ripping off the people,
the queen's in the parlour consuming the spoils.
And the maid is like the working class,
its nose taxed off its face.
So this little song could be,
you know, like in South America,
where they can't really say what they really mean,
so they turn it into a metaphor,
a subversive little tune
to spread the news from ear to ear
under the very noses of the ruling entities.

> While Brian was selling the country,
> Merrily down the stream,
> Mila was out shopping,
> Life is but a dream ...

But like,
what do I know about politics?
I didn't even vote in that referendum thing.

At first I thought,
Well, yes, of course I'll vote yes.
You know—I want Canada to stay together,
even though, deep down, sometimes ...
I wish those fucking French fucks would fucking just get over it!
Oops ...
But then ...
I never actually did get around to reading the literature—
you know, that stuff we got in the mail.
I meant to, I really did ...
but like,
if they wanted us to pay attention,
why did they put it on
at the same time as the whole U.S. election thing?
I mean, it's like football—
they play a much more interesting game.
Anyway, eventually I thought,
Maybe I'll vote yes because June Callwood says to
and she's a nice lady ...
But then maybe not—
Trudeau says no,
and he's a smart guy ...
But then, what the hell,
I'm going to vote yes because the Blue Jays won.
But by then it was too late to register.
And anyway,
really,
I don't know,
I felt like any vote at all
would be like buying into the belief that it really matters somehow.
And really,
I really don't care.
Really.
What difference do they think it's going to make in twenty years

when the ozone layer's gone,
and the world population is on its way to doubling
again? ...
Have you ever looked at one of those population graphs?
You know—
it just sort of cruises along pretty evenly till about the Renaissance,
and then it starts gradually heading uphill
until, in the twentieth century, it just goes joooooOOP!
He draws a graph in the air with his hand.
And we're here.
Now.
Is there anyone who seriously thinks
that something dramatic on a global scale
is not going to happen in the next few years?
Hmm?
Think about it.
He draws the graph with his hand again.
JoooooOOP!
Now, when that happens,
whatever *that* is,
do you seriously think it's going to matter
whether the signs in Montréal are written in French or in English?
I don't know ...
But I do know that it is not the national anthem in my head.
No.
I think the really important fight
is here,
inside,
in the kingdom of the heart,
where time sits cross-legged,
reality curves,
and love is the power to choose;
and a blackbird is really a peacock in winter,
without the fancy feathers.

He takes some black make-up out of the pie, smears it on his eyes, cheeks and lips, then puts it back in the pie. He then takes off his shirt and finds a red feather in the pie which he puts in his hair. He grins.

Do you think I'm getting carried away?

He picks up the veil and begins to play with it.

It's just ...

I think you have to be accountable for what goes on inside your head.

You know?

I mean suppose someone catches you off guard and takes your picture

when your hair's all greasy, and you got a big zit

and spaghetti sauce on your T-shirt.

And you look at it and say,

"Well that's not really me."

And I guess it's not, really.

But at that particular moment it was.

And that particular moment might live on in a shoebox

at the bottom of someone's closet,

maybe longer than you will.

And then who's to say that wasn't you?

Well, what if someone took a picture of the inside of your head?

And maybe on the surface you're just walking down the street, but inside your head ...

He begins to dance with the veil, singing a Maxipad commercial. Repeating the verse, he builds into a dance with the veil and then stops.

Where was I?

Oh yes, the queen ...

The inner queen ...

Well, everyone has an inner queen,

as well as an inner king ...

and I don't think that means,

you know,

that you're gay or anything,

just because part of you is a queen.
I don't think …
He drops the veil.
I test myself sometimes.
I imagine a good-looking guy in front of me,
slowly taking off his clothes.
All he has on is a pair of overalls,
no shirt,
and he unclips the straps at the front
and the whole thing falls in a heap at his feet.
He undoes his pants, lets them fall, and stands there naked.
And he's standing there totally naked
giving me this look.
I walk over and I try to stare him down,
like he doesn't get to me at all.
He stares.
But then I decide to smell his sweat before I walk away,
just to prove I don't like it.
And before I can stop myself,
I'm licking the hair on his chest flat,
running my hands over his buttocks
to find the warm sweaty place under his balls,
my penis hard against his,
sparring with him …
He falls to his knees, picks up the black veil, and puts it on like a dress.

> The queen was in the parlour,
> Eating bread and honey …

This reminds me of when I was little.
My poor parents,
they used to wonder why I took so long in the bathroom.
I used to take off all my clothes and play with the towels—
dress up in different ways …

I'd make one into a skirt with a slit up the side
and show my legs in the mirror ...
He briefly exposes himself.
Well, you know what they say about big hands ...
big gloves ...
He takes off the veil.
But I don't know,
I mean, who needs a big monster snake coiled up down there?
This is classical, like those statues, you know?
They don't have gigantic shlongs hanging down to their knees.
Am I allowed to do this?
It's certainly not in very good taste though,
I know that ...
I don't know why,
it's just a penis after all.
Half the population has one ...
But you're not supposed to look.
I don't think I really looked at mine till I was at least twenty-five.
I mean, I knew it was there, but I was too polite to really look.
It's sort of like a sausage and two golf balls, isn't it?
Can everybody see?
Does anyone have a bigger one they could show us,
so people could see from the back?
And the sausage has two parts—
a head—
which looks something like a plum ...
And the shaft.
And if it is circumcised like mine,
you've got this loose skin around the head
that looks something like a lion's fringe
or a clown's collar.
Kind of like pets really, aren't they?
"Good boy, there's a good boy ... "
A personality all their own ...

And they're an independent lot—
up and down whenever they feel like it ...
He does a few steps of a ritual-like dance, shaking and making faces.
He sings:

> When the pie was opened,
> The birds began to sing!

He poses like a totem pole.
I have these dreams.
A bunch of guys in a big underground shower:
differently shaped rooms and hallways
covered in slimy green-coloured tiles.
None of us have any clothes on
and everything is warm and wet.
And I get an erection.
So I lie on my stomach in a puddle of water
and try to look inconspicuous.
He lies on his stomach, slides over to the pie, and pulls out a G-string.
He puts it on under the mass of veil and then peeks out one of the folds.
On Himalaya Boulevard,
down from the house where I grew up,
lived a woman named Mrs. Bellamy
who was always peeking out her curtains.
She must have thought no one could see her, but it was very
obvious—
fingers clutching the edge of the curtain,
half a face,
and one big eye staring out at the world ...
I don't think she ever did anything else.
At least, every time I went past her house,
she was there taking everything in,
thinking no one could see her.
All these women who sit and watch:

the woman behind the curtains,
the madwoman upstairs,
the old woman knitting ...
What is it with them do you think?
Are they plotting and planning and hatching little schemes?
The queen in the parlour ...
He arranges the veil around his shoulders.
One thing happens here,
the maid loses her nose.
Why mention the queen if she's not involved?
So I'm wondering ...
What if the maid and the king are having a fling?
I know it doesn't say that directly anywhere,
but look at the imagery:
the billowing white sheets the maid hangs on the clothes-line,
which then become bespattered with her blood.
I think we're talking the loss of virginity here, don't you?
Maybe even rape.
And if the maid and the king are having a fling,
maybe the pie is made by the queen?
And I know she's not the cook either,
but she's the queen, so she can do whatever she wants.
He covers his face in the veil with gestures that become identified with
the queen.
The invisible presence behind the scenes,
pulling the strings,
shaping the destinies of all who cross her path,
silently working her revenge on the king who's betrayed her
and the tart he scooped up out of the kitchen.
The little wild flower he found in the garden
when he once looked up from his bags of gold ...
He lets the veil fall to the ground.
And the maid ...
You can see her looking up at this king,

refined and manicured,
not at all like her father,
with his greasy hair and a big zit
and spaghetti sauce on his T-shirt.
Does the money make the man?
Or does the maid?
And this is the money that made the king
that made the maid that washed the clothes
that lived in the house that Jack built.

Along came a blackbird,
And pecked off her nose.

"The Maid and the King."
Act One: Flirtation.
He takes a pink feather duster out of the pie and begins provocatively dusting the stage. Miming, he bends over to reach something low and far away, reacts to a pinch on the bum, realizes it is the king, and curtsys. He then mimes the king giving the maid a wink, and walks away.
Act Two: Proposition.
He mimes the maid bringing the king a letter. The king responds:
"Thank you, Mary. It is Mary, isn't it? Please. Relax. You don't have to be shy with me. You're very lovely. Here, I want you to have this."
He mimes pulling a jewel off his cloak.
"It's just a world-famous emerald that's been in the family for generations. It matches your eyes."
Act Three: Intimacy.
He mimes the king counting his money, then the maid playing with her feather duster. She is bored, doesn't quite know what to do. She looks up at the king.
"Your Highness? Can I get you anything? Tea, tobacco, chocolate?"
"Umm ... A Coca-Cola. Could you get me a Coca-Cola? There's

that little store about three blocks away. I think it should still be open. You want some money? No? Okay."

The king continues to count his money. The maid comes back with the Coca-Cola.

"Thank you. Oh, but hey. Do you think you could put some ice in it? Lots of ice. I like my Coca-Cola with lots of ice in it."

The maid comes back while the king plays with his money.

"Thank you. Now put it down anywhere, and whatever you do don't bother me. I'm counting ... Oh, but you *could* do something for me. Do you think you could rub my feet? They're so sore. I think it's the new royal boots. The royal boot-maker should be flogged. Ow! Not too hard. Gently. They're sensitive. That's it. No no no no no! Can't you do anything right? Now just lie there and don't move. If I even hear you breathe I'm going to chop off your head. I'm counting!"

End of "The Maid and the King." He puts the coins back in the pie and picks up the veil as the queen.

And off in another part of the castle,
the queen smiles over her toast and tea—
Queen Maya—
weaving together illusions
spun from our deepest fears,
throwing up blackbirds in our paths
and songs inside our heads.
She dangles the keys in front of your face,
but she's loath to give them up.
He drops the veil.
I feel her there beside me when I'm walking alone at night,
behind a row of trees,
standing there all stiff and still
like they could wait forever.
And a dead cat lying in the grass,
stretched out on its side all matted and wet,
its paws reaching out for its final breath ...
And the face is familiar:

the wide staring eyes
and the twisted leer on its mouth
that's not really terror or pain so much as an overwhelming energy,
almost a laugh,
hysteria.
He imitates a dead cat.
Like a picture of someone you used to know but now you can't
remember.
He imitates a dead cat.
If I could just ...
Sometimes,
I think if I could only catch myself off guard,
surprise myself in the middle of another thought entirely ...
He shakes out and springs into the dead cat again, trying to surprise
himself.
Sun.
He springs again.
Clouds.
He springs again.
Rain.
He springs again.
Cat.
He springs again, sings a few lines of the Maxipad song, then trails off.
You're not straight ...
You're not straight ...
You're not straight, you're not straight ...
He tosses a lot of books out of the pie until he finds the right one.
Freud!
He finds a quote.

    ... One of the first questions which he addressed to
    his Nanya—

This is one of his patients, right?

—was whether Christ had had a behind too. His Nanya informed him that he had been a god and also a man. As a man he had had and done all the same things as other men. This did not satisfy him at all, but he succeeded in finding consolation of his own by saying to himself that the behind is really only a continuation of the legs. But hardly had he pacified his dread of having to humiliate the sacred figure, when it flared up again as the further question arose whether Christ used to shit too.

I'm sorry, I'm quoting here ...

He did not venture to put this question to his pious Nanya, but he himself found a way out, and she could not have shown him a better. Since Christ had made wine *out of* nothing, he could also have made food *into* nothing and in this way have avoided defecating.

A young, inquiring mind to be sure ...
What does Freud say?

... We catch a glimpse of his repressed homosexual attitude in his doubting whether Christ could have a behind, for these ruminations can have had no other meaning but the question whether he himself could be used by his father like a woman ....

Really?
No other meaning?
Well, that will teach you to ask questions!
I think it's a good question.
What about Christ defecating?

And what about his penis?
Did Jesus have a penis?
Getting hard at embarrassing moments?
Wouldn't that be something,
in the middle of the loaves and the fishes routine?
And by the way,
is it not significant, Dr. Freud,
that he is distributing "loaves" and "fishes"?
Could it not be symptomatic of repressed desire,
to be handling a type of food
traditionally associated with female genitalia,
that is to say, "fish"?
And is it not also possible
that the "loaves" represent his penis,
which he secretly desires to put in everybody's mouth?
No,
oh no,
the horror, the horror,
it's too dark entirely,
better to cut it off ...
*He takes Joseph Campbell's "The Hero with a Thousand Faces" out
of the pie.*

The twenty-fourth—

Two-four, four and twenty ...

—of March was known as the Day of Blood: the high
priest drew blood from his arms, which he presented
as an offering; the lesser clergy whirled in a dervish-
dance, to the sound of drums, horns, flutes, and
cymbals, until, rapt in ecstasy, they gashed their
bodies with knives to bespatter the altar and tree with
their blood; and the novices, in imitation of the god

whose death and resurrection they were celebrating,
castrated themselves and swooned.

*A knife has been holding his place in the book. He raises the knife over
his head and whirls like a dervish. Suddenly he freezes. He drops the knife
into the pie, picks up the veil and transforms into the queen.*
But that's only one out of twenty-four.
There are twenty-three more of them
down there still in Pandora's pie.
There's one called "Death."
And one called "It isn't fair."
And one called "I've fallen and I can't get up."
They're all still cooking away down there
and they all want out.
Dropping out of the veil, he imitates a dead cat.
I can feel them in my body,
like butterflies in your stomach,
only all over,
behind my face,
in my legs,
my hands,
struggling to break free,
they shoot out of the pores of my skin,
fly up and perch in the branches of the trees:
singing and squawking and ripping and tearing,
my body blown apart in the joy and the confusion.
He is moving his arms like wings ... he picks up The Hero with a
Thousand Faces *and rests it open on his upturned face as if the pores on
his face are soaking in the words. He kneels and recites the following as his
arms move like the dance of an Indian idol:*

> And in the same spirit, the king of the south Indian
> province of Quilacare, at the completion of the
> twelfth year of his reign, on a day of solemn festival,

had a wooden scaffolding constructed, and spread
over with hangings of silk. When he had ritually
bathed in a tank, with great ceremonies and to the
sound of music, he then came to the temple, where
he did worship before the divinity. Thereafter, he
mounted the scaffolding and, before the people,
took some very sharp knives and began to cut off his
own nose, and then his ears, and his lips, and all his
members, and as much of his flesh as he was able. He
threw it away and round about, until so much of his
blood was spilled that he began to faint, whereupon
he summarily cut his throat.

He falls on his face.
The king is dead, long live the king!
He jumps back onto his feet as a blackbird.
Okay, who's next?
Yes, I know, it's only a twelve-year contract,
but just think, for those twelve years ...
You can have whatever you want!
Your word is law.
Your thoughts are the truth.
Your desires are divine inspiration.
Your comfort and well-being
is the comfort and well-being of the whole realm.
You catch my drift?
We're talking absolute power here.
He picks up the veil, covering his face with it, and he becomes the queen,
laughing.
But we know who's got the real power, don't we?
The queen caws like a crow.
"Caw! Caw!"
Dropping the veil, he becomes the king again.
Yes, Ka,

divine spark of the Pharaoh,
carrying immortality from one king to the next.
Why is it so easy to believe that the king is somehow at fault here?
When the pie is so full of his familiars?
Somebody's got to count the money.
Things have got to be counted
and accounted for.
Just think if no one was counting the animals
on the endangered species list.
He begins putting the books and props back into the pie.
What about this frivolous queen,
who finds no earthly purpose but to stuff herself with sweets?
Maybe the beast with two backs
is born of the maid and her.
His hand gets pulled into the pie and pulls out a bloody handkerchief;
his hand goes to his nose. He screams and pulls his hand away.
Guilt ...
The sympathy scene ...
But every queen was once a maid,
and how can anyone plant the seeds unless they pick the flowers?
He wipes his black make-up off with the handkerchief.
But kingship lost all credibility
when Henry VIII reinvented the church so he could divorce
Catherine.
And then that business with Anne Boleyn.
Up comes the veil and he becomes the queen.
And out of their union was born a queen,
whose power was greater than any man ...
As the king again, he stuffs the veil back into the pie.
Elizabeth, the virgin ...
then Victoria, the patron saint of prudes.
What an inspiring alternative ...
But the whole thing was merely political by then.
He puts his clothes back on.

It used to be that
the king, or queen, was God's representative on earth,
the link between the community and all that lay beyond.
And when the old king died he knew,
in that moment of final surrender,
that a new and greater synthesis would move in to fill the void, like
an old idea that breaks apart and forms anew in a younger mind.
But what does it mean to be half divine, now that God is dead?
Never mind.
Now it's all just a thought.
You could never have a person who was king.
Or queen.
They'd have to be too large,
too all-encompassing,
to link together all the different parts:
the one with the many,
the present with the future,
and the spirit with the flesh.
*With almost everything packed away back in the pie, he picks up a
plum.*
And it was only after I got the story to here
that I finally found the key.
As it turns out,
it is about that moment when kingship fell apart,
and we lost that most important piece of our cosmology …
You see, when Henry VIII created the new church
so he could divorce Catherine,
he incidentally confiscated much of the church's wealth,
filling his counting-house to the brim.
On more than one occasion,
the deeds to church properties
were presented to him literally baked inside a pie.
Some kind of custom …
And as a matter of fact,

one of these concoctions was delivered by one Jack Horner,
whose thumb, rumour has it, on the way to see the king,
found its way beneath the crust
long enough to filch out a juicy little property,
which set him up nicely for the rest of his life.
The Abbot of Newstead sent Henry a pie
containing four and twenty deeds,
for properties rich in fields of rye.
Henry got his divorce
and married the maid he'd spied in his garden,
all decked out in the latest clothes from France.
And, well, we know what happened to her.
And this little song is a time capsule meant to be opened now.

REFERENCES

— Cecil and William S. Baring-Gould, Eds. *The Annotated Mother Goose, Nursury Rhymes Old and New, Arranged and Explained* (New York: Bramhall House, 1962), pp.26-27.
— Sigmund Freud, "From the History of an Infantile Neurosis (the 'Wolf Man')" in *The Pelican Freud Library Volume 9: Case Histories II.* Trans. James Strachey (London: Pelican Books, 1979), pp.298-300.
— Joseph Campbell, *The Hero with a Thousand Faces* (Princeton, N.J.: Princeton University Press, 1973), pp.93-94.

PERFECT PIE
Judith Thompson

PERFECT PIE
Judith Thompson

An early April evening in Marmora, Ontario. Light snowfall.
Patsy, a tired-looking woman in her late thirties, sits in her kitchen
expertly kneading pastry dough. She is making a steak and kidney pie from
scratch. She presses the record button on her tape recorder.

Hello, Marie? Is this Marie Charles—from Marmora? Are you— sitting down? 'Cause when you hear who I am you might uh, you might want to be sitting down. Marie, shall I talk for a while and see if you can figure it out? Well, I got a hold of your address Marie, and I just uh, really, wanted to say hello. Like after so many years. What is it, about twenty-three or so? I know it's bold of me really, you're likely so busy and all, in Toronto. Do you know who I am yet? Do— you know my voice at all, Marie? It's not the same, that's for sure, it got broke, eh, with smoking cigarettes and drinking rye and ginger and having two wild boys I had to yell at all the time for eighteen years. Yes, I got two, Johnny and Darren, eighteen and seventeen, living with their girlfriends now, you know how the kids are. Marie can you believe that we're two years short of forty? I can. I got grey hairs all over my head and love-handles on my hips!

Well you must know me now, eh? Three guesses and the first two don't count, right? Patsy—from Marmora! How are you? I bet you didn't expect to hear from me, eh? After all this time? So. How are you? I uh, been thinking about you, you know, ever since I seen you on that commercial, on TV, the one for the Niagara wine?

I'd just put a meat pie in the oven, I been working a lot on my meat pie, eh, on account of the County Pie contest coming up next week, and so I'd just put one in the oven and sat down with a cup of tea to watch my shows when your wine commercial come on. At first I didn't know it was you, eh, but I thought to myself, That woman is familiar somehow, then you spoke, eh, and I go, Oh my God if that isn't Marie, and I'll tell you, it was like when our pipes burst last winter and all the water come through the wall, all these memories I thought I clear forgot, come soaking thru. It's the two of us, painting our bikes yellow and getting them straw baskets for the front, it's you and me holding hands going to first-day grade one together, and you won't go in the school, it's the both of us getting the strap from Mr. Doyle for smoking in the washroom at Holy Name grade six, it's sleeping over your house, watching the late show, getting kicked out of the I.G.A. for scoffing chocolate bars, laughing so hard in the parking lot there we peed our pants remember? Had to go home on the bus like that; weren't we, we were best friends but I do wonder if you remember me, for I am an ordinary person. I have not achieved nothing in this world not one thing at all. I have stayed in Marmora, I live in the house I was born in. I haven't even been to Toronto, and I don't think I ever will. For one, I don't like to even leave the house, for two, I won't drive on the 401, and for three, I have heard that it is not friendly. Don't get me wrong, I'm not putting down Toronto, I know it is your home, and I respect that, I'm just saying, I am not a city-type person. You have to be in Toronto, you got your work and that, and there's no reason in the world you would be thinking about me. I am a common person. You are a TV professional and I'm very proud of you and to tell you the honest truth the main reason I wanted to get in touch with you was to tell you congratulations; I think your acting is very good, very professional.

She finishes rolling the dough.

And you look very attractive, Marie: the only suggestion I would give, if you were to ask my opinion, is that I don't think that hairstyle perfectly suits you on account of you do have the high forehead, and you need to soften it up with some bangs; just a soft fringe, you know how I am about hair, Marie, I was always right about your hair. Because I care about your face. I see it in the kitchen window lately, early in the morning, when I get up to make my dough.

Branches of a tree brush against the kitchen window. Patsy gets a meat mixture, brings it to the table, puts the meat in a baking dish, and takes the empty bowl to the sink. She starts assembling the pie, rolling dough over the top of the dish, sealing the edges, trimming off excess dough. She brushes the top with beaten egg and cuts in steam vents.

And I wonder if you have any plans at all to visit Marmora at all.

I wonder if it's likely you'd even stop here to get gas. Because you likely feel uncomfortable of Marmora. Of the people, eh? Like, I was thinking, especially the kids, from school—I mean they're all growed up now of course—but that you may run into them. This is a small town after all, and if you have to run into the IGA to pick up some shampoo or some Kotex you could run into them, I mean Nancy Tanks works in the IGA and it might bring back some not very nice ... memories for you. Like the—uh, time in math there you were picking at your hair. You used to do that, remember, just pick and pick away up the front of your head, like a personal habit. Well I'd get after you for it, but you wouldn't listen to me, you'd pick away all through class, on account of you were concentrating so hard on your studies, you were like in another world, really, and the one time you had a scab from all the picking, but you kept on at it anyways, and it was a geography test and it was all about glaciers, eh, and the formation of the earth, and I was on question four about the ice-age when you picked it right off. You picked the scab off and the blood dripped right down your forehead and down your face but you didn't do nothing. I guess you thought it was sweat so you didn't bother with it, but before long every kid in that class had put their pencil down and they was looking at you. Well I just got up and took you by the hand right straight down to the nurse's room and I laid you down and I cleaned you up. You must've cried all the water out of your body you cried so hard, honest. I didn't think you'd ever get over the embarrassment, and them girls didn't help any, the way they'd talk about you in the warshroom after that; the things that come out of their mouths, concerning you, I don't know. So poison, honest to God, I looked over once and I thought I seen spiders falling out of Nancy Tanks' little red mouth, I remember coming out of a stall and going to warsh my hands, and Margie is putting on her blush and Joanne runs in shouting, "Oh my God! Oh my GOD," she says, "Did you see her HAIR today, she looks like such a HOSE," and Margie goes, "I know, I know, she's so GROSS," so I turn around and I says, "Joanne, you better look in the mirror at your own hair before you go putting down others," and I slammed the door behind me. No I didn't, I just give 'em a dirty look, no I didn't, pretended like I didn't hear and just walked out. No I didn't do that either, you know what I did? I TOLD. I TOLD—That. Your secret. I know. I know, I promised you, I swore on the lives of my future kids, I would never tell a soul as long as I lived and I never planned to tell at all, Marie, not at all. It just spilled out of my mouth. Like organ meats. I don't know why, I'll never know. Joanne and Margie pulls me by the hand to the cafeteria over to their group, with Steve Hurley and them, and she goes, "Patsy, Patsy tell Steve, Steve, listen to this you'll *die*"......... Remember how Steve and them started calling out dirty words at you all the time from then? I remember once you asking me, "Why are they calling me those words?"

And I said I didn't know but I kept telling your secret every time Joanne or Margie would ask me to, like a jack-in-the-box, got me invited to a few of their parties, great, sitting in somebody's rec room watching everyone else neck all night. I never fit in with that crowd, that was me, jack-in-the-box, and soon the whole school knew about you and your secret just 'cause of me, you are, like, tattooed in Marmora. You'll never show your face here. And who's fault is that, eh?

She puts the pie in the oven and starts to clean up: excess dough in fridge; bowls, etc. to sink. She wipes the table clean with a J-cloth.

I work with those girls, what picked on you so, with Joanne and Nancy and Marg and even Steve, at the Soup, you know, the Lipton's

Soup factory over in Belleville? I even stand beside Marg on assembly, eh, putting dried noodles in the envelopes, all day long eight hours a day minus half an hour for lunch. We don't talk about you.

She pours herself a cup of tea.

I was just a little disappointed when you didn't come to my wedding. I'm sure you were busy or you wouldn't have missed it. That's what I kept telling my mum, but she wouldn't listen to me, she went and put a place card for you, at head table. She kept turning her head to the door, all through the ceremony, all through the food. I went up to her, I told her to stop, but you know Mum, you know how she was. Yes, I did say was, Marie. I think it's only fair to tell you that Mum passed away. Just eighty-two days ago, after a real long and too brave for words fight with cancer. You know I was always very religious, Marie, I always had a lot of faith, and I prayed all the time from when she first took sick.

She had cancer in her kidneys, eh, so her body was just filled up with poison; I never realized how important our organs are to our life, Marie. My mum was throwing up bile, Marie, bright green like paint. And when she did pass away, on that afternoon we were all in the hospital room, Dad and me, and the boys, and Rick of course, we were talking about my son Darren's wedding plans for next year, Mum loved to hear wedding talk, when suddenly Mum took some kind of convulsion. Her face sort of twisted and her body jumped up in the bed and I started screaming, Marie, they had to take me out of the room.

I kneeled down in the waiting room and I prayed and prayed and I was sure that she'd be *okay*, because I was praying so hard, and then after a while I saw my dad and my brother, Gary, coming out with Mum's coat and her things. My first thought was that Mum was coming home, I just thought thank you God, thank you God for letting her get better and then I saw their faces. Then I knew. It was stupid of me to think that she'd be coming home after I'd just seen her the way she was but that's what having that much faith does. I think you were right in what you said, Marie, that there may be no God at all. "See! I will not forget you. You are carved in the palm of my hand."

So this is, like, what I'm doing now ... anyways, just a quiet Marmora housewife, making my pies up and talking on the phone, I look at the paper, and watch my shows, hours and hours I watch, at night, like the statue in the park being snowed over, eh, the snow falling and falling and falling till you can't see the statue no more, just the snow, that's me, a statue covered in snow, just sitting there, watching the news shows, the little kids in Buffalo standing on the dresser drawer their whole room on fire, being saved by the 911 crew, and the mother of the murdered girl in Pennsylvania vowing to see the man that stabbed her girl fry in the electric chair, pointing at him, this is the drama of my life. And that's the way I like it.

I don't like change. Like, like okay ... I have been very content with things between Rick and me, right? He has always been gentle, and caring, and never presses the sex on me more than once a week: he always wants to know if I've had my pleasure, and I always tell him I have had, although I never have and wouldn't want to have, although I know all those talk shows go on about a woman is supposed to be all sexy these days, and be having the orgasms. I hate that word don't you because it always makes me think of an animal's organs, that slide out of your hands ... but I never really cared if I had them or not. I would have been quite happy to give the whole thing up. I wouldn't never tell Rick that, it would break his heart, 'cause he feels that's where he shows his love.

But then, last Thursday, something uh, happened, Marie. My son, Johnny, see, his girlfriend was over to her Mum's for the night so he brung over this friend of his, Mark, a fellow he works with, you know, just his age, eighteen, over just for the evening, to have one of my meat pies, you know, and to play cards and watch the hockey game.

And this Mark, he is a quite nice-looking guy, you know, about nineteen or twenty. And he looks at me when he talks to me. And I liked being near him, even though I did feel strangely nervous. And when I was serving him dinner my hand brushed against him and I felt: like a shock—in my privates, and my breathing was like ... high. When I spoke, I spoke high, like a ten-year-old girl, I couldn't even look in his eyes no more when he talked to me. And here I am thirty-eight years old. And then they took off down to Morrison's to catch last call, eh, 'round about midnight, and I said goodnight, and I went off to bed, Rick was out and I just lay there and thought of this Mark, okay, I thought of him putting his arms around me and lifting his shirt and my shirt and pressing his chest to my chest and my whole down-there like JOLTS. Like an avalanche, or something, eh, when the snow moves—DOWN, I never felt nothing like it, all in my down-there, my whole WOMB, just lying on my bed and thinking of this young man. I don't know why that happened but it makes me feel very embarrassed. It made me feel not myself. I don't know, you are the only person I could've told that to. You are the only person who wouldn't think the less of me.

Marie, this morning I woke up and the way the light was in the room I remembered the time we woke up; you were sleeping over at my house, I believe, and we woke up and it was early light just coming out, and we looked out my bedroom window and it was all ice outside, everything was ice, because it had been wet the day before and then it had froze, and we didn't even have breakfast, we just put our jeans and our coats on and our shoes, not boots, and we skated around the whole town.

I think of these things, every evening when I'm waiting for my pies to cook. The window you remember, it faces out to the train tracks, so in the spring—right now, right? Well right now, Marie, the light coming through that window ... it's so—beautiful, and when that train come it's like the dream of falling and there's no bottom and the air is like the oranges from Loblaws, oranger, and the sun coming off the train, it's so bright in my eyes I can't see the counter nor the clock on my stove, it's all train, and orange.

The sound of a train going by is heard.

Marie, listen to me for God's sake, even if you had lived you wouldn't have made it out of Marmora. You were marked, like for different, it was coming out of your skin like a bad smell, although I never did think you smelled, I argued that, but the point is you were out of the crowd—you were marked. But I loved you, I did love you, my best friend. And I feel cold to think that all that's left of you is some bones and a skull. I'm glad you are there, on the way to the highway after the Tim Horton's, it's nice, it's pleasant to think of people eating doughnuts and having a coffee as they drive by where you are, on their way out of town, Marie.

Marie, I don't think it would have done any good if I'd kept the promise and stayed on the track. I mean, Marie, if I was lying beside you, a skeleton, holding hands with your skeleton, we couldn't talk, or tell stories like we was on a sleep-over, we'd both be bones. And all the things I done and the sons I had and the church suppers and the pies, none of that would've been done.

My mum said for me to watch her meat pie, Marie. She counted on me, she instructed me to turn that oven off *in sixty minutes' time*, oh orange light, it is snowing outside, over the tulips out back, and the snowdrops, the fat flakes coming on down, we lie on the hook rug, the TV's on, just a laugh-track, we're eating chips, sour cream and onion, we're sharing a large bag, and we got the Tabs and we're just, like, talking, about nothing, about if we should get our hair cut short and how come I get cramps so bad on my period and you look at me and you say, "Patsy, I would rather die than have my life here, in Marmora," and I go, "Well Marie, you don't have to have your life here, my sister took off out west when she was sixteen and she's doing fine," and your face goes purple, I mean purple, and you look right at me in my eyes and you go, "Patsy, I do not have the heart. I do not have the heart to leave, I do not have the heart to stay." Then you're taking me by the hand, you take me out the back door and we're looking at the sun going down over the tracks and you whisper to me, "We'll be martyrs, Marmora martyrs," and I thought you were kidding, or talking like poetry in English class, but you keep on, "They will build a statue of us in the park," you say, "in stone," and I follow you up to the tracks and the snow keeps coming down, we're standing on the tracks in our running shoes with the snow all swirling round; my feet's getting freezing, I got no socks, and the light from the house and the orange, and the coppery smell of the pie burning; it's burning, oh my God my mother's pie! And then I hear the whistle, and I remember I forgot to take the pie out, and you squeeze my shoulder and you say, "See you after, Patsy, in the hand of God," and then I seen it, coming, bigger and bigger the train so loud so black, screaming screaming, "There it is, right there right there." I try to pull you away, off the tracks, like, "Come on, Marie, *Marie* are you crazy, come on the train is coming, my mum's pie, I gotta get it out, the pie is gonna burn," alls I wanted in the whole world was to save that pie, I was gonna get in deep, my mum hated the way the smell of something burnt stayed in a house for so long, she hated it, and alls I could see was that pie turning black, I flew off that track.

You should have come with me; jump off the track, roll down the hill, hit the rocks, gash; you should have come with me.

There wasn't no statue, Marie. Just a article in the paper. And I'll be honest with you, I haven't heard anybody even mention what happened for, oh, I'd say ten years. So as far as Marmora goes, you are gone. You're gone. But as far as I go, well, I'll tell you, this is gonna sound mental, but some times when I make my pastry, I think I'm making you, kneading the dough till, till my hands they are aching and, and I, like, form you; right in front of my eyes, right here at my kitchen table, into flesh. Looking at me, talking soft.

Marie, along with this tape you will hopefully find one frozen steak and kidney pie. I just hope it don't break apart in the mail but if it does just shove it in the microwave, it'll taste just fine.

If you ever need a break from the big city we'd just love it if you'd stop by for a visit. We've got a spare room now that the boys are gone and you would be more than welcome to stay overnight. Well, anyways, Marie, I'll let you go. Please do drop me a line, and I hope you don't mind my being so bold and all, sending you this letter by a tape. I hope that we will start up being in touch, you know, maybe just Christmas cards, or whatever, and please do enjoy the pie. Oh … Your best friend, Patsy.

She reaches over and turns off the tape recorder.

POSSIBLE MAPS
Edward Riche

POSSIBLE MAPS
Edward Riche

A large projection screen sits centre-stage. Concealed behind it is a ladder leading to the top of the screen. A cassette-tape player rests on a pedestal upstage right. Upstage left there is an illuminated drafting table, behind which are suspended three illuminated globes. Down-stage right there is an armchair and a lamp, and another suspended globe.

The performer enters. He holds a small remote-control unit with which to advance or reverse his slides. The first slide, a tourist map of Moscow, appears on the screen.

• *Tourist map of Moscow*

You find yourself in Moscow!

It is your intention to return from the Kremlin to your hotel, The Cosmos on the Mira Prospekt. Unfamiliar with the city, you consult your official city map. You determine a route. Perhaps the most efficient, perhaps one designed for the purposes of sightseeing, most likely one marrying both purposes. But, Comrade, you do not reach your destination. The official city map of Moscow has been drafted deliberately in error. You see, it was thought unwise to provide enemies of the state with an accurate aid to enterprises of sabotage, to Western imperialism.

The performer pauses and examines the map briefly.

But I don't think it's a bad map. It's a map of the reality of Moscow, the headquarters of a great madness. These truly are Stalin's streets, his avenues, his prospekts.

• *Black slide*

My father was a cartographer. Actually, he had started out as a cartographer, reputedly quite a good one, but had gone on to the more esoteric reaches of the study of geography. He had acquired a Ph.D. in geography when sociology, anthropology, literature, history and so on were all collapsing on one another. He and his peers were consumed in the vortex caused by this intellectual calamity. Somehow though, because of his attachment to maps, he was still tied to the idea of places, of this being related—in a real way—to that, of something being deeper or twelve kilometres higher than a point of reference, of annual precipitation in the Congo.

• *Annual precipitation in the Congo*

The turmoil that eventually became post-modernism was, to him, the grinding together of tectonic plates, the implosion of a star, ideas crashing around.

As he speaks, he changes the slides, with the remote-control clicker held behind his back …

• *Tectonic plates*
• *Starscape*
• *Ideas crashing around* [*slide of the performer's face*]

I'm not being very graceful here. Of course he was more than the ideas he was surrounded by. I suppose he was. No, I'm sure he was. It's just that the thought of him brings his ideas, or those ideas, the ideas that were going on around then, to mind. He had staked a lot on them. They were his means; in many ways, his life. Maybe that's the right place to start after all. Certainly ideas were his undoing.

• *Black slide*

I blame ideas.

Ideas used to occupy a very exclusive terrain. Ideas were privilege. I'm one of the generation of children whose parents were part of the great idea-grab. Any middle-class kid with the inclination could go off to a university and gorge himself on ideas. My sister has a doctorate in history from Harvard.

• *1910 map of Yugoslavia*

She teaches at McGill University in Montreal. I was halfway through my doctorate in English at Cambridge—contemporary post-colonial drama, no less—

• *Cambridge*

… when I bailed out.

• *Black slide*

Ideas were so easily had that people took them for granted. My father's generation gravely underestimated the price that would be exacted by these ideas.

The maps. The maps. The maps. Tell about the maps. My sister and I grew up with maps. All the games we played at home were constructed around maps. Easter eggs could not be found without the aid of a legend.

• *Easter-egg map*

We would go on trips to the woods and, to our terror, Dad would abandon us, leaving us only a map with which we might find him. Darkness would be upon us, the fog creeping in, and we would be shaking as we studied our laminated page, consulted our compass. We hated the game, we were horribly frightened. We wanted to say: "Daddy, this is scary. It is not a good game for children. We could get lost. We don't want to play it ever again." But could never bring ourselves to temper Dad's pleasure ...

• *Map of bog*

... when we found him in a bog. He was so proud, so happy.

But Dad got less pleasure from his work. He wasn't engaged in anything so simple as the charting of bogs.

• *Black slide*

Father was publishing papers with titles like "Maps, Meaning and Colonialism: Re-reading Reports to the Royal Geographical Society 1782-1824." When I was younger, when I was about twenty-two years old and a genius, with razor-sharp critical faculties, I would ask my father about some of these articles, ask him to explain them to me. I did it because I knew it drove him crazy, because I knew he had doubts about many of the things he was saying. What had he really discovered? I would ask him to be smart. I would ask him so that he would never answer.

He steps off-stage and returns with a lectern, which rocks precariously.

I apologize for the lectern. I don't give lectures. I don't mean this to be a lecture. My father gave lectures and the few I saw, I found incredibly tedious. I always thought that he used a lectern as a prop that lent credibility to statements that he, himself, was beginning to doubt. It was a crutch. Earlier in his tenure he would stand behind it, straight as a whip, only lightly resting his hands on it, using it to hold his notes. As he got older though, he would hold his full weight up against it. He seemed to be unsure of himself, suspected himself a fraud, mumbled, lost his place, avoided looking out into the auditorium lest he be detected, revealed. In this way, with this performance, he gained more and more credibility. Slouching, incomprehensible, he became an important scholar.

He would occasionally host a cocktail party. Our house would fill up with his colleagues and their petty rivalries. Only the younger ones talked shop. They would grow animated after a couple of drinks and talk excitedly about this idea or that. My father pretended to be encouraged by their interest and energy. Pretended ... His head was actually full of fantasy. [*angry*] I'm sure he believed that one day he would be called on some great expedition to map the interior of a newly discovered continent, one that had somehow escaped our notice until now. Daddy wasn't a university professor, Daddy was a fucking adventurer. I grew up believing that ... and maybe that's why I gave him such a hard time later, because he was a university professor.

But any hopes my father had left, all the illusions of great adventure, became a weightless cargo aboard a *Voyager* spacecraft.

• Voyager *spacecraft*

He watched in astonished disappointment as the vessel flashed back photos of Jupiter ...

• *Jupiter*

... and Saturn ...

• *Saturn*

... before tumbling into the darkness of deep space.

• *Black slide*

He stared into his drink and muttered that there was nothing left to map. He would never confess it, but I know that he was disappointed to have missed the crazier days of intellectual activity in

Europe—the days when there was a new "movement" a week, camps formed around a new theory, headquartered in one café or another. But those days were gone. Instead of sipping coffee with Dr. Freud or Lenin in Vienna ...

• *Vienna*

... he was listening to Dr. Peterson complain about his insurance premiums at the Science Building cafeteria.

• *Science Building cafeteria*

He started feeling sorry for himself. He moped. He drank a lot while parked in front of the television. Drunk and sleepless, he made embarrassing long-distance phone calls to old buddies.

Then one day, after this long interval of solitary depression, my father suddenly seemed to perk up. He seemed to once again have purpose. He woke early and worked late. He seemed—driven. This was new ... and ... unusual ... and probably should have set off a few alarms among his family and friends. But we were exhausted by the weight of his melancholy and felt it best if we left what seemed well enough alone. There is a natural human tendency to do that kind of thing, accept a trade-up for a better kind of madness, to be thankful for a change from a dark, introspective insanity to a happy, stupid insanity. Some prescribed medicines offer just such a deal. Dad was smiling as he slogged away at a new series of maps for the Government of Newfoundland.

• *Remote-sensing technical map*

Improved remote sensing techniques had provided new and more accurate data, so charts of the interior were being revised. Dad was on the team. Three months later, one week after the "new" maps were released ...

• *Dad's trick map*

... news came of two anglers out of St. John's who had become lost in the woods for three long days and nights. Nocturnal gloom and a deep fog had descended upon them so they were forced to guide themselves home with the aid of one of the "new" maps.

• *Zoom-in on Dad's trick map*

These men were not novices. They had experience in the bush. They were familiar with maps. The map that had led them astray wasn't so in error as to elicit any grave doubts. There was nothing so strange as the reporting of a non-existent hill. A large marsh [*he points*]... seemed ... to be ... pretty much where you expected it. The map was only slightly ... skewed, there wasn't the proper "balance" of things.

• *Further zoom-in on Dad's trick map*

A pond that should have been two miles to the east south-east [*points this out*] turned out to be three miles directly to the south-east. [*hushed*] The anglers never suspected for a second that the map was in error. They imagined that they must have made a minor miscalculation. They trusted the paper over their considerable common sense. "There it is—on the map," despite what they might have seen. They staggered around in the deepening murk growing more confused by the moment, under the spell of a horrible hallucinogen. They bickered: "It's this way!" "No, it's this way!" They seemed to have found their place: "We'll see the river and the bridge—

The performer goes behind the screen, climbs the ladder, and appears on top.

—from the top of this hill." But no river, no bridge. They spent the first night in the woods—cold, hungry. They had taken a wrong turn. With daylight they would go to the nearest peak, look over the land, consult the map and find their way. It wasn't any kind of emergency. It was just a shame that their families would be worried. They were embarrassed at the prospect of a search party. Well, they woke and soon situated themselves and set off, deeper and deeper into the wilderness. Dad claimed to have been without malice—it was a game, a puzzle. He was sorry for the great anxiety he had caused: the wives in tears; the children worried and confused; the men hungry, in a panic. Dad just couldn't believe that they had kept believing in the map. He had imagined that users would spot the obvious errors and then try to decode his puzzle. What did they think they were doing? They could be playing a game on the barrens, leisurely working on the crossword, searching for buried treasure. The world was too small; everybody knew everything; it was a noble project—creating a new world. Those anglers were explorers—they were more than that, they were primitive men struggling against a malevolent god. Their world a dark mystery.

He prepares to descend.

Dad felt as though he had given these men a gift—he had written a wonderful story for them.

His head pops up.

An adventure.

And yes, they could have solved the puzzle.

He begins to speak in a singsong voice.

For every second of latitude you travel north you must shift the longitude by 1.5 seconds to the east.

He laughs.

It becomes increasingly complicated if you choose to travel in something other than a straight line.

He assumes a BBC announcer's voice.

Yes, the map is simply a tale, a primitive simple story—one person's version of the world. Not to fault them, but those unfortunate anglers had assumed the map was the world. It isn't even a picture of the world—it's merely a report, a simpleton's story, told in ... [*drops BBC announcer's voice*] monkey language ...

He has a revelation.

Yes, monkey language. Monkeys do speak, you know. They squawk nouns at one another. They scream, "Lion!" "Hill." "Python!" "Tree." My father was an extraordinary teller of stories ... in fluent MONKEY! [*pause*] We've got ourselves in a lot of trouble lately placing too much faith in stories, mistaking them for the world.

He moves towards the armchair and resumes the slide show.

This is not the world ...

• *Peeters Projection map*

This?

• *Upside down world*

This?

• *Map of Quebec incorporating Labrador*

Is this the world?

• *Mercator projection*

This is the where I went to school. Where I went to school, the distance between Head Smashed In Buffalo Jump, Alberta, and Kyzel, Autonomous Soviet Republic of Tuva, is almost the same as the distance between Ouagadougou, Burkina Faso, and Christmas Island, Kiritimati. Such is simply not the case.

He goes to the globe down-stage.

This string connects Head Smashed In Buffalo Jump to Kyzel ... This string Ouagadougou to Christmas. And ... with a twist of the wrist ... Ta da!

He shows the strings to be of different lengths.

You've got to pity the poor crow that flies.

The notion that maps should pretend to be accurate representations of the world is a new idea. This is the world—according to the Christian church.

• *Early Christian T-O map*

Maps were, first, simple guides to get you from one place to the next. They were there to help you if you had lost your way.

• *Black slide*

Lost ...
What a horrible thing—to be lost. My father was lost, as I'm sure you've been. He knew where he was but didn't know where to turn. Perhaps he didn't know where he was going, or what that place might be.

• *Maze with "You are here" twice*

Perhaps he knew where *he* was but didn't know where that "where" was?

• *Black slide*

Stanley found a Livingstone who wasn't lost at all. Having lost track of the man, his sponsors merely assumed he had disappeared. But Livingstone knew precisely where he was. It was presumptuous of England to imagine otherwise. In darkest Africa, England was lost.
He extends his hand.
"Dad, I presume."

• *A young woman*

Oh ... Ooops ... that's not right. It's ... it must have ... this is the wrong slide, it must have been left in the tray ... anyway, moving along ...

Flustered, he mistakenly goes backwards in the slide-tray.

Oh dear ...

   • *The young woman again*

It's a curious coincidence but this is a photograph of an old lov— ... girlfriend of mine, and she's made reference to a little later ... in a map story. It must have been left in the tray. Janice. I saw her when I was studying in England. I'm going to skip ahead ...

He races through the next slides, the first of which, a title card, announces the titillating theme of the section.

   • *BURIED TREASURE*
   • *Series: Maps of St. John's*

The maps obviously show locations of buried treasure but they are passed over so quickly that it is difficult to make sense of them. The next slide shows a crudely hand-drawn map on loose-leaf paper. It directs the user to an English country place.

   • *Byron's map*

This map has tormented me for years. It is so poorly imagined and executed. The scale changes randomly as you cross the page. The junctions are ambiguous. It almost compels you to wrong turns. It directs prospective revellers to a party being held at a country estate. I was invited. So was Janice. The party was sort of a send-off for her. She was continuing her studies in Canada. I saw the event as my last chance to profess my love for her. JESUS, this map! It was fashioned by the host—a twit named Byron. You may have guessed by now that I am not fond of maps, that they irritate me. I have drawn only one in my entire life. This ...

• *Performer's first accurate map*

... is an accurate map of the area, with appropriate indicators to guide travellers. It even warns the motorist of prospective traps, of treacherous forks in the road. Forks like that one. [*points*] Perhaps if I had been guided by this map, my life might have taken a different turn. That fork in the road! I took a wrong turn. I drove abandoned country roads for hours. Like those ill-fated anglers, I panicked. I attempted short cuts rather than retracing my steps. I got lost. Horribly lost. And finally, like a proper idiot, I ran out of petrol. My car came to a halt on a lonely one-lane road winding through endless hectares of flax. I filled the tank here. [*points*] I've reconstructed the entire affair.

• *Previous map with circuitous route superimposed*

My Vauxhall's tank would have carried me seventy-two miles. So it was here [*points to an "X"*] that I staggered into the flax and howled, in despair, like a dog at the moon.

She was in Ottawa for two years ...

• *Ottawa*

... and then moved to San Francisco.

• *San Francisco*

I tried to contact her there one night but she had moved on. A mutual friend met her while vacationing in Antwerp ...

• *Antwerp*

... and said she asked about me. I wonder ...

• *West Coast*

... where ...

  • *Four states*

... she ...

  • *Arkansas*

... is ...

  • *Ontario*

... now.

  • *East Coast*

But no one else got lost that night.

  • *Byron's map again*

They all made it to the party ... no problem.

  • *Dad's trick map again*

Dad's trick maps were withdrawn from circulation, at considerable cost to the taxpayer.

  • *Black slide*

To avoid facing criminal charges Father had to be examined by a physician who testified that he was suffering from ... "nervous exhaustion." Folks at the university were not amused. They were particularly sensitive to mad-professor stories floating around. My sister was mortally embarrassed. Dad was placed on sick leave. Strangely, he didn't claim he was sane. Dad claimed that mental illness was simply an incredibly common disability. There were provisions to protect people with disabilities. They couldn't fire someone for having lost a leg. How could they fire him for having lost some of his mind? Lost? We allowed him to make a fool of himself, writing letters to the paper demanding rights for "the emotionally dysfunctional"—that's what he called it. We didn't try to stop him because we were filled with dread at the prospect of him having to spend all his time at home: we desperately wanted him back at the university. Even if you love your father—think of him being around ALL the time. Think of your poor mother. Our mother was quite terrified at the prospect of Dad hanging around the house. Only a couple of days after his dismissal, he started to talk about "systematizing" the workings of the household. I think everyone's father likes to imagine that he's "handy," despite all evidence to the contrary: the shed ...

- *The shed*

... the bookcase ...

- *The bookcase*

... the workbench ...

- *The workbench*

Growing up, I remember that every dad in the neighbourhood ...

- *Map of neighbourhood*

... attempted to put a wet-bar in the rec room.

- *Map of neighbourhood with X's*

Seemingly as an afterthought, he points to one of the lots on the map.
That's a nice property, shows beautifully, old mouldings, lots of
"character."
He laughs sardonically.

• *Black slide*

Clearly my father would have to be kept busy. There was a brief and
failed effort to find for Papa some kind of hobby. We could never
suggest such an idea outright. We reasoned that he would feel,
justifiably I suppose, that he was being treated as an invalid, and that
we had concluded he was never going to return to the university. I
attempted to lure him into the pleasures of tennis, but I believe he
understood it as a rather pathetic attempt at closer father-son relations,
and so he went along with it briefly. But I also think he pitied me and
was even embarrassed by my efforts at intimacy. He was soon making
transparent excuses not to play. My sister and mother thought that
gardening might be the ticket, but Dad showed interest only in
drawing plans.

He was testing our patience. We tried to help him but he refused
to cooperate. As feared, he became a burden and a torment. Though
they had been happily married for years, my parents began to fight. My
mother would call my sister and I at all hours, often in tears. One of
us would have to go over and attempt to straighten things out,
awkwardly. Long-established roles were now reversed. Dad and Mom
behaved like children. My sister and I had our own lives and little time.
We began to fight over who would go this time, each of us arguing that
we had put in more hours of service, even insinuating, strangely, that
the other had more responsibility. We didn't get along all that well, my
sister and I. I think she was embarrassed by me. She had become a big
deal at the university and I … I sell … "real" estate. After … my …
problem … [*loudly*] PROBLEMS … at university I … I had to do
something. She resents the fact that I make so much money. Do you

know something: when she and her husband were looking for a house in St. John's, when she moved back, they didn't call me. She said it was a bad idea to involve family in financial matters. Too bad, eh? I could have sold them THEIR DREAM HOME!

• *Drawing and plan of dream house*

What a beauty this is going to be. Look at the size of that kitchen. Planning for kids, are you? Lovely yard. I think there will be a lot of young families on this street. [*pause*] Of course the trees aren't there yet ...

• *Same drawing without trees*

... and that man there, [*points*] he's your neighbour. He's two storeys tall. Big guy.

But my sister wouldn't have me sell them a house. It's odd that she would be so cautious about real estate; after all she is the historian, she's the expert on real estate. That's all history really is, isn't it? One great series of tragic real-estate deals.

We've both carried on the family business of maps, of boundaries, of lines drawn in the sand, if only in the abstract. Perhaps my "problems" at the university were propitious.

I suppose you think I'm being facetious, that I'm bitter over my sister's success. Not so. I'm much happier in real estate than I ever would have been in the academy. I deal with *people* now instead of characters, people as real as you and me. Deep in my studies I think I'd lost the ability to separate the two. It was easy to think of every person you met as a player in some drama. I would never admit to having held that view. It was so modernist, so trite, so naïve. Obviously though, given my exploits in England, I had cast myself as the lead in a great tragedy. I was bound up in a ridiculous story. Young people do this.

Today I have fewer illusions. I am intimate with the "real" in real estate. I do love the business: talking on the phone, zooming around town, pressing the flesh, getting inside people's lives. Moving is very traumatic you know! Every deal I make is a big deal for somebody. What's "real" about real estate? A home to raise a family; increasing property values; a starter home you can't go wrong with; the foundation is everything; kitchen with built-ins; on lease-hold land for a century. What's the point of an outdoor pool in Newfoundland? Awfully near the "Circle." You can tell by getting on a ladder and poking at the eaves with a simple screwdriver. A MAN'S HOME IS HIS CASTLE!

What do they buy? Not those lovely fireplaces or the eat-in kitchen. They buy the fence, my friend. They buy the dimensions on surveyors' documents, their piece of history, they buy the line on a map. So I'm very much my sister's brother, very much my father's son. And perhaps that lineage was the root of my ... "problem."

• *Black slide*

He pauses to reflect.
Yes, my "problem." I'm well enough now but I ... got "unwell" over in England. I thought I was in love with Janice ...

• *Janice*

... but really, I had hardly ever spoken to her. Let's be honest. I did try to call her, that's true, but I think my friend only said that she had asked after me in Antwerp to be nice.

• *Black slide*

And I screwed up my doctorate. I drank a lot. WHOOOW, spooooky. I got into drugs. Because I began to hate myself, I picked fights with giant fuckers who would inevitably kick the shit out of me. Because I was so unconcerned over whether I should live or die, I jumped into my trusty Vauxhall one evening after having put away a quart of whisky—Irish—and several pints of lager—British—and I tore around London like Mario Andretti until finally ... here ...

• *Map of London*

... I collided with a parked ... building.

• *Black slide*

What an asshole.
He takes a deep bow.
When I came to ... days later! ... who, with my one remaining eye—
He covers the lost eye with his hand.
—did I look up to see hovering over me? Dear old Dad, of course.
Thanks for the guilt, Dad.
He turns as if to continue on another tack and then halts.
This eye?
He removes the cupped hand.
I've seen you looking at it. It's the first success story in an innovative transplant procedure. This ... is ... a baboon's eye. The eye of a monkey. Slide!
Finally the top blew.

• *Mount St. Helens*

An argument erupted that shook the very foundations of my parents' marriage. I suppose every family has a dark area. Sometimes it's politics, or the man one's daughter married, an abortion, a divorce. There are those silences when a visitor mistakenly brings the subject up.
He turns on the cassette player: dramatic Japanese music is heard.
In 1976 my father attended a symposium in Kyoto ...

• *Kyoto*

... where, during a banquet, he fell under the spell of sushi. Yes,

Dad was hypnotized by Japanese cuisine. Yes, the subject that always brought my parents to paroxysms of acrimony was the proper preparation of seafood and, in this instance, the appropriate cooking time for lobster. I know this sounds trivial but after his return from Japan, Dad insisted on serving fish that was virtually raw. We all hated it. It was more than unpalatable; it was sickening. You would think that he would have been satisfied to have his fish raw and to serve ours fully cooked, but no, he insisted that we would grow to like it. He was self-righteous.

The first great affray in this gastronomic dispute came when my father prepared halibut for my mother's sister and her husband who were visiting from England. Slabs of gelatin graced their plates. Mom just got up from the table and went to the kitchen. Aunt Alice and Uncle Byron—yes, he was a Byron too—were left in the difficult position of, out of courtesy, having to eat dad's preparation. They were deep in the jungle among strange natives who might be dangerously insulted if you didn't eat the grub stew. After having collected herself, Mom stormed back into the dining room. The ensuing fight ended with my aunt and her husband feeling it best to leave, my mother in tears, and my sister and I confused, and Dad—why was he being such an idiot? It was a lie to say that he thought they might have enjoyed fish prepared properly. Why was he so selfish? Didn't he think of anybody but himself? How could he have ruined her sister's visit? There was a torrent of tears. There was such deep despair, such disappointment. I remember going to bed that night and listening intently to the mumbles coming from down the hall. I couldn't make out a word, but I was riveted, worried that Mom would leave Dad because he was so selfish, worried that … MOM WOULD LEAVE US WITH DAD, that we would no longer be lulled to sleep by the sound of her playing the piano downstairs, that comfort and common sense would finally concede to chaos. That we would have to grow up once and for all.

He looks around hopefully.

Mom? [*pause*] But in the morning we woke up and it was as if nothing had ever happened. My parents were conducting themselves at breakfast in such a manner as to suggest that we should forget that anything had happened. We could tell from how meticulously the table was set ...

• *Meticulous table setting*

... that no questions should be asked. We could tell from the fact that we were having fresh-squeezed orange juice instead of frozen that we would never say to our Aunt Alice, "Remember when Dad served you raw fish?"

• *Black slide*

We could tell that if anybody ever brought up the topic of sushi that we should all contribute to a collective effort to change the subject.

But this time, years later, it was lobster. When I arrived I could see the detritus of battle. The scene of the crime!

• *Schematic of kitchen crime scene*

There was a partially cooked lobster in two pieces on the kitchen floor. Father had evidently only plunged the crustacean in the boiling water for a moment for it still exhibited vestigial motor capacity.

He mimes the lobsters' claws moving.

The victim was in the bathroom being comforted by my sister. The tone of their discussion suggested to me that my sister had broken a solemn pledge. She was taking sides. My father, the perpetrator, was sitting at the dining room table. He was eating one of his *Homard à la Japonaise* with the affected nonchalance of an idle *boulevardier*, discreetly wiping the corners of his mouth with a linen napkin, washing it all down with a flinty Chablis that had been put away for a special occasion. I don't know whether this was out of spite or simply because he didn't know quite what else to do. And the lobster ... the white flesh was ... difficult—runny, gelatinous. The meat, or organs, within the body cavity, the portion my father was eating when I found him, were something else altogether ... black. Black slime that dripped and splattered on his plate as he spooned it into his mouth.

• *Black slide*

And I don't know whether I imagined it, but the antennae of the poor creature seemed to be moving. The sight held me in terror for a moment. I hadn't considered, really, that he actually was insane. But then, as he ate that black goo ... I was frightened by my own father and suddenly overcome by anxiety about my own mental health. How fragile is the mind?

Black slides and blank screen rapidly alternate as the performer stands in front of the screen for three "mug shots" against the white light.

• *White light*
• *Black slide*

Was I governed ... was I governed by an inherited gene that had, one day, years ago, at Cambridge, started sending confused messages to my brain? I wanted to say something to him. But what? I should have understood. I walked to the living-room and collapsed in a chair. I was paralysed. An hour or so passed, the light waned. My sister found me and began a tirade. "I" had to do something about all this! It was my job to confront Dad! Why? Because I was the son and therefore somehow more "like" my father? I would have argued and refused but I was so stunned that I let her lecture me. I sheepishly nodded in agreement. It was all I could do.

I found him in his study. It was a room I had rarely entered. From the time I was a child I always found the room unsettling. The focus was a large drafting table on which my father worked, on which he drew maps. The walls were covered with my father's favourite maps ...

• *Aerial map*

- *Franklin expedition*
- *The North Pole*
- *Hell*
- *Newfoundland*

... or maps of some mysterious significance. Nothing was familiar. There was no map of anything I knew, no Mercator. There was an ancient map of Newfoundland but it offered no relief, no firm ground. When I was a child I couldn't understand what was wrong with it. It didn't resemble Newfoundland at all. Where was the truth? Who was lying to me? There were maps of unearthly scale: 10,000 to 1. But how could a picture of something be larger than the thing itself?

- *Black slide*

My father was at the window. I was lost for words, so I awkwardly looked around the room, poked at things.

"I'm mapping the north-west passage for Franklin," he said.

I was relieved that he recognized the gravity of the situation and had some sense of humour, however morbid, about it all. I didn't do as well. I huffed or snorted or whiffed or something. I went "Phuffh." I kept my head down, avoiding eye contact. I looked at the big map on the drafting table and feigned interest. I didn't recognize the terrain immediately but there were familiar elements ...

- *The bog map*

... familiar landmarks.

- *Dad's journey* [*big map*]

A journey was being charted. The expedition had evidently found themselves in some trouble for they were now encamped at one of the lowest points in an immense maze of canyons.

• *Maze of canyons*

The sides were incredibly steep. The path of an extinct river winding madly; dinosaur bones. You couldn't see where you were going. Perhaps they had lost their way. They appeared to have been travelling in circles. I snuffled or piffed again.

"I've got to find a way out of there," said my father. I was taken aback. What was this map?

"Out of where?" I asked.

"Despair," he said. "Labyrinthine canyons of despair."

A long pause.

"Humph," I said.

• *Dad's journey again*

"Back there." He pointed to a high plateau. "It seemed so clear. Things had gone so well that I became over-confident. I charted a much too perilous course. The journey bogged down here, in the badlands outside Disillusion."

"Disillusion?"

"It's an abandoned mining town. Bad decisions were made and I ended up in the Despairs. We seem lost, there may be mutiny."

"What's your plan?"

"I could continue through Despair and hope to come out here, but it's a long journey and there's a desert to cross after that."

"Any other options?"

"Yes. I could attempt to scale the canyon wall. It would be tough and we would have to change our course and choose a new destination, but if we got up there it would be an easier journey. I'm getting old and tired. I don't know if I could make it through a desert, most likely alone."

"The canyon is deep?"

"Deep."

"How deep?"

"Thirty thousand miles." He laughed and said "But these are very unreliable charts."

What a journey.

• *Heart Laid Seige by Love map*

An incredible battle took place here, The Heart Laid Siege by Love, repeated assaults to the front and flanks. The heart abandons its fortress and flees, love in pursuit. The heart takes to the hills and then, surprisingly, mounts a counter-assault. But love triumphs, the heart eventually surrendering after 487 days. I believe I was conceived here, at love's encampment, where the treaty was signed.

• *Dad's journey again*

The terrain grows rough then … there are treacherous swamps where the mission can bog down, illness—fevers … they give way to rolling hills, to the mountains and the great plateau. The plateau was not without its pitfalls. There are sudden drops—Buffalo Jumps—despairs, griefs.

To the east, Father's map began to lose detail. Features of the terrain were accompanied by question marks. There were vast blank zones, reports describing the area were unreliable, speculative. These lands were peopled by hairy ape-men—the fearsome flax people; there were bottomless lakes—home to beasts.

He stops; his eyes glaze over.

Eyeglasses rest on the yellowing pages of a journal: "I'm growing weaker." A pair of boots hang from a strange tree with blood-red leaves and poisonous black fruit.

• *Son's map*

Terra Incognita. I choose to leave the expedition before the Despairs. These lands are mine. They are anything but featureless. The journey seems as perilous as my father's. Many times I've thought of turning back ... but ... I might get lost and ... what would I find?

The walls of Dad's canyon were successfully scaled. The expedition proceeded. Dad found himself with Mom in the Great Valley, which offered a wonderful opportunity to regroup, take on new provisions. The remainder of the journey was being charted when, quite without warning, my father perished.

The light on the projector screen fades out.

Though he seemed in good health, I guess the Despairs and the difficult climb had taken the good out of him.

He left this.

He holds up a piece of paper.

A last navigational aid. It reads simply ...

The lights fade. On the floor of the stage, an X-shaped pool of light appears. The performer steps into it.

"You are here."

ANNE MARIE'S BEDROOM
Jennifer Ross

ANNE MARIE'S BEDROOM
Jennifer Ross

Anne Marie, a heavily tattooed woman, sits on a platform bed surrounded by a sultan's tent of netting. (Note: When Anne Marie speaks about her tattooing experiences, the text is italicized.)

This is where it starts: here, above the hip. An ivy, creeping its way over here and then circling the navel, before climbing its way up to here, the nipple. This I had done when I was nineteen so I could mark my body before anyone else could: to say, this is my body to do with as I please. In the time since, I have added to the ivy various things at particular times. A hummingbird after I had my baby Anna. A honeysuckle to cover a surgery. A hurricane to fill in some space between my navel and my breasts: space that got larger as I got older. What does a hurricane look like as a tattoo? What indeed. You would really have to see it.

Fuck, I blew it. I knew there would be hell to pay—he'll never trust me again. I shouldn't have gone. I *had* to, that's all there is to it. I mean I couldn't pass up an opportunity to get away from here—if only for a weekend. No, I had to, I had to go. But now what's he going to do? He is going to be here any minute; he is on his way *now*. I've blown it. The needle. Oh fuck.

The house I live in has ten men and ten women and my room at the top of the stairs is the largest room. I am the only woman who does not have to share, they say because I am mean, no one would want to share with me, I am crazy. But we are all crazy in here. That is the point.

No, the reason I do not have to share is that I am the Queen, the Sacred Whore, the Madonna, the Ancient Babylonian Love Goddess. *You* call me Anne Marie.

People said, once you have one you won't be able to stop.

To my private room at the top of the stairs, the men of the house come to visit. You may say they are not much to look at, I don't mind, it is no insult to me. After all, it is me they are lining up for, me. I am their soft pillow, their Milk, their Mother, their Solace, their Lover. And when they come, they come as I have told them, bearing gifts and sacred offerings. John: a comb for my hair, mother-of-pearl. Dick: a pair of silk garters and push-up bra, crimson red and lacy black. Roger: a bottle of No. 5. and lacquer for my nails. And Ed, my main man: a two-six of lemon gin and a soft pack of Camels.

Everybody told me, once you get started you won't be able to stop.

And what do I care that they make no money, that they have no money to give me. I say, it doesn't take any money, honey, to bring Anne Marie a present. So I make the suggestion, I tell them what I want. And they come, they stand outside my door, shifting or still, until I tell them to come in. I tell them, loosen up your belt and slacks, but don't take them off. Come over here and lie on top of me. Lift my skirt but don't take it off. Do it until you come, while I watch TV. But don't take too long, or I might not ask you back. Okay then?

Once you begin there's no turning back. When they are finished, I ask them to wipe me gently with a Kleenex from their pocket and to take the Kleenex with them as they leave. I tell them, on their way out, don't say anything about me to the other guys, don't say my name outside this room. I don't want them taking my name in vain.

I was well warned. People said, you will regret it, there will come a day when you want to settle down—we all do sooner or later—and no decent, god-fearing, hard-working, family-loving guy will want to marry you then. And I said, is that right?

I lay down the rules; it frees them up and lets them breathe, lets them love me like a whore. And don't forget we all have to live in the same house together. We can't afford to have petty jealousies or any of them proclaiming they've fallen in love with me.

The only one who doesn't appreciate this arrangement is the housemother, the one who gets paid to run the joint, only you'd think she's doing it because she's a *saint*. What can you expect of someone who cooks and cleans for a house of twenty loonies? This is not a field with room for advancement. She *hates* me entertaining the guys in my room, says its sinful. She's a Christian Fundamentalist. She complains to my social worker about me, says: "We've really got to do something about that Anne Marie, her atrocious behaviour is corrupting the household." But I really don't see why it is any of their concern.

If you do it, they said, you will be considered a freak.

But they make it their concern. So the social worker has to come and visit me. Poor Ron, he is *such* a loser, he's so burnt out and he *never* gets laid at home. How useful must he feel after visiting people who despise him, every day for ten or fifteen years. He will parallel-park poorly, climb the stairs to my room wearily, poke his curly perm around my door, and say: "Anne Marie, you aren't angling for a re-admission to Bellevue, are you? Funny, I wouldn't have thought you'd want to be going back there. And yet, judging by your behaviour as of late ... "

The first one felt so good, but if you weren't involved in it, if you hadn't chosen it and someone was, say, twisting and pinching your skin to make you feel that way, well then I suppose the pain would be intolerable. But it wasn't that way for me. It was like getting a thousand bee stings, like getting a bee sting every second for three or four hours and—well—I guess I got hooked.

So now the social worker has assigned a summer student to me and she comes three times a week. The other day she came to my room and sat at the foot of my bed. I noticed the blouse she was wearing was too big in the bust. There were sunken tents of cotton where breasts were meant to be and it made her seem like a child playing someone else. She talks looking down at the hands in her lap. At least she doesn't constantly force eye contact. During her visit I snooped through her briefcase and read she was working on my "Grooming and Personal

Hygiene" with me. So she says: "Well hello, Anne Marie, how are you doing? Oh I see you've been making yourself look pretty." Which really cracks me up because when I do my face I really paint it; I mean I put on butterflies and blossoms, whatever catches my fancy. And as the day wears on, I just keep adding more and more.

I mean, she'd float away if you breathed on her. Looks like she'd crack if she spread her legs. And she's coming around telling me how to do myself up—barely nineteen. But I go along with her because I get a chuckle out of her being so sincere, imagining her going back to the social worker and saying: "I sure am making progress with Anne Marie." So I'll let her say to me: "Gee, Anne Marie, you sure are looking pretty these days. But I have a suggestion for a way to do your make-up that would be real flattering to you." And I'll let her spend an hour working on my face so that it will look like no one has worked on my face. And I'll say, Boy, doesn't that look nice.

I don't really see what the big deal is. I mean if the body is only a car, and you had to drive the same car for, say, sixty or eighty years, would you rather be in a Volkswagen covered in primer, or a Thunderbird in candy-apple red with gold metallic flakes and 3-D decals?

So last Thursday the clothing allowance cheque came in—*fifty dollars*—and it was time to hit the Bi-way. We get there and Sunshine is being real sweet. She's terrified to have me out in public, poor kid, and why shouldn't she be: I am a huge responsibility.

It becomes immediately obvious we both want to get the shopping over with as quickly as possible. I cannot think of anything that appeals to me less than wrestling with someone's grandmother over an item of sale clothing in a pastel colour. And Sunny says: "Hey Anne Marie, here's a nice dress," and holds up one of those duster numbers, you know, almost like a muu-muu. The dress is sort of four pastel colours but at the same time no colour at all—like porridge with violet flecks. So she holds it up and I say, Yeah that's real nice, what size is it? Great, that'll be just great.

Then we're moving back to where they have ladies' shoes and she grabs this pair of mules and says: "Oh these look comfy, don't they

Anne Marie?" I look at the pair of grey plastic things she's holding up and say, Yeah they look real comfy, what size are they? Great, those'll be just great.

So with all that settled, we make our way up to the check-out and there's a really long line—the welfare cheques have come in—and Little Sunshine says: "Well I suppose you can wait in line by yourself. You don't mind, do you, if I go back and look at the ironing boards?" Mind? Go ahead, look at the ironing boards, of course. As she bobs away, a picture of Sunny wearing freshly ironed pyjamas in a polyester pinstripe, legs sharply creased, pops into my head. The door of her closet glides open to show hanging sheets of crisp tissue, separating one stiffly pressed blouse from the next. No sooner has she disappeared than I'm out of there like lightning, cheque in hand, merchandise tossed behind me as I go.

People said, it may seem like a fun thing to do now but you'll regret it later. Try picturing yourself as an octogenarian grandmother with your doodled elephant skin. I imagined my skin shrunken and withered, slack and sagged, or muscled and stretched, and realized that the pictures would distort accordingly, and I liked the idea. I thought about being sixty or eighty with this map of marks all over me and grandchildren saying, "What's this, what's this," and I loved the idea. It might remind them and me I've come from somewhere.

I cashed my cheque at the Money Mart and took the streetcar to the Woodbine Bar out by the track. I like it out there because if the guys are doing well, they'll keep you watered all night. And if they're not, well then I had my own money to spend.

I didn't come home for *two nights*. I partied with this Stan guy—and had a whale of a time until my money and his whisky ran out.

Guys don't know how to take you, I mean they are not accustomed to a woman who looks like this. And people just assume you are bad, nasty, a deviant. They move away from you on the subway, give you a wide berth. And I say, Gooooood.

I once had this little canary, Puff. I bought her one winter, seduced by the promise of waking to a sunlit bedroom and a merrily trilling bird. Everyone insisted the bird was no more than a common finch. Look, canaries have yellow breasts and puff their throats when they sing. This bird is shades of brown and its neck is still. No, I said, this canary is just a baby that hasn't yet reached maturity.

I went to the pet shop in the mall and bought an expensive vitamin supplement in liquid form. I was advised to add the prescribed amount, 0.6 millilitres, to the canary's drinking water, fresh daily. If the bird was indeed a canary, the vitamin would help bring up the yellow in the feathers and bring on a strong song.

Through the winter I fed the bird the vitamin in her drinking water. The bird didn't change. I added more and more of a dosage until the bird's water was now bright yellow, as yellow as a canary's chest is meant to be.

I suppose the enriched water tasted too peculiar for the little bird, because she went off it and later—although I did not know it at the time—stopped drinking entirely.

One evening I came home to a quiet, dark apartment and found her, legs in the air, dead on the floor of her cage.

I buried her in a Tetley box.

Sunny is in a pretty pickle over my escape. She came in to visit me this morning and because she was carrying a Bi-way bag, at first I thought she'd bought me the muu-muu and mules herself. So I let her sit at the foot of my bed, and after shooting the shit for five minutes she said: "Well Anne Marie, I know you are out of clothing money, so I got you these underpants that were on sale."

I took them out of the bag and I could not believe my eyes. Seven pairs of extra large, one-hundred-percent cotton briefs, all in baby pink. I don't even wear underwear—what's the point unless you need something to stick the maxipad onto—and if I did it sure wouldn't be this kind. I said, Well thanks a lot, I just didn't know how I was going to get along without decent underpants. Sunshine takes this opportunity to suggest I might want to do some mending, to make the most of the clothes I still had. A stitch in time. She left me with some needles and a spool of white thread, saying she'd be back to check on me in a couple of hours.

Listen, I have never stitched a seam in my life. But that pile of pink briefs gave me an idea. I went to the closet and pulled out a housecoat I hadn't worn in years—a fuzzy yellow number with black rickrack around the neck and zipper. I took a pair of nail-scissors and yanked off all the rickrack, then took the scissors to the pile of underpants and snipped out the crotches from each and every pair, leaving a clean little oval. I took the rickrack and pressed it into place, around the openings, and sewed it on. And what a sight they were. I pulled a pair onto my head, another over my dress up around my hips, and the rest I flung on curtain rods and door handles. For a while I pranced around like that, a ballerina on a high wire.

Right on schedule—four o'clock sharp—Sunny patters in. Well she looked like she'd swallowed a bird. But Sunny Honey, I said, you know you gotta cut a diamond for its light to shine through.

What if my scribbled leather skin won't be appropriate then? But an aged, infirm body isn't appropriate to anyone, anyhow. If by then the only thing I have to regret are the marks, then I'll have done pretty well, I figure. No, by then they will just be relics of a former life, as will my uterus and other parts for that matter.

He's not going to do it. He just threatens. He said himself I manage without the 'promazine. Everyone is afraid of the stuff, right, you can watch the guys of the house line up for their needle and, week after week, grown men, they will faint—wither like cut flowers in a too-hot room. I can't remember anything from back then, all that got erased. Oh the bastard, the pasty, mealy little crustacean. I would rather *die*. I won't, won't. I won't let him come near me. He'd better stay clear of me.

I blew it with that little binge, but it was real sweet to come home to the guys again. Someone had started the rumour I'd eloped with one of the cashiers from the Sev' at the end of our street. Well *that* would be an attractive prospect. They had missed me something awful and I found them lined up waiting for me. The hall outside my bedroom was like an over-booked doctor's office. There they stood, backs against the wall, five against one wall, five against the other. They were all smoking their Player's filters and the smoke hung above their heads in a single cloud. As if they were sending their prayers to heaven in the smoke, the cloud read "Anne Marie." Actually Harry, who has never said two words to me in my life, got it in his head to spray-paint my name blood red down the corridors. Through all the smoke it was a neat effect.

I shouldn't have taken off ... Ron will ... Oh God, the needle ... I'll be the same, same as the others ... loss of sex, hunger ... twenty different people, the same person, seem like the same ... sitting on bed, head in hands, legs like poured concrete ... Oh God, so weak like you need a transfusion ... weak like you haven't eaten for days ... I shouldn't have gone ... Ron is gonna ... no memory, a day a week ... if I can't remember I can't decide ... I'll be the same ... but by then, too late ... afraid *not* to take the needle ... too afraid not to ... I know I've been told ... my mind works against me ... I've been told, I'm my own worst enemy ... I'll *never* be well, my mind keeps me ill ... don't know any more, which is worse ...

I wanted something to look at, and their being so permanent was the whole idea. Thinking of the skin as a scrap of paper, I wanted to decorate it in a pleasing way. Might as well if I am to have it before me all the livelong day. And all these years, they have been the only things I have owned. Of course they could never rob me of them. For this reason they have made me feel reassured and more permanent.

Well the body gets its battle scars in the course of living and all of them unpleasant: pock marks, a Caesarean, melanomas, liver spots. So, I thought, why not add *some marks: good marks, amulets, marks of my choosing? And, not scars, they would be badges, brooches to ensure distinction and safe passage through these events of life.*

Across my midriff a hurricane rages, strokes of red and green, so passionate, the perfect work of a master Japanese tattooist. Some have called them waves and others flames, but all have said they sound, and their sound is that of an inferno. As I grow older, the strokes have stretched, having more skin now to cover. But they cover, they do not leave me bare. Where once they were deep and ferocious, now they are soft like petals. What does a hurricane look like as a tattoo? You would really have to hear it.

LA DUCHESSE DE LANGEAIS

Michel Tremblay

LA DUCHESSE DE LANGEAIS
Michel Tremblay

translated by John Van Burek

A terrasse de café. La Duchesse de Langeais, an aging queen about sixty years old, vacationing somewhere in the sunny climes, is seated in front of a half-empty bottle of Scotch. She is already visibly under the weather. La Duchesse is as effeminate as can be: completely, perfectly… and touchingly. No wiggle of the hips, wave of the hand, or "wink perverse" is spared. She often tries to speak à la française, but her "joual" origins always show through. She is wearing dreadful American summer clothes: powder-blue chino trousers, a three-buttoned shirt of the same colour, and white straw shoes.

La Duchesse is resting her head in her left hand, her elbow on the table. With her right hand she is toying with her empty glass. She seems very much preoccupied. After a moment, she smiles sadly and pours herself a hefty drink. With dignity, she stands and walks about, her hand raised as if in a toast.

Tonight, we don't make love, we get drunk!
She empties her glass in one shot.
That's right, girls! Fini, l'amour, fini, fini! The final strains and then no more!
She staggers a little.
Jesus, that's strong! Garçon!
Very woman of the world.
Garçon, what have you put in this drink? It's dreadful! Oh, silly me. The garçon has gone for his "siesta." There are no more garçons.

She sighs.

You're all alone, little girl ... No wonder, hein? Who else but you would sit on the terrasse in heat like this? Hélas, a woman of the world is a woman of the world. One must maintain one's "standing." Besides, sonny boy, I just woke up, so I'm hardly gonna take a nap now! Barbarous custom! God, are you stupid! Une vraie folle!

She laughs.

The queen of the Nellies. Good thing I know it, hein? ... I may not know much, but I do know that! No one can say I don't. For forty years I've been telling the whole world!

She plants herself full front, à la Marlene Dietrich.

That's right, your Honour, forty years of service with the best of references. À la française, à la grecque, tout ce que vous voudrez. And première classe!

With a big dramatic laugh.

I am a praying mantis, a devourer of males.

Another big dramatic laugh.

When they talk about me, they say, "La Duchesse? A raving queen! The biggest faggot that ever came down the pike!" You think I give a shit? I know it. Doesn't bother me. Not in the least. And the people who say that aren't any better. They're powdered up, queen-faced faggots. That's all. Oh, they can all go ...

I'm thirsty ...

She struts back to the table, wiggling her bum, and pours herself a drink.

No more ice. I have to drink it straight? Yech, sick to my tummy. Oh, what the hell, you can do it! Allez, allez, allez. Bottoms up, ma chérie. Give the monsieur a glimpse of your talents ...

She holds up her glass, then howls like a circus barker.

Ta-raaam! Et voilà! La Duchesse has just consumed a disgusting glass of disgusting booze in one unfaltering swig POUR-LE-MONSIEUR! Ta-daaam!

She drinks it down, then falls onto her chair under the effect of the alcohol.

Ouais! … Pixie, you're really overdoing it.

She throws her head back.

That sun is like Chinese torture! … That's okay, it's good for you. You'll be all tanned and beautiful.

She wipes her face.

That's not true, 'cause all you ever do in the sun is turn red as a lobster. Oh, a lobster! Mon Dieu! C'est masculin! Am I gonna start referring to myself au masculin! Quelle horreur! Of course, there must be lady lobsters, but still … Oh, go on, have another drink, chérie, then we'll go cruise for a bit, see if we can't scare up some game in the underbrush … Ouais ben, don't waste your time. At this hour, the beaches are deserted … Goddamned "siesta!" I am so fed up … Ah, the men must all be sleeping now, their tails gently resting … "Softly draped upon the thigh," as I would say if I were a poétesse …

She sings:

La poésie fout le camp, François Villon!

Of course with me, poetry hasn't descended into the streets. It's descended into the shit!

La poésie fout le camp—

That reminds me … Mon Dieu! I haven't thought of him for ages.

She laughs.

Aie, you must be plastered to have him come back to mind, the little worm … Well, well, well, this calls for another drink!

She performs the same routine as at the beginning.

Tonight we don't make love, we get drunk!

She drinks. Coughing mixed with laughter.

Careful, Marguerite … Mon Dieu, mon poète … That goes back a long, long time.

Very woman of the world.

Tucked away in the depths of my memory, like a precious jewel …

With a great dramatic sigh.

The stupid twit! ... Let me see, I met him ... that was way before Sandra's club ... I think I found him on the street ... Nice girl, as usual ... right in front of le Cinéma de Paris where la Vaillancourt was taking tickets ... He'd play the poor suffering poet and while la Vaillancourt would tear your ticket, he'd tear your heart out! Hah! All he needed was a pair of big ears to make a perfect Gérard Philippe ... Oh, what was his name? ... Search me ... Not too far, hein, you'll get me all excited ...

She laughs.

At your age! Tsk, tsk, tsk! You're so pretentious!

A wink, a little squeal, and a wiggle of the hips.

I called him "my lover with the brazen shaft." I don't know why. Guess I thought it sounded nice. God knows, that was the only thing about him the least bit hard ... On the circuit they called him "Bite my shoulder" because of a poem he wrote for me ... Can you believe it? "Bite my shoulder!" And I was stuck with the pisspot for two whole months ... He couldn't do a thing! Rien! Had to show him everything! Toute! From beginning to end! Mon Dieu, the things I've done in my life. No one in Montréal has had more "aventures stupides" than me. I could entertain you for weeks, my darlings. No one has known more people than me and fucked more people than me in the whole of Montréal in the last forty years! I've spent my life at it, girls, my entire life. Never anything else ... Fucking, fucking, fucking ... Mon Dieu! You're so vulgar! If the vacationing CBC Nellies heard you! They'd swoon on the spot! 'Cause, believe it or not, nowadays when they meet me, they're ashamed!

Very woman of the world.

Eh, oui! They told me themselves, like this, their lips all pinched, pinkies in the air ... "We'll have nothing more to do with you if you don't clean up your act. You call yourself 'Duchesse,' you should set a good example." Aie, whoa, hein? Nothing but snotty ladies! Bloody bitches! I'd scratch their eyes out if I still had my nails! They make me sick, lying around on the beach, playing Madame ... Like they were

queens of the world ... They've got as much class as ... And they don't
have two cents to rub together, hein? Oh, I know them all, those CBC
sluts who come down here on vacation. Queers, tapettes, every one of
them! Cocksuckers, all of them! Toute la gang! A few of them try to be
males, but all they look like is constipated whores. Who do they think
they're kidding? I can smell a queer a mile away! That means I've always
got a noseful, but that's another story ... Yesterday, mes chers amis,
they were eating les fruits de mer, sprawled out on the beach, pinkies
in the air, yeah, in the air, and they'd coo with pleasure and roll their
eyes every time they'd pop a weird little fishie into their mouth ... But
back in Montréal, they'd die of fright if they saw a fly in their soup! Aie,
whoa, hein? There's ridicule and ridicule! I wasn't born yesterday, and
these "princesses" from Montréal, Canada, haven't impressed me for
a long time. Look, I've got forty years' experience and a few thousand
men up my ass, so I can afford to play "la Duchesse" ... But them,
they're not even thirty and they want to play woman of the world.
Between you and me, hein? ... All they manage to look like is cheap
little Jewish ladies coming out of the five and dime ... Their petits
bleached hairdos, their petits fingernails all filed, their petits bikinis
transparents and their cutsie, cutsie petite walks ... that they copied
from me ... Aie, whoa, hein? Grow up a little first, sister, then come
see ma tante. You can play the ingénue all you want, but not la femme
du monde! If it's lessons you want, I'll give them to you, free of charge,
but don't try to pass for a pro. Not in front of me! Okay? ... Tiens, my
glass is empty. God, the way this stuff disappears! Maybe there are
ghosts, eh? Like "le Horla," by de Maupassant ...

Very woman of the world.

I'm very well read, you know? Garçon, un autre drink. Si señorita.
Merci.

She starts to pour herself another drink.

Keep going at this rate and the poor dears will wake up to find you
under the table.

Again, the same routine as at the beginning.

Tonight, we don't make love—

She stops suddenly.

Love! Shit! I'd almost forgotten it!

She runs to get the bottle and comes back.

Tonight we get drunk! Paquetée! Blotto!

She drinks. A long silence. She paces about like a lion in a cage.

You think I'm gonna start bawling like a fat Italian mamma, throw myself on the ground and tear out the last three hairs on my head, hein? Well, you're sadly mistaken! You won't see me cry. The way I feel right now ... Take a good look, hein? ... The way I feel right now, I am unhappy like I've never been unhappy in my life! And you know why? Yes, that's right, my little lambies, you've guessed it ... Love.

She climbs onto a chair and lifts her arms in the air.

La Duchesse de Langeais has a broken heart.

Tell it to the firemen, they'll piss all over you! La Duchesse, heartbroken? Impossible! After forty years in the business? Yeah, that's what I always thought, too, that after forty years, you had no more heart. Well ... When, after forty years' experience, you realize that you still do have a heart ... Stop it, Alice, stop it! That's sentimental shit. Don't tell me you're going to get shitty. A woman of the world never gets shitty in public. A woman of the world shits on the public! I shit on the whole world!

She drinks, choking a little.

Amen.

She gets down off the chair.

I'm drunk as a baby after its suck! If only I could have a good burp and fall asleep. Sleeping Beauty.

In a neutral tone, without conviction.

Last year I went to a costume party at la Choquette's dressed as Sleeping Beauty. I never saw people laugh so hard.

She sits down.

Sacrée Duchesse, I love you anyway ... You're the most beautiful, and the most loveable ...

She gets up suddenly, her arms in the air.

Aren't I beautiful? Maybe not any more, but I used to be. Oui,

monsieur! I was stunning! With the whole of Montréal at my feet. I
won't tell you what year that was, but it's true. All of Montréal, at my
feet! When I started doing la Duchesse, they came from miles to see me!
All the men, the real ones, the males, the bulls, would crawl before me
in the hopes I would deign to look at them. I'd push them, like this,
with the tip of my foot ... In those days I was a star ... Une grande
artiste, in my own genre ... Even today, when I put myself to it, I can
make a small crowd drool! Men are so demanding, you never know
what they're going to ask of you. That's why I've always had a
répertoire. A répertoire of star performances ... Look, when you're
good enough to make a man think that he's sleeping with a famous
international star, while she, his international star, is really just a man,
because it's with a man that he wants to go to bed, well, hat's off to
Mary! And those of you who've got hats, you can take them off to me,
okay? Yeah, I know, nowadays it's Sophie Tucker, Marlene Deitrich
and Josephine Baker, but in the old days, dans ma jeunesse ...

Very "actrice."

You should have seen me doing Edwige Feuillère in the final scene
from *La Dame aux Camélias*!

She throws her head way back and coughs a little.

I was sublime! I used to do that for my ice salesman ... He wept
buckets, the poor dear, enough to tear your heart out! Then he'd hand
me twenty-five bucks! For my roller-skating dancer, it was Esther
Williams. You should have seen me in my bathing suit! A real siren!
Who didn't end up in the tail of a mermaid, believe me! The towel
around the head, the whole bit! ... For my actors ... 'cause I had
countless actors, countless ... I had two numbers that were show-
stoppers like you've never seen! Now get a load of this ... The first was
Marguérite Jamois—she was a great French actress, long before your
time. You don't know her—in *Britannicus*—that's a play by Racine.
Wow! She was *Agripping* all over the place, okay? Nails this long, the
jaw way out front, bust three feet in the air, nostrils flaring ... I was
géniale! "C'était pendant l'horreur d'une profonde nuit ... " No, wait
... That's from *Phaedre*! No, it's not that either ... Anyway ... the

second number … Are you ready for this? … This was my masterpiece … Sarah Bernhardt en personne playing Hamlet! Complete with the wooden leg! That good enough for you? I even had a little sword … It was incredible. I almost looked like a man. And the quotes! I'd spout speeches one after another. And if it had been the style, I'd have had posters printed too … Of course, I had other imitations for my less important lovers … Greta Garbo in *Camille:* "I vant to be alone …" Bette Davis in *The Letter*! My eyes were big as saucers and I'd walk all crooked … Barbara Stanwyck, Michelle Morgan, Mae West, Arletty: "Atmosphère, atmosphère … " When I felt like a real queen, I'd do my Shirley Temple. The frizzy wig, the whole bit. I've even done Galina Ulanova in the dying swan!

She crouches, more or less, into the dying swan position from "Swan Lake."

At the end, I had it all in my little finger. I could die like no ballerina ever died before … Now one thing you've never seen is my Claudette Colbert in *Cleopatra*, in my milk bath. Seventy-eight bucks worth of milk in my tub! And in those days, seventy-eight bucks, hein? … As the old whores say: "Those were the days … "

She sings:

C'était dans ma jeunesse, du temps que j'étais slim …

I did cabaret too, you know … back in the fifties … at Tampico … *Laughing.*

What if I told you that Pierre Mac Orlan wrote a number for me?

She goes towards the table, pours what's left of the Scotch into her glass, and drinks it down in one shot.

Get a load of this … Maestro, musique, s'il vous plaît …

She sings the first stanza of "La Chanson de Margaret" by Pierre Mac Orlan, and sits down.

Yep, even Mac Orlan knew about me … 'cause Tampico, hein, I was there … Eh, oui. Then for six months I was assistante striptease at a cheap club in the red light district … I caught the clothes when the broad tossed them off.

Dreamily.

Of course, all that was before I became la Duchesse. I wasn't yet a woman of the world ... But, you know, that's where I met my first real millionaire ... A German playboy with looks of a god, who'd never slept with a man. But once he'd been cuddled in the arms of yours truly, he swung the other way like that! He's the one who showed me the world ... Like I always say, through him I learned the first rudiments of my future career as Duchesse. It was him who took me on my first trip to Europe! Eh, oui, l'Europe! Until then I didn't believe it really existed. But, after three or four countries, I got bored with my German god. I did the rest of the tour "freelance." When I came back to Montréal, I was walking on air. A woman of the world in every wonderful sense of the term! I started giving teas for my lady friends on Sunday afternoons ... My Sunday teas; all the royalty of Montréal was there: la Choquette, la Dubeau, la Rolande Saint-Germain ... She was crazy! ... la Steeman, la Rochon ... Every Sunday afternoon they'd arrive at my place, all girdled up and dressed to the nines, floor-length gowns, high heels, you name it ... La Rochon would show up with her mink stole, even in the middle of August ... We'd sit there, stiff as boards, and sip tea with our pinkies in the air. Then we'd play chamber music! La Rochon played the flute, la Steeman, the violin, la Rolande Saint-Germain, crazy as ever, played the French horn ... We called her "le fond du cor au son des bois" ... La Dubeau, the mandolin, and me, your humble servant, played the piano ... What music! Unbelievable! A ladies' orchestra like the world had never seen, before or since! Aie, and no nonsense, hein? We meant business! If anyone acted up, she'd hear about it for the rest of the afternoon. Once we even played in a charity ball ... We called ourselves "The Ladies Morning Club, Junior." An unprecedented success! The men clapped so hard, they got blisters on their hands! I know, 'cause my sister, Robertine, was in the hospital then and I spent the night with her husband ...

She shrugs her shoulders and laughs.

It's awful when I think of the things I've done in my life ... I've almost gone around the world ... On my ass! Rich as Croesus or poor as Orphan Annie … Of course with a life like that, you never know what will pop up between your legs … I worked like a goddamned slave to get where I am today. I don't regret a thing, hein? Not a thing! Whatever I did was because I wanted to. I has no intention of spending my life as a two-bit queer in Montréal, Canada. Not me! My ambitions were of a larger scope … For starters, international whore. After that, Duchesse! Do you know, I've fucked on four continents! America, Europe, Asia and Africa. Australia? Ah, I never found it … Oui, quatre continents! I've seen all colours and all sizes, if you know what I mean … But I like it that way. I chose my profession! And I've had one beautiful life! Okay, so now I usually pay for a screw, but that's only lately. Furs, jewels, limousines, la Duchesse had them all! Aie, when I got taken out, it wasn't to some chintzy movie, hein? Oh no, Her Highness always chose the most expensive and the most exquisite. And not many dared refuse, hein, because her anger was infamous and they knew what would happen if they said no. And it was like that for years! Oh, oui, for years!

That's right, mes chéries, la Duchesse is a somebody! And she has no regrets … Except this one goddamned little thing … Attention, Duchesse, you're getting mushy. Stop it this instant!

She looks at her bottle.

Ouais ben, the "siesta's" not over and my bottle's empty … which means la Duchesse is gonna go find another one … And while she's at it, she'll also powder her nose … In other words, she's gonna take a piss, like the most common of mortals … And if you want to do the same, now's your chance. See you later …

She goes out "with dignity," albeit tipsy, the empty bottle under her arm. A strong baritone voice is heard singing "Take Me Out to the Ball Game."

•

La Duchesse returns, a bottle under one arm, a glass in one hand and an ice bucket in the other. She is all dressed in white.

Dear Lord, make my heart as pure as thine! Ouf! I'm drunker than ever after I piss ... can't understand it ... I'm twice as bad as before ...

She sets the bottle on the table.

Aie! Mon amour, if you get to the bottom of that one, it's not dead-drunk they're gonna find you, but drunk, dead! ... I'm pooped just trying to open it.

She opens the bottle, pours herself a glass and starts doing the same routine as at the beginning.

Ah, shut up, everybody knows!

She drinks.

Mmmm! On the rocks, it's divine! Can't stand it straight ...

She looks into her glass and plays with the ice cubes.

Clink, clink, clink ... That is the most charactis— ... characteristic sound of a woman of the world! The tinkle of ice cubes on the rim of a glass ... When I hear that, I get the most wicked thoughts ... You know something, my lambie pies, I have drunk whisky in every conceivable, possible position.

Very woman of the world.

Mine is a life of ice cubes tinkling in whisky glasses. Whisky and men, they'll be my perdition!

A big perverse smile à la Marilyn Monroe, a little cry and a toss of the hip.

There was a time I drank my whisky with a straw 'cause it looked chic ... Aie, whoa, hein? That does get you plastered! And it tastes like shit! ... For forty years, and then some, la Duchesse has been ingurgitating this miraculous elixir, which makes her so voluble and interesting, as you have no doubt noticed ... I say forty and then some, because the first time I ever drank whisky was at my First Communion. My big sister Robertine was trying to be funny ... Me, I was sick as a dog ...

Laughing.

My First Communion! For a little girl making her First Communion, I was horrible! What a pain! Ugly as a monkey's ass scratched with two hands, my armband all crooked, and my eyes in cousin Léopold's pants. Eh, oui! Déjà! People are always surprised when I tell them that, but what can I do, it's the truth. Cross my heart. Cousin Léopold started on me when I was barely six years old. It's true! He didn't just go for the young ones, he went for the babies! He was really crazy! He died in the nuthouse, you know ...

She drinks.

I mean, he'd suck me so hard I'd have spasms and I'd scream 'cause it hurt like hell. Of course I couldn't ejaculate, I was too young ... I didn't even know what was happening to me ... All I knew was, I shouldn't say a word to anybody ... But before long, I started to get a kick out of it too. Must admit, I was always a bit of a masochist ... I love it when males hurt me! Sometimes I'd even tease cousin Léopold to make him crazy so he'd hurt me more ... His eyes would get all red and he'd come charging at me ... Six years old! And already I was depraved!

She stares for some time, then sits down.

I know, I know. It's disgusting.

When la Duchesse thinks of all that, she doesn't care if she gets mushy ... Because la Duchesse, too, has started running after the young ones!

She pounds her fist down on the table.

Oh! Oh! Temper, temper! Don't break anything, dear, especially your pretty little hand. You're still going to need that ... Here, have another drink and forget all about it.

She drinks.

After all, you're still a woman of the world! Pull yourself together. If you can't hack it any more, go back for face-lift number four and die on the operating table. C'est toute!

She drinks again.

Later on, after cousin Léopold, when I really started to enjoy it, I'd let people feel me up at the movies ... Gosh, did I love that! I'd sit near some guy who looked game and I'd stare at him ... When he'd get the picture, he'd come and sit next to me ... I was so excited, I'd shake like a leaf ... He'd rub his knee against mine ...

She wipes her hand across her brow.

How old was I then? ... Maybe twelve ... Usually, we'd go finish up in the toilets ... Sometimes we'd go to his place, but not often. Men were always scared 'cause I was so young. I was dangerous!

Suddenly changing her tone.

Mais chérie, you've always been dangerous. And you still are!

She pours herself a drink.

So that means I've gone without men for five years of my life ... the first five.

She makes a face and drinks. She looks worn out and crushed, like a drunken old whore. Suddenly, she reacts.

I want a Peruvian sailor in my bed tonight! I've just decided and I won't go to bed till I've got a Peruvian sailor by the tail ... That will get all this crap off my mind.

Very woman of the world.

I've always adored sailors. They're my soft spot, vous savez?

Speaking naturally.

For a while I kept a record of my sailors ... I stopped at two hundred and thirty eight ... I lost my notebook ... It's unbelievable, the money I made with sailors. They must pay more than anyone else ... No wonder, hein, they go for months without seeing a woman. I remember in New York, the whores hated me ... Can't blame them, hein, I stole all their meat ... Of course, I was a lot more woman than they were!

She staggers to her feet, her arms in the air.

I've always been more woman than *all* the women!

She falls back into her chair.

You'd better stay seated, dear, the floor wants you.

She pours a drink.

A toast ... Yes, yes, a toast, Duchesse, a toast. You do it so well ... To the health of ... Mon Dieu, everything's all red. I am plastered ... I drink to the health of ... Once at a party at the end of the war, I came in nude, my body covered with Heinz ketchup. I was the widow of the Unknown Soldier ... Quel succès! I made quite a mess of Monsieur's maison, but what the hell ... seems they even found ketchup on the handle of a vacuum cleaner ...

She breaks out laughing.

What was I saying? ... Oh oui!

She gets up with difficulty.

To the health of l'amour with a capital *A*.

She drinks and sits down again.

Peter! Peter! I don't believe it.

She tries to get up. Unable to make it, she puts her forehead on the table. She tries to speak rapidly, but the words get mixed up and she stutters.

A Peruvian sailor! I need a Peruvian sailor with his pants full of goods, a big bundle that I can grab with both hands!

She lifts her head but keeps her eyes shut.

Yes, with both hands! Then allez-oup, into the sack.

She opens her eyes.

Let me tell you something ... Even if I look like an old bag, a man doesn't get bored with me in bed. Far from it! Far from it! La Duchesse is still capable of outdoing the kids of today. Just tell Auntie what you'd like and she'll take care of the rest. She'll even throw in a little extra, free of charge!

She closes her eyes.

Come on, lover boy, come with me, you'll have the time of your life. Show me your pecker so ma tante can gobble it up.

She opens her eyes.

I do "fleur de rose," you know? Yes, I've tasted shit, but only because I wanted to! Because I like to please when I make love.

She jumps up.

Love. Never say that word again, Duchesse. Never.

She sits down.

Say "fuck" all you want, but never that word. From now on, my darlings, your woman of the world is gonna fuck and that's all.

She leans her head on the table and murmurs.

La Duchesse de Langeais has a broken ...

She raises her head.

Asshole! That's right, Duchesse, and you'd better get used to it. At my age, to think I have to change my vocabulary because of some shitty little worm! When I met him, around here, in one of the cafés, I asked him, with a little pout naturellement, a woman of the world is a woman of the world, I asked him what he liked to do in bed? He looked me straight in the eye and said, "I'm a fucking buck-driver-buffalo!" O, mein Gott! I almost had heart failure! I was frothing at the ass! In the wink of an eye, we threw ourselves into each other's arms ... I had no idea this could happen to me. I thought I'd been immune to that bug for ages! You can sure fool yourself, hein? You think you have no heart left, and you wake up to discover that that's all there is. Within three days I was head over heels in love. I'd have done anything for him ... And he'll be twenty years old next month.

A long silence.

Ever since then, I've been taking care of him. I feed him, I wash him ... Oh, he loves it when I wash him ... I wipe his nose, I take him out, I run along before him ... Yeah, I run in front of him because I love him! I love the little bastard. Why shouldn't I say it? That hasn't happened to me for forty years!

Very woman of the world.

I guess that's what they call "décadence!" Love with a capital *L.* I've reigned for too long not to know how revolting it is to stoop before someone ... and to serve ... But I can't help it. I can't help it. I'm in love like an eighteen-year-old girl who's still got her cherry. And it's not as if he's good in bed! 'Cause he isn't! I don't know what it is, I don't know! But I can't stand being without him. It's ... It's as if he were my child ... What I feel for him is almost pure!

A long silence.

He's been gone since yesterday. He left me a good-bye note! A polite little "mot d'adieu"! To me, la Duchesse! No man has ever run out on me. Never! Oh, I've made lots of them suffer, but nobody could ever brag about making me cry. Well, I cried my eyes out, all night long! And if he doesn't come back, I know I'm gonna die like an old bitch.

I know he won't come back ...

She pours herself a drink and drinks it.

If the vacationing CBC Nellies could see me now, they'd be happy as pigs in shit. I don't care. I'll never sober up!

Very woman of the world.

Who gives a shit about them?

What's more, he left me for an eighteen-year-old beauty. A "native" that he picked up on the beach! Duchesse, your pride should rise up in your throat and choke you to death! After two bottles of whisky you haven't got much pride left, hein, ma chérie? Everything's flown the coop. Even your fake love for Peruvian sailors has taken off ass-end over tea cups. So suffer, you bitch! It's your own fault. Paye, ma câlice, paye! You're always bragging about your forty years' experience, why didn't you do what experience taught you? So, die, goddamn it! Die! Don't fight it, it's no use ...

Very woman of the world.

Sure, I know, nobody dies for love any more ... but when they find my body ... That's a pile of shit, Duchesse, and you know it. You're not going to die and that's what's so horrible. Ben oui, it hurts now, but it'll pass. You've seen worse. So fini, l'amour? Hein? Good! Have a good cry, roll on the floor, then ... Then, do what you've always done ... Tell yourself you're the most beautiful, the most loveable, and the world is full of men just waiting for you.

She struggles to her feet.

The men are at your feet, Duchesse!

She falls heavily onto the table.

Who gives a shit? I don't want them anymore.

The bottle gets knocked over, splashing la Duchesse in the face. She doesn't move.

They call me "la Duchesse de Langeais" because I've always dreamt I'd die a Carmelite nun ... sipping tea!

CAVEMAN RAINBOW
Caroline Gillis

CAVEMAN RAINBOW
Caroline Gillis

The stage is lit by two lamps: one, stage-right, with a blue light; the other, stage-left, with a red light. Under each lamp is a podium. At centre-stage, two ropes hang from the ceiling, with clamps on the end on which to hang various props, which are leaning against the wall. On the back wall of the stage is a blackboard. Marie-Lissa, a woman in her early thirties, enters carrying a medical book which she places on one podium and a journal which she places on the other podium. She reads from the journal.

One a.m. Alone.
Looking for a rainbow to chase the caveman out.
Yellow rings the inside of the toilet.
Saliva floats on top of the water.
I want to be sick but I can't.
My stomach's holding everything so tight.
Posters cracked and sagging from the walls.
Peppermint foot lotion unopened on the floor.
Shower dripping from the rusting head.
Cheek to tiles … nose at pipe.
I feel so afraid.
Looking for a rainbow to chase the caveman out.
If he would just touch it.

She closes the journal, then goes to get a map of the world which she begins hanging from the ropes.

I love that.

You know what I love?

I love when you're in a restaurant or somewhere and you think that someone's looking at you and you find out that they really are looking at you. I love that.

Like most of the time you're wrong.

You think they're looking at you but they're really watching a dog pissing on a fire hydrant out the window back of your head or something.

That I hate. I hate that.

But I love it when they're really looking at you.

I also love slow dancing with a guy in my living room if the guy I'm slow dancing with is the guy who's singing on the tape machine.

I love that.

That I love as my fantasy.

But if then he stops dancing and gives me flowers ... that I hate.

I hate him in the fantasy if he's got flowers.

Flowers are easy.

Flowers are for funerals or for saying good-bye.

She pin-points a place on the map.

Reykjavik. Iceland. Too cold.

You know what I hate more than flowers for presents?

I hate when guys pretend to be fighting over you and they're really fighting over beer.

I hate that.

And I hate those guys who—he sees you and right away loves you and wants to have kids with you and quits smoking.

I hate that.

I didn't ask him to quit smoking ... I never said I wanted kids.

She pin-points a place on the map.

Abuja. Nigeria. Maybe. Uh uh.

I hate when people secretly start making you do all this stuff that you never wanted to do.

You know what else?

I have this fear of oil trucks. Oil trucks.

Every time I walk by an oil truck I'm always sure it's going to explode and I'll be blown into a million pieces.

So I try not to release those hormones or pheromones that might cause an oil truck to explode when I pass one.

She pin-points a place on the map.

Buffalo. Uh uh. Anywhere I can get to by bus doesn't count.

Another thing about me.

I never tell anyone to "drive carefully."

I think it's a bad omen.

It was Christmas Eve at my Aunt Virgine's place and when my Uncle Murray is leaving she says, "Murray, you drive carefully."

It was snowing.

Murray had a couple of rum and egg-nogs before he left.

Dead instantly.

Wrapped his car around a pole.

Ripped his head right off.

Car was unrecognizable.

Of course everyone who was at the party, all they talked about for the rest of their lives was how they almost got a ride with Murray that night but changed their minds at the last minute.

He was only driving a Toyota Tercel.

He woulda had to have been driving a bus for all those people to have fit.

She pin-points a place on the map.

Mar del Plata. Argentina. Mar del Plata. Wasn't she in that movie with Al Waxman?

But.

People do get feelings about these things like "drive carefully."

There are feelings you can feel about things like that.

Like dying.

Like Natalie Wood.

She pin-points a place on the map.

St. John's. Newfoundland. More bars per square foot than any city in Canada. You wouldn't think they'd be so thirsty with all that water around.

Natalie wouldn't go near the water ... terrified of it.

Then one day she goes out in this boat and she drowns ... she drowns.

Her fear came true.

It's kind of neat, really ... I don't mean neat *really* ... I mean interesting. It's interesting.

Like can you bring something on just by fearing it?

I'm not afraid of water though.

She pin-points a place on the map.

Granada. Spain. Granada. Home of the Alhambra.

She recites haltingly.

> *L'Alhambra! l'Alhambra! palais que les Génies*
> *Ont doré comme un rêve et rempli d'harmonies,*
> *Forteresse aux créneaux festonnés et croulants,*
> *Où l'on entend la nuit de magiques syllabes,*
> *Quand la lune, à travers les mille arceaux arabes,*
> *Sème les murs de trèfles blancs!*

By Victor Hugo.

She takes the map down.

Granada. Spain. There's two Granadas. There's one in Spain and there's one ... somewhere else.

This is the Spain Granada.

She writes "Granada Spain" on the blackboard. She lights a cigarette.

It's a secret that I smoke. Nobody knows.

Smoking's my mystery.

It's hard to feel mysterious when you have strangers looking into every hole in your body and staring straight out through the other side.

I know that smoking's bad for you.

Makes you sick. Gives you wrinkles.

But you can get sick even if you don't smoke.

And who said that wrinkles are ugly?

I don't believe that someone would want to get rid of wrinkles.

It's like getting rid of fingerprints.

It's like you got your own personal map of everything that ever happened to you.

Every time you laughed or cried or just stared at something for a long time.

Every emotion from your whole life is recorded right there.

You could take a walk through the wrinkles around some people's eyes and at the end of that walk you'd have a story of a whole life. And the stories on every face would be different and the stories on every face would be good.

You could be walking through this deep straight wrinkle looking at all these raspberry bushes or something and all of a sudden you fall down this gully where it's like a dent where somebody slugged that person one night.

Why would you want to forget about something like that?

And I bet when you think about it … I bet when it comes down to it … like if you had to … you wouldn't want to forget about anything if you had to.

She reads from the medical book.

> A prime characteristic of living things is change. Every living cell is in a constant state of flux from the moment of its birth. Thus, every organ of the body is different from one minute to the next, though the difference may only be microscopic....
>
> The delicate mechanism of the cell is subjected to constant strain and stress in its perilous journey through life. The outcome of this struggle depends on the power of destructive forces and the strength of the defensive mechanism.

She closes the medical book.

These are the people that I know.

Please pay attention. There will be a test afterward.

Not hard.

She brings out a large picture of a woman and hangs it on the ropes.

Marcy. Marcy who's about my best friend of a hundred years. When she was eleven she said if she didn't have a boyfriend with a 1968 silver Chevy Malibu convertible by the time she was sixteen she'd kill herself. And she's way past sixteen and she's single and she's still alive.

Marcy doesn't live here anymore. She moved to Bathurst, New Brunswick, about two years ago because New Brunswick is the kind of place that people just drive through to get somewhere else. So there's more chances of a '68 silver Chevy Malibu convertible pulling up on her doorstep. She sends me one postcard a month to keep me updated on her progress. Lately the postcards have been pictures of these buxom blonde movie stars so that I can pick out a new pair of tits if the time comes.

When we were kids we used to swing off the maple tree in front of my house. Jumping off the concrete steps at the end of the walk onto the sidewalk. Holding onto the tree's branches. The branches sliding through our hands ... pulling off bunches of leaves in our palms ... I can still see the green from the leaves, imbedded in my palms. Marcy's standing at the end of one of those paths. Her saying how she wouldn't like me anymore if I ever cut my hair. I can hear my mother yelling bloody murder out the window about killing the tree. I can see Marcy running home. See ya later alligator. In a while crocodile. Call for you tomorrow.

Marcy.

She takes the picture down and hangs up a Sting poster.

Emil. He's about my best friend after Marcy.

Emil says the only kind of true love he believes in has a moustache and doesn't stay for breakfast. Emil's gay. He thinks everyone is gay. This isn't Emil. This is Sting. Emil hates every picture ever taken of him ... so Sting, standing in for Emil tonight. Making friends with Emil was about as easy as sitting in a chair.

He lives across the hall from me in this apartment building, and the first time I met him, about three years ago, he came to my door to borrow some tea. When I brought it to him he said, "Do you mind if I drink it here? There's a guy I don't know wearing my bathrobe and squeezing fresh orange juice in my kitchen." Emil's an assistant art director for films, which is different than a set decorator for movies, apparently, which is why he's always bringing me books it takes three months to read, and making me eat those smoked oysters that come out of those cans with the keys on them, and taking me to see "films" with subtitles. I dozed off at them at first but Emil says taste is something you acquire, not buy at Honest Ed's.

One of the best films was *Time of the Gypsies*. By Emir Kusturica—he's Yugoslavian. I was always crazy for gypsies. When I was in junior high I always wore those really soft Indian dresses that you could see through, and of course I worshipped Stevie Nicks. It was a beautiful movie ... but sad.

Beautiful and sad at the same time.

I never knew things could be beautiful and sad at the same time till I met Emil.

Emil.

She takes the poster down and hangs up a large picture of her mother.

My mother, who you would call Evelyn because she insists.

When I started my period at around eleven, twelve, fifteen, she said, "You're a woman now, honey. Call me Evelyn. Your pal. I'll call you Marie-Lissa."

Evelyn. My pal.

I always wondered what it would be like to have to whisper about things like periods or boys or the first time you let him put his tongue in your mouth. I never had to.

When Evelyn told me about sex she said, "Don't let him stop till you've had an orgasm." Yeah right, if I took that advice I'd've had to have had sex from 1976 straight through to the mid-eighties. The first time I got drunk I came home and puked while Evelyn played George Jones because she said she always found him most soothing when one was nauseated.

Evelyn always knew everything I did. She still does.

She thinks it's wonderful that I have a gay friend.

But Emil tells her it's not "gay" anymore. It's "queer" now.

But Evelyn can't get her head around that because "queer" is like her favourite adjective. Queer fella, queer hairdo, queer colour, queer taste, queer turn. Queer turn. That's like being sick. People are always having queer turns at the old-people's home she works at. She's like, "Mrs. O'Neill had a queer turn when she ate the lime Jello in the cafeteria because the Cool Whip had gone bad," or "Lois had a queer turn when we were playing forty-five last week. I think the pretzels were old."

I'm not exactly sure what a queer turn is, but I know the person is always perfectly healthy right before the queer turn occurs. Food has usually been consumed right before the queer turn and a person having a queer turn usually turns a queer shade of green or yellow as the turn sweeps over their body. Also the person usually doubles over at some point during the said turn.

Emil finds this hilarious and says, "Fag, homo, fruit, pansy, queer —when it comes right down to it who cares as long as you get laid."

He's always telling me that I should try taking a queer turn myself some time. Then he sticks his tongue out and waves it around in the air like this.

She demonstrates.

Emil ... my mother.

I mean Evelyn, my mother.

She takes the picture down.

Emil thinks Sting's gay.

Emil thinks everybody's gay. Maybe he's right.

I mean, it's crossed my mind.

Maybe it would be easier with a woman.

Maybe there's some things she might understand better.

Like now.
She reads a second passage from the medical book.

> One of the most insidious and mysterious of stresses
> to which humans as well as other living things are
> subjected is cancer. The secrets of its cause and how
> it performs its deadly work still elude us. Much
> research is being carried on in centers all over the
> world directed toward solving these mysteries, and it
> is the profound hope and expectation of all mankind
> that this work will lead to a complete understanding
> in the near future. As of this writing, however, all we
> have are hopes and a few very promising leads.

She closes the medical book.
Evelyn gave me this medical book.
It was supposed to be a medical dictionary but she couldn't afford one.
She also got me a date with a lab technician.
He was supposed to be a doctor but she couldn't find a single one in
the hospital cafeteria.
The date.
I meet my mother for supper.
I meet him for supper.
Surprise.
First of all, I don't know about this date.
Second of all, I don't want this date.
And third of all, five minutes after we sit down my mother has to
leave for an appointment she forgot about.
An appointment.
My mother's never had an appointment for anything in her life.
Except maybe for her hair.
Seven minutes.
I am now alone with him.
He brought me flowers.

Ten minutes.

He orders for both of us.

Twelve minutes.

Introductory conversation.

The weather. We agree on the moderately cool condition of the evening.

Fifteen minutes.

Drinks.

I sip beer. He sips Chardonnay.

Post-introductory conversation.

He tells me about dead family and acquaintances.

Dead people.

Twenty minutes.

He works for a coroner.

Twenty-five minutes.

Books.

His favourite.

Jonathan Livingston Seagull.

Thirty minutes.

Dinner is served.

Two midget-sized chickens with their little legs sticking straight out of them.

Forty minutes.

I eat some of the midget chickens.

Forty-five minutes.

Another beer.

Forty-seven minutes.

The midget chickens are coming alive in my stomach.

Fifty-five minutes.

I go to the can.

Sixty-two minutes.

I return.

He's wearing this oily little grin on his face.

I can see the chickens screaming between his teeth.

He's ready to go.

Sixty-six minutes.

I bid him a polite farewell outside the restaurant. He insists on kissing me.

All I can think of is screaming chickens.

Sixty-eight minutes.

I jump in a cab.

I arrive home and beat myself over the head with a spatula.

Seventy-five minutes.

True love eludes me once again.

I only ever had one true love.

Very very tiny perfect true love.

I think love has to be tiny for it to be truly perfect.

May we please have the tiny perfect love mood-lighting and music please? Thank you.

She brings out a large red cardboard heart and hangs it from the ropes.

The Varsity Restaurant.

I'm trying to eat a fried-egg sandwich, and just as the middle part of it falls onto my plate I see this guy looking at me, really looking at me.

He's not beautiful ... not handsome.

His hair wasn't shiny. His jeans didn't fit right.

But for some reason at that particular point in time he seemed beautiful to me. It seemed right ... him just looking at me.

Then he smiles and I smile back.

I take a sip of coffee ... he takes a sip of coffee.

I look over my shoulder to make sure it's me ... he looks over his shoulder.

He takes a drag off a cigarette: I don't smoke in restaurants.

He's still looking at me with this kind of secret smile on his face. Me smiling back. Feeling silly but liking it.

She goes behind the heart.

I'm trying to put my sandwich back together, and then he gets up and comes over and says to me in this deep voice from way down inside him, "You will."

Then he leaves.

She releases the heart from the clamps and it falls to the floor.

All my relationships have been short-lived.

But maybe that's what true love is.

I don't know.

Maybe I wouldn't know true love if it hit me on the head.

Maybe I can't love someone till I know what I want.

You gotta know what you want before you can find it—find it on the outside or the inside.

And to get there you need the power.

So make sure you use your power while you still have the chance.

She reads from her journal.

There was this huge hand covering my face ...
this huge rubber hand covering my face.

And I would try to pry the fingers away but I can't feel them.

And I look up at the face to see if it's smiling or sad but it's all covered.

I can feel the lines of the palm against my chin and the tip of my nose.

And I can smell the rubber of the palm.

Last thing I remember is this rubber smell like something bad burning.

I'm not catching ... I'm not catching.

Take off your gloves ... take off the mask.

You can't catch it from a spot on a screen cause the spot's deep inside me.

It's in me.

It's in me.

She looks up from her journal.

And then I scratched my head.

And I looked at my fingernails. And I could see the white skin from my scalp underneath them.

And then right before my eyes these flowers grew out from under my fingernails.

These little white flowers.

She closes the journal. She picks up the heart.

Emil doesn't believe in true love.

So he says.

But if that's true, how come he spends all his money on fashion clothes and getting his hair dyed a different colour every week? And how come he's got that special bank account so he can get his eyes lifted or tucked or pulled or whatever?

I think his eyes are fine.

I think his eyes are beautiful.

But Emil says, "I'm not trying to look younger. I'm just trying to stay the same."

How come people are so scared of getting old?

For some people getting old would be a prize.

It's just skin, after all.

If I had that money I'd do something self-improving.

Like one time I almost went to live with a family in Quebec to learn French, but I couldn't because I didn't finish high school, and I was too old for the bursary program, so I'd have to pay for it myself, unless of course I'd been on unemployment for six months prior to the course, in which case I'd be entitled to a bursary, but I'd have to take high-school upgrading at Continuing Ed., which I'd have to pay for myself unless I'm over sixty-five. Then it would be free.

Then I could quit my job, wait eight weeks, go on unemployment for six months, and then I could take the course.

Shit.

You gotta be under twenty-five or over sixty-five to use a friggin' HELP LINE in this city.

I can't even rent a VCR in my own neighbourhood like a normal human being. To rent a VCR I've got to give the guy a credit card or three-hundred dollars.

But I can rent a video by just giving him a phone number.

So I can get the video but no VCR.

What am I supposed to do with the video?

Throw it on top of the TV and hope for the best.

And even if I said what the hell, and even if I had three hundred dollars in my bank account, I couldn't take it out anyway because someone at the bank decided that I was only allowed to take out sixty dollars a day on my CONVENIENCE CARD.

Every person behind a counter or a desk is the same person.

You look at the Post Office some time.

Don't they all look related to you?

No wonder there's so much unemployment these days.

There's only one person got the same desk-job all across the whole country.

No wonder my mother never owned a car and I never owned a car, and my kids, if I had any, would never own a car.

There's someone out there afraid we might just drive right out of our place in society.

I could always rent a car I guess, but to do that I need a credit card, a full-time job and my name in the white pages of the phone book for a full year.

Shit.

I mean, basically, right now I've got absolutely nothing.

No kids, no husband, no car, no VCR.

But ... I've got great hair.

What if I were bald?

She reads from her journal.

If a caveman came to your house what would you
do with him?
A big mean stupid caveman.
You never invited him.

He just walked in.

You didn't even know he was there till he showed up as a spot on a screen.

And this numbness ... and this pressure.

Pressure in my head ... on my back.

Through my arms ... in my eyes.

This numbness in my fingers and when I touched my lips I got this numbness on my lips and when I closed my lips I got this numbness in my mouth, on my tongue, down my throat, in my chest ...

And this pain ... this pain in my armpit.

Will I be bald?

Will I be bald?

Will I be bald?

It's like that cavemen dragging me home by the hair but he's pulling me from the inside of my scalp.

A caveman has no manners.

Doesn't wait for an invitation.

Won't take no for an answer.

And the only way he'll go away is if you bombard. Bombard. Bombard.

I want my hair.

I got great hair.

Imagine if it was gone.

Imagine if I didn't have any.

I feel okay.

There's nothing there.

Fear gives you a bad state of mind.

"Do you live alone?"

"Do you live alone?"

"Do you live alone?"

Yeah I live alone.

"Close your eyes."

"Don't fall asleep."

"Don't fall asleep."
"Close your eyes."
"Don't fall asleep."
"Don't fall asleep."

She closes the journal.
I won't fall asleep but I'm already dreaming.
She hangs a hospital shirt from the ropes.
I'm dreaming.
I'm standing outside, up against a brick wall ... on a roof somewhere.
I'm wearing a denim jacket with a rip in the right elbow and the side torn out.
And underneath that: a wedding dress.
The dress is all tight across the back, and I can feel it stretching across my shoulder blades.
This guy is taking my picture and saying, "Think about roses."
And I'm thinking, I don't like flowers, and then I'm thinking, I don't have a denim jacket.
And my mother's there, Evelyn's there, wearing a T-shirt that says "Mummy" and she's laughing.
Laughing like she laughs at the reruns of "M*A*S*H."
And this guy keeps taking my picture ... flashing ... flashing and the flashing turns into clapping.
Flashing.
Clapping.
Flashing.
Flashing.
And in my head this George Jones song is playing over and over: the race is on ...
And then I'm at the hospital and my mother is saying she's sorry but she thought that I'd be more artistic.
More flashing.
Clapping.
Flashing.

Pictures of my insides ...

Pictures of my outsides.

I feel like wax paper.

You can see right through me except for a denim jacket and a white dress.

And roses.

My mother laying roses on my chest.

I don't like flowers.

Flowers are for funerals or saying good-bye.

I don't like flowers.

Flowers are for funerals or saying good-bye.

I'm not going anywhere.

She releases the shirt from the clamps, and it falls to the floor.

The farthest I've ever travelled is down to the walkway over the Gardiner Expressway on my way to Sunnyside Beach.

I love it there ... on the walkway.

It's always windy.

It's always noisy.

Noisy with cars and the city.

You can look down at Lake Ontario from there and imagine that the water is still pure and clean.

No toxins in the water.

No syringes scattered in the sand.

When you turn your back to the lake you can see this huge billboard for the Journey's End Motel.

I like standing out there.

It makes me feel alive.

A part of something ...

A tiny speck on the map of the world.

I stand right there in the centre looking down at the expressway watching the cars going in both directions.

Speeding into the city.

Speeding out of the city. But now ...

I can feel a straight line through the middle of my body, through my forehead, under my chin, over my throat, between my breasts, down through my pelvis, splitting me completely in two.

The two halves pull me hard in different directions.

When I look down at the cars now I wonder if it might just be easier ...

She reads from her journal.

So I've got this thing of caveman.

There's this spot, this place, this thing in me, and the doctors say it's bad and shouldn't be there, and maybe it's weird but I think of caveman.

So I try to think of something good, something beautiful to kill the caveman, cover him up, chase him out, so then I think of rainbow.

But then I find out that rainbows aren't necessarily good.

There's all kinds of dark and forbidding stuff written about them.

Like they're demons ... they're these dangerous demons.

Anyone who dies suddenly or violently is supposed to be the victim of a rainbow.

If you get touched by a rainbow you're almost guaranteed to suffer some kind of serious misfortune.

And to point at a rainbow is bad news.

Very bad luck.

But there are some good things about rainbows.

If you wish on a rainbow your dreams will come true.

And rainbows are bridges ... bridges to heaven.

Whatever that is.

Until you reach it, heaven is just a word.

Rainbow's just a word.

Caveman ...

No one really knows what he is or who he is or
how he looks.
A caveman is whatever you make him.
So it's caveman or it's rainbow
But either way it's this spot.

She moves to stand centre-stage.

And my body orbits around this spot inside me.
Waiting.
Waiting for bombardment.
Maybe it's simple and nothing.
If you blew on it … it would be like blowing the
fluff off a dandelion weed.
This tiny spot …, half an inch in diameter …
Controlling my body.
Controlling my life.
Making my decisions.
But it's up to me.
And Emil gives me this map to find a place to run
away to.
And Marcy sends me jokes.
And Evelyn plays for rainbows.
But it's up to me …
To chase out the caveman or bring in the rainbow.
I've … only got me and my will.
I will. I will.

*She pulls down the ropes. A voice-over of a woman reciting "L'Alhambra"
in French. Then Marie-Lissa recites the poem in English.*

The Alhambra! The Alhambra! Palace that the
genies
Gilded like a dream and filled with harmony,

Fortress of festooned and crumbling battlements,
Where at night magic syllables resound,
When the moon shining through a thousand
    Arab arches,
Spangles the walls with white clover!

A voice-over of the following list by Marie-Lissa is heard.

I will ... swim, write, drink coffee, snowshoe, shop, cook, recycle, sing, tap-dance, take pictures, snorkel, pick skin off my feet, I will ... clean, put things in alphabetical order, count, hunt, toboggan, water ski, belly-dance, fix pipes under sinks, collect coins, paint, walk, skip rope, skip stones, I will ... cut my own hair, drive, play golf, eat spinach, squeeze blackheads out of my chin, dig through garbage, pull white hairs out of my head, I will ... ride the Queen streetcar all the way from Parkdale to the Beaches, busk, pet cats, grow plants, pick strawberries, join committees, build ships in bottles, mountain-climb, sail, have sex, mow the lawn, I will ... answer chain letters, smell old jars in cupboards, answer personal ads, fence, bowl, fix chairs, I will ... chug beer, talk, make long-distance phone calls, masturbate, cart-wheel, travel across the Atlantic in a row-boat, needlepoint, and grow little white flowers.
    I will.

She reads from the medical book.

Until we learn how to protect ourselves against the onset and development of breast cancer, we must continue to use improved methods of detection and treatment to cure the disease more often. We must also tell more women that much of their protection lies in their own hands.

She reads from her journal.

Seven thirty-seven a.m. Alone.
Distant smell of the Mediterranean in my head.
Short hair, long hair, no hair.
One breast, two breasts, three breasts.
Breeze from the sea clears my head.
I am the Alhambra.
Chasing the caveman out.
Making my own rainbows.
Orbiting my own body.
In 1493 the Alhambra began to crumble.
It's still standing.

REFERENCES

— Victor Hugo, *Les Orientales*, "Grenade," 1829.
—- Philip Strax, *Early Detection: Breast Cancer Is Curable* (Toronto: Fitzhenry & Whiteside, 1974), pp. 45-46.

THE COCKROACH TRILOGY
Alan Williams

For Mike Bradwell

THE COCKROACH TRILOGY
Alan Williams

The performer sits at a table. On the table in front of him is a bottle of whisky, a cheap video-camera, and a large kitchen knife.

There's that crow again. Never see that crow for weeks on end and then it's around for days and days.

This is better, this being on my own.

Ever noticed how movies these days are all lousy? I know, I work in a video store. All they are is people having sex with their clothes on and getting shot through the head. Why? Because movies are made by people who hate people, in the sense that when you're a kid there's two types: people who like people and people who hate people, and people-likers spend their childhoods on street corners hanging out with ... well, people, but people-haters spend their childhoods in attics with little Stanley knives carving up expanded polystyrene to make a new hill for their train set. But movie-makers are the worst. They are the ones who hate people but pretend to love them. They say, "I want to testify for humanity, state my feeling and vision of them," but the only "humanity" they meet is a few actors that they bark orders at for a few weeks, and then they go and sit in a room for six months with a little Stanley knife, editing.

I always wanted to make, you know, a movie that was really about people and not about Stanley knives. Unfortunately, I don't know any people so ... I suppose I could make one that wasn't about Stanley knives.

He points the camera at himself and turns it on.

Dear etcetera … Thank you for the book. Great to see it after all these years: *The Village Voice Reader,* published in 1962. It gives a picture of that rather interesting era during the 1950s when, I suppose, Jack Kerouac was wandering around, and all those free-jazz people like Pharoah Saunders and John Coltrane—and Charlie Christian was recently dead I suppose. I have to say I never liked any of those people's music, it always sounded to me like Superman rubbing his fingernails over a blackboard at Superspeed, but there's something I admire about their spirit, and the book's good because it describes all these odd things, funerals and weddings and arguments; and really it's just a bunch of people that for some weird reason, as opposed to us or me or something, thought it was worth writing down what they did: stuff happened and they wrote about it.

As for me, life is sort of fine. Every day brings nothing fresh, except this, which I have to wonder why you sent. I hope everything is going well for you and all your successful friends and they're all making billions of dollars. Unfortunately, I will have to send the book back because I intend cutting my throat tonight.

Picking up the knife, he makes as if to cut his throat, then stops and checks the camera.

No batteries.

Close, too close.

Quite interesting all that 1950s stuff really—never liked it at the time; mind you, I never came across the beatniks, the white hipsters and the jazz players—all I met were the Teddy Boys, the Greasers round our way, and I used to fucking hate them. I remember they were the school bullies, and they were older than me—which, of course, is how you get to meet school bullies—and—oh I remember, yeah! At a certain age every time I saw a Greaser I used to abuse Green Lantern's sacred trust. See, Green Lantern was this Superhero, and he'd been given this Magic Ring by some Cosmic Rotary Club called the Guardians of the Galaxy, or something like that, "On the condition that he fought evil in all its forms throughout the universe and never harmed another human being!" Well, he only had ten adventures a year—one a month except January and March—so the rest of the time this ring wasn't doing anything and he used to lend it to me. I would walk downtown on Saturday afternoons, and when I saw Teddy Boys I'd change them into harmless identical androids pzzzzt!, in the winking of an eye.

Actually, I used to be a Superhero once. Don't ask me who because obviously, "My efficiency as a crime fighter relies on my identity being kept a secret!" And anyhow, I wasn't a very good one. I was young for the job—eight—and I didn't have any super powers except I was a bit precocious at chess, so I had to stick my chest out and try and make like Batman. But Batman, although he had no super powers, was not just a blowzy amateur, oh no, he didn't get where he got just through bluffing his way through to his own TV series and two of his own comics for fifty years. No no! *Hard graft* is what got him where he got. First, he had his parents shot by muggers—he was orphaned in front of his very eyes by criminals, and that's what gave him the steely determination to fight crime, which is something that you need if you're going to be a Superhero, otherwise, you're out there, it's a rainy night and you'll think, "Fuck it, I'll go home." Plus, he had about a million-and-a-half gadgets which he used to cram in this really svelte, really Carnaby Street type of belt, you know? His Utility Belt. And he was super, super, super, super fit. And, um, he was a genius as well, intellectually speaking.

Well I thought I could muddle through on the genius bit but the rest of it did present problems. See, I didn't really think it was in the spirit to hire a hit-man for my mother, but I was fortunate there, actually, because my father was not around. I never saw him … never saw my dad. So it was the easiest thing in the world to have him garrotted in Venezuela by the International Brotherhood of the Puce Quadrangle.

Oh! I used to have this thing, right, where I would be lying in bed at night and this Being used to float into my room with robes on and lights glowing in his eyes and weird little balls rotating around his head, and he would come to the end of my bed and he would go, "You have been chosen, O Wise Before Your Years One, to fight evil in all its forms throughout the universe and be a member of our eternal brotherhood even beyond the veils of death, death, death, death …"

And I would prevaricate for a bit. I'd go, "I don't know. What about my homework?" And he would tell me how my Old Man had been murdered and I would leap out of bed full of steely determination and take the vow there and then … in my pyjamas. And sometimes he would tell me that my Old Man had in fact been leading the criminal syndicate and would I like to join the Cosmic Brotherhood to atone for his sins, and I would. I didn't mind.

I met him years later—my Old Man that is, not the Celestial Being—he was a really nasty, boring, stupid, little jack-in-office with ridiculous ideas about himself, and I told him, I said, "It's a real shame I met you, actually, because you used to be this really exciting thing in my head, but to meet you're just a boring little jerk." I told him that.

But anyway, to return to my sojourn, pyjama-clad, with Celestial Beings: I did a couple of circuits of the garden and I reckoned the best way to get super, super, super, super, super fit was to have a couple of strenuous adventures. Oh! The real drag was gadgets. See, I don't know if you know this but Batman's secret identity was Bruce Wayne. Oh, damn, there it's out. And he's like a multi, multimillionaire. Now, this turns out to be just as well because a Bat Plane, a Bat Copter, a Bat Submarine, a Bat Forensic Laboratory, they all cost money … and the Hot Line, there's another bill. I had a fish slice that I nicked out of the kitchen. Captain Fish Slice. "Who dares challenge Thorg The Magnificent?" [*mumbles*] Captain Fish Slice. "What? Speak up man!" Captain Fish Slice.

Oh, God, I was stupid, wasn't I! In fact, looking back, I was very lucky about the advent, in 1963, of Merseymania, when the whole world went insane. Working on the principle that the best place to hide a nut is in a fruit-cake, it was the best possible thing for me, because everyone went crazy for Beat groups from Liverpool doing simple little tunes, like they were some kind of revolutionary thing. I look back, I can't imagine why. I mean, they were all right, sort of cheerful, little dapper fellows in identical suits singing about nothing, but at the time I thought: THIS IS IT!

Ridiculous. The only thing I still remember from that period with any kind of affection is my Little Dancette, my little Woolworth's record player. It was so bad you used to have to put a threepenny piece on the arm to stop it skidding off the records, but it helped me get over all sorts of little privations, all the minor tragedies of being young, like having to wear short trousers until I was thirteen and having to watch "David Copperfield" on Sunday afternoons on the TV—OH GOD! And ... my mother's nose!

God, that amazing appendage comes coursing through the mists of time at this juncture. See, my mother had this nose—not unusual in itself I know—but the thing about this nose was it was so noisy. On a good night it used to sound like the sea. On a bad night it used to sound like a death rattle when she breathed in, and a fart, a long, dry fart when she breathed out.

Some nights she wouldn't let me play my little record player, and we only lived in this modern post-war apartment with little thin walls, just the two of us, and I would have to sit there all night listening to her in the next room: Death rattle, fart. Death rattle, fart. Death rattle, fart.

But even when she wouldn't let me play my record player, I would sit there and I would turn it on, and just watch the turntable going round and round and round and round and round and round and round. Loved it. I think I preferred it to the records, actually. I think I sensed, even then, that the spirit of rock music was better than the reality.

You know, I used to sit there and I used to think: One day something from OUT OF THE SKY is going to come down on this machine and it's going to be incredible; it's going to be like ... those old Jack Kirby comics that you used to get in the sixties, you know, with these huge figures, their faces all rigid and powerful and all this black flame playing inside their mouths and their eyes and from their fingertips would pour these torrents of power, great untrammelled floods of beautiful blazing power—that's what I used to think the rock bands of the future were going to be like—except in sound, of course. I had this thing about the sound of an electric organ floating so raw and piercing and throbbing it would actually tear through the dark, black concrete of the buildings, huge towers of masonry toppling down on thousands of upturned screaming faces.

I had clues, just little touches on records by the Yardbirds and the Byrds, and by 1967 I had built up this whole theory. It was something to do with … history, I reckoned, was like a set of rituals, invocation rituals. Take an example: Germany after the First World War, the Weimar Republic. Everything's in pieces, right?, the whole society, so they've got to start from scratch, and, just like a ritual, everybody takes on a role—roles like "We're the government and you're the poor." And they stick to these roles, no matter how uncomfortable they are, because they are a protection from the unknown. See, all they know is a few things they don't want, like the plague or foreigners coming in, and a few things they can't do, like fly, so it's all ad hoc decisions, mutual understandings, and there's no need to say what they got in that instance, but the thing is, nobody actually knows, in these rituals, how it's going to turn out, but all of them so far had been SENSIBLE rituals, FAIRLY well made plans, FAIRLY well carried out, based on existing models, and each one of them had degenerated into evil and weakness … and what rock music was supposed to be was like the first NONSENSIBLE ritual, where you purposely did everything for no reason at all, or even better, the wrong reason, and God help the next few years. Let's see what we summon up. That's why so much of what went on then seems silly now. It wasn't what it was but what it would conjure that was the point. And we felt like there was something. For about six months people were looking up as if they expected to see giant faces form in the clouds. I mean, Hendrix could play a simple twelve-bar and it sounded to us as if he was tearing the clouds apart, man.

That theory came to me one night when I was stoned and this guy had asked me why I still had the first Strawberry Alarm Clock LP. He fell asleep by the time I finished telling him. And when I got to the bit about purposeless extreme activity, I used the example of killing him. Stabbing him while he was asleep and helpless, because he'd made fun of the Strawberry Alarm Clock. Always wanted to do something like that.

"Excuse me mate, have you got the time?"

"Uh, no mate. Sorry."

"SORRY'S NOT ENOUGH. AGGGHH!"

I did like all that stuff then. I used to be in a band myself called Remo and The Juggernauts. We were great. We used to do "Substitute" on kazoos. We used to do "With God On Our Side." That was great, that was the number I used to do my free-form guitar solo on, which was great, and for the gigs, because we couldn't get all the feedback and distortion that we really wanted, in order to beef the sound up we had to borrow my mother's Hoover.

OH GOD! And we used to do "Wild Thing"! That was great because I remember, second gig that we ever … No, last gig that we ever did … well both actually … and we had this singer on who had a range of half a tone and a voice, "mememememe," like that, and this is way before Elvis Costello was ever big, so this guy wanted to sound like Captain Beefheart, the now forgotten psychedelic hero. "Arrrrrgh! Arrrrrgh!" Like that, right? So we're at the front doing the chords, and this guy's lurching about the back of the stage, doing his psychotic and interesting number, and he lurches down to the microphone and he goes, "WHHAAALD TH—!" AND HE THREW UP! A MARS BAR AND TWO TABS OF ACID DRIPPING OFF THE MICROPHONE. All the groupies he got.

And we had a drummer as well, called Jim Morrison, which was a great name to have in those days, but unfortunately, he was four-foot-ten, with pimples the size of golf balls and no personality. Oh! We had a bass player called Roger Harris as well!

Yeah, Roger Harris. When he was growing up, he'd always wanted to be Jet Harris, the bass player from the Shadows, and the kids at school called him Wet Harris. "NNNNNNYUUHH Wet Harris!"

Oh and his dad was a vicar! I remember because we used to rehearse at his house, and when we got bored we'd run round the house drawing upside-down crosses on the walls. Roger Harris.

Anyway, they all died shortly after.

No they didn't.

Yeah they did.

No. No, they didn't. No. Sort of.

I first knew it was kind of coming to an end when Roger and me started this alternative magazine round about the turn of the decade and it was going to tear the lid off Western Civilization and pour the contents out all over the floor. It was going to be experimental and it was going to be called *Probe*—terrible name, really. But we did put out one issue. It was thirty-two pages long, and in the middle was the front cover (because it was experimental), and there was sixteen pages of Roger Harris's girlfriend writing this tone poem about dawn over Chipping Sodbury, and there was fifteen pages of Roger Harris being rude about his mother, and that left one page for me to tear the lid off western civilization, pour all the contents out all over the floor. I mean, you see my problem: not enough, is it?

We never got the second issue out. He went mad. He'd always been strange. He used to like to wear long, black cloaks and carry a sword, but the first sign of him going *completely* was when he elected a tree to the editorial board. I tried to talk him out of it but of course I got outvoted, and then he had this whole political thing, that he wanted to make historical reparations to the trees on behalf of the magazine industry, all these trees being cut up in order to make paper. "Time to stem the tide!" he said. "Next issue comes out on human skin."

The night he went insane, he spent a hundred and fifty pounds on the telephone trying to call long-distance to ask Captain Beefheart what to do about the end of the world. Captain Beefheart was out. And they carried him off.

The next years were just full of disappointment. Remember the Maharishi? God, that was awful! It was about 1972. You'd just get on a bus and you'd see someone you hadn't seen in ages, you'd go, "Oh hi. How are you?" And they'd go, "... hi," and you'd look down at their lapel and there would be this greasy, fat toad beaming out of all these multicoloured lights. There's another one gone, you'd think. And that's when I realized that the revolution was not going to happen in the way they said it would, because these people were too weak.

I blamed the rock stars. I wanted to kill some of them. Thought it would make people think. For some reason my mind locked particularly on George Harrison. Finally I just roamed round the country for a couple of weeks, determined to make something happen, and one night in Wolverhampton I remember walking around the part of town where all the factories are, and it was really dark, really black, really silent, nobody around, and all of a sudden, I could see this giant insect, about fifty-, sixty- feet tall, eating the building, giant insect mandibles slicing through the dark, black concrete, huge insect tentacles punching through the windows pulling people out and just *gulping* them down.

I was delighted. I thought, This is the way the world ends, not with a bang but with giant insects eating the buildings, but I did suspect that this apocalypse was somehow tied up with my chemical condition, so I went to this nearby pub, which I knew was a good pub for scoring pills, and I burst in there, in a good mood for the first time in years, and I'm lurching around going, "Hey, fantastic! Have you heard?" And they'd go, "Oh, no. What?" and I go, "You'll find out!" But I didn't want to buy a drink, so the landlord started getting heavy with me, you know, you've got to buy some drink in a pub, and I wasn't taking any of that, not tonight of all nights, so I picked up this chair, threw it through the window, one of those smoked-glass windows with the name of the pub on.

I remember thinking, You know, I might have gone too far, and I actually said, "Well, I think I'll be off now."

They got hold of me, dragged me down to the floor and kicked my head in. Just pounded the crap out of me.

And they put me in a loony bin.

After they let me out, it seemed I had more problems than I'd gone in with. For one thing, I'd acquired a tormented, paranoid fear that I was going to be murdered by rock stars. We still had the same violent relationship, just that now they were coming for me. I dreamed it was Stevie Wonder once, and then another time Roger Whittaker disguised himself as a gardener at Hampton Court and when my back was turned for a moment, he drove this garden rake into the back of my head and buried me under a privet.

Just thinking about it makes me nervous. Brings back the old fear. Don't like this feeling. Uh ... What'll I do about this? I know. I could take one of my pills. That's what I'll do. I'll take a pill.

Hmm ... That's better. That'll calm me down.

Wonder what it is? Might be an upper... or a downer ... placebo ... milk of magnesia ... I hope it's not acid. Last time I took acid was horrible. I became convinced I was the Department of Health and Social Security, and it wasn't just a trip, you know, it went on for weeks after. It got so I wouldn't answer people's questions when they asked them. "We'll let you know," I used to say. "But I only wanted to know the time!" they'd go. I'd say, "I'm sorry, I can't tell you that over the counter. We should have something to you by about Thursday."

That's a really stupid thing though, isn't it? Taking that pill. I mean, here I am, all alone in the middle of the night, thinking about the big issues, and I don't know if I'm going to be speeding, sleeping, hallucinating or shitting. I mean, what if, in about an hour's time ... when I might be peaking OR I MIGHT NOT because I don't know ... what if the Bee Gees were to come in here disguised as picadors on horseback, with little picador spears, and they murdered me? I wouldn't know! I'd think I was tripping. I'd just go, "Oh wow! Far out!"

And I'd be dead!

No that's ridiculous, that's pathetic. I haven't had this fear in years. I got over it ... The night I got over it ...

I spent the last few hours of the 1970s miles and miles and miles and miles away from civilization, near Bolton in Lancashire. I was sitting in my apartment and I was really cold and really miserable. I was so cold and so miserable, I thought of sharpening the butter and stabbing myself with it.

See, I don't know if you remember but around about 1973 this whole set of people started to disappear off the scene, people like the guy with the big, black beard that used to turn up at parties with a mandolin in a bashed-up case, hoping someone would ask him to play it, all those women with little mirrors on their dresses, and Grateful Dead fans, you know: "I can play 'Ripple' on the tambourine." Suddenly you stopped getting into conversations about whether Carl Jung had actually had a prophetic vision of the Beatles, and the scene was full of rugby players in Aladdin Sane make-up talking about the gear change on their new Simcas. Suddenly, everybody was into Led Zeppelin, table football and projectile vomit, so what happened is all the purists moved out of town. They loaded up their dad's station-wagon, that they'd borrowed for the day, with their half-hundred-weight bags of chickpeas and their Fabulous Furry Freak Brothers comics and their alternative-technology handbooks, and they drove … out of town, to the hills beyond Oldham, the moors past Burnley, to tiny, obscure, rainswept towns of granite—kind of places where it was front-page news if the wind stopped—places so dismal and grey, you had to take acid so you could remember what colours are!

And that's where they all went, it's true: The Lost Tribe of Dylan. They've all been sitting there for the last twenty years.

But anyway, I was part of that little migration. I went because the rents were cheap, but once you get to those places, you can't leave, and this is how I came to be celebrating the New Year—nay, the new decade—in this little furnished fridge halfway between Bolton and Rawtenstall, and I was getting into this long, philosophical discursive look back at the 1970s and my part in the advancement of culture during that period, which is a bad sign, so I started to turn my mind to where I could go out for the evening. It so happened I'd got three pairs of socks for Christmas that year, so this meant I didn't have to go to the laundromat until after my unemployment cheque came, which in turn meant I had another seventy-five pence to play around with.

The town was mine! But the only place to go was this New Year's Eve party organised by the local alternative bookshop: Bilbo's Underpants. That's not the real name of the shop, it's just that people started calling it "Bilbo's Underpants" and "Bilbo's Underpants" stuck—if you pardon the iconoclasm, I mean the name stuck to the shop—and it's this really horrible place run by these three ex-hippies who stand around all day talking about "creating viable alternatives," when in fact they make their money selling Dashiell Hammett books to skinheads from the Further Education College up the road, and *Watership Down* to vicars' wives from Radcliffe, and one of them's really, really fat and the other two are really, really thin—have you noticed how hippies are always either overweight or underweight? It's weird—and the fat one's called Fat Packer and the thin ones are Ray and Pat Smudgley.

Oh! This shop used to be even worse! It used to have this hippie with pimples working there who always used to pick on you if you bought the wrong book. He'd go, "YOU DO REALIZE, DON'T YOU, THAT THIS BOOK IS ABOUT A CRYPTO-FASCIST, REVISIONIST, ELITIST EPHEMERA ISSUED TO BOLSTER THE MISPLACED AND CRUMBLING CONFIDENCE IN IMPERIALISM AS IT EXISTS WITHIN THE IDEOLOGICAL SYSTEMS OF THE AMERICAN BOURGEOISIE? EH? THOUGHT OF THAT, HAVE YOU? EH? EH? EH?"

And you'd be looking down at this copy of Erle Stanley Gardner's *The Case of the Perjured Parrot* that you had absentmindedly picked out of the second-hand bin and you'd go, "Well I don't know till I've read it, do I?" And he'd say, "A LIBERAL IS A NAZI IN HUSH PUPPIES! TWENTY-FIVE PENCE, PLEASE. NOW GET OUT OF THE SHOP!"

He was horrible. In the end he had to leave because people kept dropping Solzhenitsyn books on his head.

He indicates that it was he who did the dropping.

Anyway, so I can go to their party but it's going to be awful, in this huge, freezing church-hall, with just one paraffin heater in the corner, and about eight people huddled around it, and five of them'll be sensitive bad folk guitarists all hoping someone will invite them to play, and the other three people'll be, like, two will be the local radical feminist collective and the other'll be that damn vicar with his practised Irish twinkle and his bottle of Glenmorangie. And there'll be a doorprize for some shop-soiled Kurt Vonnegut books.

And when I get there Ray and Fat Packer from the shop are on stage singing their long, whining rendition of an old Rolling Stones song, "My Sweet Lady Jane," which Ray dedicates to an ex-girlfriend whom he compares to one of the minor characters from *The Lord of the Rings*, but I happen to know ran off with a set of his headphones, and I know that next they'll steam into their flaccid rhythm-and-blues medley. I'm weary from this set. They've been doing it as long as I've known them, and each time they come up after and ask me, "Uh ... What did you think of the set man, you know? It's a shame we didn't get to do the encore 'cause the audience wasn't very receptive, you know?" Forty times I've seen them play and I've never heard the encore.

The real problem is that something had changed while I was in the bin. Before, I would amuse myself by criticizing everybody. I could meet anyone and just go, "You know, you are emotionally, politically, intellectually, artistically screwed. You don't know what you're talking about, and you're making life miserable for yourself and everyone around you." I didn't have to know them, I just assumed, and what's amazing is you're almost never wrong ... all right, I was a bit tough on a couple of babies, but you know ...

But after my therapy I couldn't any more. When I met people I just wanted to hide. They frightened me.

So this was just depressing and I went across the road to the pub, thinking I'd go back in a bit to see if I won a door prize, but the pub is full of all these people with Mohawks and weird clothes and things sticking out of their ears and rings through their armpits and so on, and I recognize them, it's the New Wave contingent from the Further Education College up the road, and the one closest to me I recognize, this guy in this green vinyl jacket and a polka-dot kilt with an arrow through his head, and he's the art teacher from the Further Education

College from up the road. He's always trying to keep in with the students, you know? He's thirty-five, he's got Johnny Rotten's autograph, poor sod, so I say to him, "Hey Henry, what are all these post-new-wave-sub-post-modernist-fringe-pre-new-order business studies students doing at the wake for Donovan's reputation?" And he says they've all come here because there's this band playing at the party across the road later on.

I ask around and it turns out it's true, there's a fully fledged, fully professional rock band, with a recording contract and everything, playing at this party. Amazingly, I've even heard of them, it's a group called Trevor and the Golden Gates of Despair. I go back over the road to the hall and above the door is this huge banner announcing the name of the band. There's trucks parked outside, people carrying equipment in, guys selling programmes. And by the door are pinned up these recent reviews of the band, blown-up so you can read them from a distance, I guess—or whole gangs of you, happy fans, can all stand around and recite these reviews in unison, or something. I go over and I read one of these reviews. *The New Musical Express* of October the 17th, 1979, had this to say: "Trevor and the Golden Gates of Despair play Dadaist rockabilly with a difference. They redefine, reprocess, restructure and refurbish the traditional, non-decorative mannerisms of gloom rock. They rediscover the toy despair of Jim Morrison in angular oral puns. With one hammer-blow of joyous, baroque, wittily uninventive twelve-bar they show us what Nietzsche would have said if he'd had pop sense. THE CLASH ARE THE PROSE, THE EVERYDAY EXPERIENCE, OF THE POST–NEW WAVE SUB–POST-MODERNIST FRINGE PRE–NEW ORDER BUSINESS STUDIES STUDENT WORLD, BUT BUT TREVOR AND THE GOLDEN GATES OF DESPAIR ARE THE CONDENSED EXPERIENCE, THEY ARE THE TRUTH ABOUT YOUR LIVES!" Or not.

I'm just thinking, Whatever happened to a toe-tapping blues chaser with nice harmonies and a message? When all of a sudden I hear these voices behind me go, "Right! Where's the chicks!" And it's the roadies.

I go back in and stacks and stacks of amplifiers are being set up, lights are being rigged. This false stage is being built. There's two road-managers on the old stage beating up the sensitive bad folk guitarist halfway through his rendition of "Alice's Restaurant" because they're trying to set up. And all the hippies are standing around looking sheepish and outmoded—looking like Aztecs in Spain, if you know what I mean. The excitement is palpable as a twelve-foot-high set of golden gates is erected at the back of the stage.

Finally, Trevor and the Golden Gates of Despair take to the stage.

They turn out to be this art student with a souped-up stylophone and a drum machine, and Trevor, who's this guy in white-face make-up who shouts out this poetry in the same sort of tone of voice as the guy shouts out scores on darts on the television: "SMASH THE SYSTEM! ONE HUNDRED AND TWENTY!"

And they launch into their first number, which is this samba—speed notch three, fact fans—in which the art student plays what sounds to me like "Let's Dance" without the chord changes, and Trevor shouts out his poetry.

> I HAVE A PLASTIC LIFE!
> I LIVE IN A PLASTIC HOUSE!
> WITH A PLASTIC MOTHER!
> I LOVE SWEAR WORDS!
> FRIEND OF MINE TRIED TO SMASH THE
>   SYSTEM!
> THEY GOT HIM!
> I WOULD'VE HELPED THEM TO GET HIM
>   BUT I WAS AWAY ON HOLIDAY AT THE
>   TIME!
> HIT IT, LEO!

Goes on for twenty minutes. Finally it stops and Trevor introduces his new single. It's called "The Fastidious Hamster Gets On the TV."

In this one, the art student plays what sounds to me like the theme tune from "Sports Night with Coleman" at quarter-speed, but they may say it's Wagner, I don't know.

Trevor shouts out his new poem and it goes:

ONE!
TWO!
THREE!
FOUR!
FIVE!
SIX!
SEVEN!
EIGHT!
NINE!
TEN! …
I AM PRODUCT!
YOU ARE CONSUMER! …
ONE! TWO! THREE!

Well, you get the rest. That's all the lyrics! TWENTY MORE MINUTES!

I'm looking around to see how this is going down: like a turd in a punch bowl. Trevor is going down very badly. All the sensitive folk guitarists, sensing that this act is doomed, are tuning up and stroking their beards expectantly. At the back of the auditorium, Pat Smudgley is absentmindedly picking the fungus off the door prize, and the radical feminists have got this really heavy dominoes tournament; but the climax of the unrest is when the vicar, who's had his share of whisky by now, shouts out, "I hope you lot can do 'Auld Lang Syne' better than you do your own stuff!"

Trevor stops, halts the band, and goes, "Shut up! You stupid vicar!" He quips wittily, "NONE OF YOU PILLOCKS'VE GOT THE GUTS TO STAND HERE LIKE ME ON THE STAGE AND TELL THE TRUTH AND CHALLENGE YOUR HORRIBLE

PRECONCEPTIONS OF LIFE! I'VE GOT GUTS! YOU'RE ALL SHEEP! SHUT UP!"

But the sensitive folk guitarist who had his fingers broken earlier for playing "Alice's Restaurant" summons up the courage to say, "I bet you can't play 'Universal Soldier!'"

Trevor turns and goes, "NOR CAN BLOODY YOU AFTER WHAT MY ROADIES DID TO YOU. HA! SEE HOW I LAUGH AT YOUR MISFORTUNE? SEE HOW I SNEER AT YOUR AGONY AND PISS ON YOUR NOTIONS OF GOOD TASTE. NOW HEAR THIS: TO ME, BAD TASTE IS FREEDOM. GOOD TASTE IS ALL ONE WITH THE INHUMAN SHACKLES OF YOUR PETIT-BOURGEOIS SOCIETY. NOW HEAR THIS: TONIGHT IS THE END OF THE END OF AN ERA; FROM THIS NIGHT ON ALL ROCK STARS WILL OPENLY AND PUBLICLY CONFESS THEIR CONTEMPT AND RIGHTEOUS HATRED OF THEIR AUDIENCES. YOUR PETIT-BOURGEOIS IDEOLOGICAL SYSTEMS LIE SHATTERED AT YOUR FEET. IT IS NIGHT AT THE GOLDEN GATES OF DESPAIR!"

I'm looking at him. His neck is bulging with hatred. Spittle is spurting out into the audience as he slobbers through his diatribe. His eyes are bulging and his make-up's all streaking down his face, with the sweat and everything, you know, making him look inhuman and weird, and far too upset for there to be any point to it, and sick, and nothing, and horrible, and spiteful, and slowly I'm getting to like him.

Well he's got style of sorts, you know? So I think, Encourage him, and I shout, "Right on, Trevor! You tell them!"

And he turns and glares, and I get this little tremor of excitement going up and down my spine ... a rock star with a couple of albums behind him and he's looking at me! Like, once one of the Mothers of Invention waved to me from the band bus, but other than that, I'd never had a single rock name at all ever look at my particular features. He might even speak—but all this goes through my head in just an instant, because a moment later he turns to me and he goes, "You! I remember you! YOU DROPPED THE ENTIRE *GULAG*

ARCHIPELAGO ON MY HEAD!"

For the first time in my life I was gob-smacked, didn't know what to say. Trevor was the hippie with pimples that used to work in the book shop.

The next thing I remember, I'm walking home. I'm so crushed and humiliated, I'm choking back the tears. I MEAN, I KNOW THE GUY'S A JERK. I remember him from when he lived round here. He was an angry flobber merchant—the kind of guy when he started talking politics in the pub you'd have to put your hand over your beer, you know? "Trot-thh-kism." You know? And then I'd think of the thrill I got as he looked at me! Since 1973—since the first time I heard the first Roxy Music LP—I'd hated rock music. I'd spent at least three hours a day being rude about it. But I realized that night that I bought the whole thing, really. At this rate, in thirty years I'd still be saving up for green vinyl retrospectives of The Clash.

By the time I got home I was in a really foul mood. I just wanted to be on my own. But I notice that the downstairs light is on, which means my old landlady is in, and I don't want to talk to her so I try to tiptoe up the stairs, but they squeak, so I get half-way up and this little, wizened, old head pops its way round the downstairs door and goes, "Hello, luv." I say, "Hello, Mrs. Neck"—that's her name, Mrs. Neck. "I thought you'd be out tonight." She says, "No, luv. They all went for a medieval banquet down the Bleeding Wolf. I don't like those medieval banquets. They just put raisins on your beef burger and charge you a fiver." She says, "How do you fancy a nice cup of tea to see the New Year in?" So, I can't turn her down—I like her actually— so, I go downstairs.

Mrs. Neck is this cartoon old lady from Lancashire: fluffy slippers, head scarf, flowery dress. The only strange thing about her, really, is her shades. She wears jet-black shades, around the house and every-where, kind of like a cross between Roy Orbison and someone from "Coronation Street." She does have other peculiarities as well, a bit of a tendency to see dead cats floating up the walls, and she sometimes goes, "Ah ha!" and "Hmm," when nothing's happening.

So this is how I see the New Year—nay the new decade—in: sitting in this little back-room in the wilds of Lancashire, surrounded by the framed photographs of the dead contingents of the Neck family, drinking this strange sherry with a sediment in the bottom, singing "Auld Lang Syne" with my arms linked to this nice little old lady from Lancashire in jet-black shades.

Shortly after the stroke of midnight she says, "How do you fancy a little bit of the ancient wisdom of Thoth?" Oh no, I think, She means her Tarot pack, her little bit of washable magic that she got from the W.H. Smith in Bolton. Yes! She's getting it out of the drawer. She's going to read my bloody fortune.

I remember ... The spooky Two of Swords and the Falling Tower and these dogs howling at the moon, and Mrs. Neck saying ...

I would bump into someone I never expected to see again ...

I would come into some money I never expected to ...

But some of my greatest ambitions would not come true.

And that night, I went upstairs and tore up my books and rammed them in the bin. Took all my records, snapped those I could and gouged the rest. Burned my posters. And that's the night I finally realized that I have no relation to rock stars. It's silly to be angry at them, and they've never heard of me.

The next morning I went downstairs and there was a parcel waiting for me. I opened it and there was five thousand pounds in used notes—

He listens for a moment.

Sorry, I just thought I heard a noise.

No, it's nothing. Yeah, it was. Yeah. It's like horse's hooves or something.

Oh there's horses coming up the stairs.

Anyway, so the next morning ... THAT'S A BIT WEIRD ISN'T IT? What're horses doing coming up the stairs? They're coming closer ... and closer ... They're going to come here, I can sense it. YES! THE DOOR'S OPENING!

Here they are!

One, two, three, four ... four beautiful, dappled mares, and each one of them is being ridden by a gaily covered paperback book: *Gravity's Rainbow* by Thomas Pynchon, *Blood and Guts in High School* by Kathy Acker, *Arthur's Britain* by Leslie Alcock and *Bomb Culture* by Jeff Nuttall. It's weird, I've read them all. Yeah, they were all published by Picador.

PICADOR!

OH NO! IT'S MY GREATEST FEAR COME TRUE! IT'S THE BEE GEES DISGUISED AS PICADORS AND THEY'VE COME TO MURDER ME!

All right! I know who you are and what you've come for! You murderous mega-stars. Finally tracked me down, eh? Take off those false front covers and reveal yourselves for who you truly are: Robin Gibb, Andy Gibb, and um … uh …

Oh no, they are! THEY'RE TAKING OFF THEIR COVERS! THEY'RE GOING TO KILL ME!

NO! PLEASE DON'T DO IT! I DON'T WANT TO …

Oh.

It's Abba.

Oh hi. I quite liked "Knowing Me Knowing You." It was a bit over-produced—*AGHHH!*

That's it, I'm dead! Might as well have a cigarette, eh? "Warning: Tobacco can seriously damage your health." Unless you're dead! Ha ha. There you go.

Trevor remembered me and how revolting I could be, so he thought I could make an alternative comic, so I went down to London. He hired me as the warm-up act for Trevor and the Golden Gates of Despair. I went out on stage and …

Nothing. It was weird.

I had an agent and everything. I'd phone up and I'd hear, "OH WOW! HI! GREAT TO HEAR FROM YOU! I WAS JUST THINKING ABOUT YOU JUST NOW! JUST THINKING ABOUT WHAT AN AMAZING, UNIQUE TALENT, A VERY

PARTICULAR VOICE YOU'VE GOT, AND IT'S REALLY TIME
WE GOT TOGETHER TO REALLY WORK OUT SOME KIND
OF PACKAGE IN ORDER TO PROJECT YOU INTO THE
PUBLIC'S MIND AND MAKE A PANT-LOAD OF MONEY!
Unfortunately, there's no one in the office at the moment, so can you
please leave ... "

At the end of my garden, right on the eastern edge of London, there
were these five railway lines. Intercity, suburban and goods trains were
forever going past my bedroom window, often making the room shake
so much the needle would skid across my records, and every night
about four a.m., clanking carefully through the darkness, a great
heavyweight tiptoeing miserably, came a train carrying nuclear waste.
It took twenty minutes to shuffle by, and seemed, when I parted the
curtain and looked out, eerily lit by ice-blue lights. One night I
dreamed that war was imminent. I believe many other people around
that time also mysteriously did.

I became so convinced, it was hard to go through London without
looking at all these lions on plinths, all these mighty crests from around
the Empire, all those bitter people, and lunatics, and not think they're
going to disappear in a sheet of flame at any moment. I had discovered
politics, something to be obsessed about other than rock. It was there
in my mind every day, to the point where I couldn't function.

It was weird being in that crowd. I remember going to this
Christmas party in London, and there were all these savage iconoclasts
wandering around wishing each other a happy Christmas. I came to
suspect them politically.

Later, in the tube station, waiting for the last train, I was half-asleep
when I heard a voice from the other end of the platform, talking to the
band, [*Glasgow accent*] "HEY, YOU! YOU, THAT'S RIGHT, YOU!
YOU IN THE PUCE PACAMAC WITH THE TEETH LIKE
TERRY THOMAS, I'M TALKING TO YOU! WHAT'S THE
MATTER? I'M TRYING TO TALK TO YOU! All I want is a light,
man! That's all I'm asking for. Oh great, thanks. What's that? I know
it's a match. What use is a match without a bloody cigarette? Don't

play the bloody social worker with me! GIVE ME WHAT I NEED! That's better. Thank you very much. Sorry I shouted. Sorry about that. Let's be pals, eh? Shake hands, eh? Eh? Let's shake hands."

Then I heard, "YAAAAAAA!" and, "That's a pretty good trick, eh? Bet you didn't realize a thumb could bend back that far, did you? Will you stop screaming, pal? It'll be a bit flappy for a month or two, but it'll be right as rain in about eighteen months. Hey, you guys students? Oh you're not. You're a band? That's great! I used to be in a band as well, I used to play the bass guitar. Which one of you plays the— Oh, you! You're the bass player! That's great! I'm a bass player too! Shake on it!"

"AHHHHHHHHHH!"

"Oh, well come on now, you're not going to be playing for a while, are you, eh? Tell you what: your bass player's out of commission now he's got a broken thumb. Tell you what I'll do, I'll join the band, we'll all get really rich and really famous and then I'll leave to pursue a solo career and your old friend can rejoin. What do you say?"

We kept bumping into this guy, whose name was Roy. One time I heard him say, [*Glasgow accent*] "Get your head around this. I used to be a burglar. I wasnae a very good one—I'd just go out and get drunk, get really pissed, and then just break into somebody's apartment—anybody's—take whatever was there. Take it down to the pawn shop. Get some money. Buy some more booze.

"One night I got really, really drunk and went off and I broke into this flat. There's almost nothing there. There's just a really old crappy TV and a lousy little transistor radio. So I thought, Oh, well. It's better than nothing. Took them down to the pawn shop. Couple of pints worth of money, you know? Drank that back, went home.

"Bugger me, I'd been burgled. Even worse, it was me that did it. Even worse than that, I went around all the pubs going, 'When I find out who burgled my apartment, I'll kick his bloody head in!' So, when I realized it was me, I did. I disco-danced in a telephone box until my elbows broke."

Another time it was, [*Glasgow accent*] "You know what I always wanted? To work in Customs and Excise, because then you'd get to meet all these famous people, like rock stars, as they were jetting about, and if you wanted you could look up their bums."

I bumped into Trevor and some others at the cinema in Notting Hill Gate to see this new release—very startling, very searing examination of human society called *Apocalypse Now*.

This movie starts off there's this bloke gets hired by the army to try and track down Marlon Brando 'cause the army thinks that Marlon Brando has gone mad. So he agrees to do it. They're in Vietnam. He gets in this boat and he sails down this river for about three hours. It's mythic, right; if you sail down a river in a movie these days for three hours, it's mythic. It's like if everybody's sitting in the same room and nobody says anything for fifteen minutes, it's claustrophobic, or if you steal bits from other movies, it's references, and if the film is too long and it's got lots of naked bottoms in it, it's either a *Carry On* film or the director coming to terms with his own Catholicism. But in this case, we're into the mythic, so we toil up this bloody river till finally we get to this weird temple affair with all these strange guys in face make-up wandering around, who think that Marlon Brando is God.

Our hero gets out of the boat and he goes, "Excuse me, can you tell me where Marlon Brando is, please?" They take him off and it turns out the army is right, Marlon Brando is mad, all he does is sit in this weird hut, sweating profusely and reciting poetry so bloody quietly that four people die half-way through a sonnet.

And they have this climactic conversation. I can't remember the exact details, but it goes something like this:

> HERO: Uh … excuse me, Mr. Brando? Can you tell me the way to the toilets, please?
> MARLON: You haven't come all this way … to ask me the way to the toilets.
> HERO: Uh … No. No. Actually, no. I came to kill you cause the army thinks you're mad. But please, it's been a long journey, I'd like to freshen up.

MARLON: Can anyone ... in this world ... really ...
freshen up? Are you familiar with the works of T.S.
Eliot?

Spot the grammar-school reference: T.S. Eliot. Trevor and all his
mates, they came out of the cinema agreeing with the film. They'd see
the grumpy guy in the box-office of the cinema who's overworked and
underpaid and go, "See? Take the mask off civilized man ... " Or these
skinheads walking down the street, "Oh, yeah. Take the mask off
civilized man ... The horror, the horror, the horror."

All the time I was wondering, Where have I seen Marlon Brando's
character before? Then it hit me: I used to have an English teacher just
like him—all right, there were differences. This English teacher did
not have a charismatic sniff and nobody thought he was God; but he
thought he was God and he used to spend a lot of the time looking out
the window reciting poetry so bloody quietly no one could hear it, so
there were similarities; and he used to have two horrible tricks. One
was, if he saw you walking down the corridor or anywhere without a
cap on, he'd shout, "YOU ARE NAKED, BOY!" Just because you
weren't wearing your cap, but he was totally convincing. You'd be like,
"Oh God." And the other thing was, he would come to you and he'd
go, "Who's your favourite Beatle, boy?" And whoever you answered,
he'd go, "Wrong, boy, they're all talentless nincompoops!" and start
jabbing this pencil in your ear. "I'm cleaning out your ears so you can
hear what talentless fools they really are!" But the point is that when
he used to quote T.S. Eliot he'd say, "Just goes to show if you take the
mask off civilized man you get *the horror;* that's why they invented the
army, and the police, and segregated toilets."

In the pub after, I'm trying to tell them that it's too easy to believe
"the horror, the horror ... " It's like, someone's parked a car over your
foot and you're going "Aaaaa!" and they go, "Listen! Those dreadful
animal cries!" "No no! Move the car." "Well, the car's obviously a
factor, we can see that." "Move the car." "Take the mask off ... "

I felt so lucid, but they weren't understanding. I was starting to feel sorry for myself, then I heard [*Glasgow accent*]:

Ah, but as for my story, it's sadder yet.
I might look to you just like a tatty looking,
pissed-up Scottish get,
but it's not always been the case.
I used to be a part of the human race,
in the big castle, loved and lazy—
not as you see me now, hated, violent and crazy.
I'm not even Scottish.
I'm Polish.
As a youth I used to bask in the reflected glory of
my incredibly talented brother, but also I used to be
a star centre-forward for Wiedew Lodz, the local
First Division soccer club.
I was terrific in the air, I was brilliant with my feet,
I was excellent at the half-volley.

And then one day I fell victim to a wicked
referee's folly.
The ball had quite clearly bounced off Grobni's
knee.
A damn, shitting, stupid, bloody CORNER WAS
THE ONLY TRUE DECISION THERE COULD
BE!
He gave a goal kick.
Boy, was I sick.
It wasn't the result that mattered, you know—we
were six nothing up with five seconds to go—it was
the SHEER INJUSTICE of the decision!
And you know, from that moment on, I've never
been able to look at a football field as anything else
but just a bunch of grass with white lines drawn on it.
I was almost bodily flung off it into a region of

total chaos.

And after that it all goes kind of weird.

I kept changing identities;

I was a fish for a bit.

I was a poodle in Splott, a little-known area of Cardiff.

I was a massive dirigible in Japan for a while.

And in case you think I'm just boasting, I'll also tell you that for three years I was also a packet of stomach powder in rural Nigeria.

1967, the Summer of Love, I was a hamburger. Grace Slick ate me. My only contact with the famous.

And then one day, years later,

I was in the United Kingdom and I happened to notice in the newspaper that Ipswich Town were playing Widzew Lodz in the UEFA Cup, so I thought I'd go and see them—see how my ex-pals from the Youth Team, who would now be in their full maturity, were getting along.

They lost five to one.

My feelings were such a bizarre mix between cosmic terror and tenderness for my ex-companions that I did not announce myself to them. Instead, I trudged wearily and sadly down to the bus station in Ipswich and there I went into the toilets and I locked myself in one of the booths leaving a sign on the door saying, "I won't come out until you make me famous."

Two weeks went by and when I came out, I was Scottish.

I said, "That's a sad story." He says, "Not really. We none of us really get to choose our nationality."

What finally tipped me over was that the next night I went back to the pub, and they said, "Not you, you stupid Scottish bastard. You're barred."

I must have gone to the bus station, because the next thing I remember I was back up in Lancashire, my career over.

I knew I had to find a way of maintaining any hope, convince myself that it was worth carrying on. And what I came up with was this story from my past that sort of did the trick.

Remember when people thought Paul McCartney was dead? Well in those days people were quite ill about the Beatles, and they discovered that if you played the last section of *Sgt. Pepper's Lonely Hearts Club Band* backwards you could distinctly hear a voice saying, "Fuck your fucking Superman."

Well, of course, then the thing came to be to listen to all the Beatles records backwards, hold their albums' sleeves up to mirrors, soak out the mysterious signals the boys had left behind, which turned out to say that Paul McCartney was dead.

Obviously there's some kind of wish-fulfilment going on here, some kind of deep-seated belief that since we know and love and are obsessed by the Beatles so much, they must in some dim, mysterious, subterranean, Jungian sense be aware of us and want to communicate with those of us who are fucking stupid enough to sit around playing their records backwards.

I had a friend who took all this one step further—Roger Harris. He listened to his entire record collection backwards, and became convinced, eventually, that the Ultimate Spinach were speaking to him— but this was different, this was him personally. He became convinced that this now-forgotten psychedelic group from Boston had involuntarily set up this kind of weird psychic link, sort of a cosmic telephone-line—to the extent that he believed the communication was two-way, to the extent that he actually believed that he had inspired their best song—to the extent that when their third LP came out and it was no good, he wrote them a letter apologizing. He said, "I'm sorry but I had exams at the time."

I learned later that the scientific definition of psychosis is this: you actually don't know what the borderline between yourself and everybody else is. You don't know what the difference is between you and everything else.

So, and this means that, for example, if you really, really want something to happen it becomes very difficult to understand that it hasn't, because the dream is in you so much that it must be in the rest of the world. And conversely, it also means that if something really awful happens around you, it's very difficult to understand that you didn't cause it. As you can imagine, this leads to some terrific mental snarl-ups.

My life was changed irrevocably one Tuesday afternoon in history at school. Old Mr. MacKenzie was droning on about the Battle of Stamford Bridge, the final battle of the Dark Ages, when all of a sudden this lad who had just arrived in the class after having been expelled from a number of very expensive public schools puts his hand up and says, "Sir! It wasn't like that at all, sir!" Mr. MacKenzie turns round and he says, "Oh yes, Harris," for it was indeed Roger Harris, "And upon what sources do you base your information?" And Roger said, "I don't need sources, sir. I was there." And he kind of made his eyes glow in this bizarre manner that he had. I was attracted to him right away. We became friends.

I remember at that time his dad was this monster of the late sixties, a liberal vicar, who actually used to appear on the media, appealing to everybody to be nice, but his big kick was being against censorship of any kind. He said, "Anyone should be allowed to read any book they want because no one is ever influenced by any book they ever read."

Now it's not a bad thing to say, but there is within it a little kernel of bullshit. But the problem for Roger was that, because he didn't know the difference between himself and everybody else, it was like he'd thought it, and he knew there was something bullshit about it, so he kept wondering why he'd invented this nonsense. It was like this little kernel of nonsense had lodged in his brain—it was like being

invaded, and it really became a matter of actually—no joking—
life and death—for him to make his dad stop saying that anybody
could read anything 'cause they were never influenced by it. At any rate
he embarked on this very, very heavy campaign to get his father to
recant it.

What he did was, he started reading books and becoming exagger-
atedly influenced by them. He read Graham Greene and become a
Catholic. He read Chaim Potok and became Jewish. Stephen King,
he read.

One time, his parents went away for the weekend and they came
back and there was Roger in the kitchen in a loincloth. Determined not
to be fazed by this at all, they said, "Hello, Roger. How was your
weekend?" He said, "It was all right ... Read *Lord of the Flies*. Went to
a party ... Ate Nigel Smiggins." "Oh yes, dear? Very nice," they said.
They had guts, his parents. They really did.

But in the end he got them. He left a copy of *The Brothers
Karamazov* accidentally on purpose in the hallway. His dad came in,
saw it, and thought, "Oh, no. What's Roger reading now?" Looks at
it. Says on the back: "Dostoyevsky's searing novel of parricide." Goes,
"Hang on. Parricide?" Dives for the dictionary. Parricide, of course,
means murdering your father.

Enough! Roger's dad went down to the police station. The officer
there was not very sympathetic. He said, "Let's get this straight,
Reverend Harris. Your son is reading a long-winded Russian novel.
Hardly a capital offence, is it?" Total defeat, but I have to say, in
defence of Roger's dad, another person might have just gone to his son
and said, "You were right, son, all along. I'm a horrible crypto-fascist
swine." But he didn't. Instead he slammed his foot down on the old
goodwill pedal.

He invited his son to come and give a talk to the Church Auxiliary,
a group of old, conservative folk who liked to sit around with cups of
tea and tea biscuits and listen to chats. "Talk about anything you
want," he says.

"All right," says Roger, "I will."

I joined him on that halcyon evening. Roger steps up in front of all this pink hair and he says, "Ladies and gentlemen, I would like to see a return to traditional British values and practices," and a palpable wave of relief goes round the room. He continues, "Traditional British values and practices like painting ourselves blue. And running up and down the hills hitting Italians in tin skirts. Traditional British values and practices like stuffing foreigners into wicker baskets and setting fire to them. In fact, I say, ladies and gentleman, let's get back to the old pagan ways!" Starts tearing at his clothing, he's going, "Ladies and gentleman, forget about this Johnny-come-lately Mediterranean god, let's get back to the old pagan days, dancing around the oak tree. I've got some mistletoe! Let's get necking." He says, "I only say this," he says, "Because I happen to be a minor Celtic deity."

Well, at this point, he's down to his underpants and his mother throws a big blanket over him and they carry him out.

After I say, "Brilliant!" I say, "Just wonderful! Particularly that gag about being a minor Celtic deity!" He turns to me and goes, "What do you mean 'gag,' mortal?"

That was the trouble with Roger. He did not know exactly what was going on, so when he said something as a joke, it carried just as much authority as if it was one of his deepest convictions. He would forget that he intended it as a joke originally. It was always continually changing, you know? Very hard thing for him to manage.

I have to say in his defence that really we're all like that—we none of us know where ourselves end and the rest of the world begins. We don't. It's just that with most of us we don't care. There seems to be some bizarre, kind of built-in, very handy mechanism in most of us for not bothering about the fact that we don't know what's us and what's everything else. But Roger never figured that out, you see? Because he just saw us all wandering around and he thought either we do know the difference between ourselves and everything else and we're not telling him for some rotten, perverse reason, or we don't and for some equally horrible reason we're all bullshitting him into thinking we do know. So he would get quite angry. Quite an angry person, bitter and paranoid.

We used to have this other friend, Jim Morrison. What a jerk! He wasted having the sexiest name in the world at the time by having just a miserable, disgusting personality and an ugly face. We only used to hang around with him because he was rich, because he'd inherited some money.

He idolized Roger and he got this awful habit of coming up to him and telling him specious lies and taking this weird pleasure out of Roger exposing him.

Like he'd say, "Ooo you know, I was playing the guitar last night and I just kind of Zenned-in on the strings, you know, and like, all of a sudden I could play really, really fast, you know, as fast as Alvin Lee." And Roger would go, "NO YOU BLOODY DIDN'T, YOU HORRIBLE, LITTLE, DIMPLE-FINGERED TWERP! YOU INCOMPETENT, THREE-LEFT-HANDED BONEHEAD! YOU CAN'T PLAY THE GUITAR AT ALL!" And Jim would go, "Ooo, you really sussed me out there."

Every time! Or he would come up and he'd go, "You know, I was smoking dope last night and, you know, and I really kind of became an unconscious mote on the wave of the universe, you know. And I could see, like, Buddha and Jesus, and stuff like that, all playing cribbage on this cloud together." And he'd go, "NO YOU DIDN'T YOU MISERABLE, TENSE, ANAL-RETENTIVE, SUBURBAN, SQUALID DROP OF DOG SNOT!" "Ooo, you really sussed me out there."

He'd do it three times in a day at times, and what happened was, I guess, 1969 to 1970 around there, we all went up north. And Roger's girlfriend got this place at the University up at Salford, near Manchester. So, we all went to live in her Hall of Residence. One little room, all of us: Jim, Roger and Roger's girlfriend. Jim was only there because he had the money.

We were there for two months and it got … people were starting to really get at each other. The climax came at Hallowe'en when we went to this place near Manchester called Alderley Edge, which is a sudden lump in the Cheshire plain, and there's legends associated with it and everything like that, so around about the end of the 1960s and the early 1970s at Hallowe'en, the ancient pagan festival, it was like bloody Grand Central Station there, it was packed with pixies from Birmingham and sort of ancient pagans from Bromsgrove and all kinds of preposterous ninnies with flutes.

You'd overhear these arguments, "Oi! What are you doing there? Our mystical cult has been celebrating the turn of the year at this sacred spot since time immemorial! Since before the dawn of time we've been coming here!"

"Oh, yeah? Where the bloody hell were you last year then?"

"Well, it was raining, wasn't it?"

You have to get there up this hill, and at the bottom is a pub called the Wizard, and we went in there first and there's all these weirdos there and this one guy comes up. He's about twenty-one but he looks four thousand years old. There're these massive patches of grey underneath his eyes and these kind of greenish, greyish, burning, weird orbs in his skull instead of eyes, and he's the colour of bone.

He comes up and he goes, "You do realize that I worship gods far more ancient than anything that can be conceived of in the narrow, petty-bourgeois ideology of the people around here, don't you?"

Roger turns to him and he goes, "Well, I suppose you'll be glad I'm back then."

What a great answer at the time! But, of course, as soon as he makes a joke he forgets it's a joke. So, we're all busy patting him on the back when we see his eyes start to glow and we think, "Oh, no, it's minor Celtic deity time again!" Sure enough.

We go up to the Edge, and there's a big rock there called Castle Rock which is in effect this short cliff, and we're standing on it, and Roger turns to Jim Morrison and goes, "Jim. With my amazing, divine powers, I can give you the gift of flight." Jim goes, "Oooo wow. Yeah, great." But senses that good will not come of this. And Roger goes, "In fact, now I think of it, poof, there you go. You can fly."

"Mmm … Uh … Thanks Roger."

He says, "In fact," he says, "I tell you what, why don't you step off of Castle Rock now and fly around a bit and show these people that there's more to life than they think?"

"Well, I ... No, it's all right, Roger."

"You don't believe me, do you?"

"Yeah! Yeah, I do. Yeah."

"No, you don't believe me. You don't believe that I have, in fact, the ability to confer upon you the power of flight, do you?"

"Yeah. Yeah, I do. I believe you, yeah."

"No, you don't."

"I do!"

"NO, YOU DON'T!"

"Oooo, you really sussed me out there."

It was the fourth time that day he'd said it, so Roger just picks up this rock and goes BOOM! right in Jim's forehead. BO-O-O-ING!!! Jim goes off Castle Rock—turns out Roger was lying and he couldn't fly.

Boof! Like that.

I mean, he wasn't dead, but he was never as friendly again.

After that, we all gradually broke up.

But the thing about Roger, I have to say, is that he was not wrong, quite—inasmuch as he was a total lunatic. I mean, here's an example ... One of his favourite books was *The Mabinogion*, this twelfth-century Welsh manuscript that's supposed to be older, and one of the big stories in there is the story of Bran the death god, who has his head chopped off in battle, and his soldiers decide to take him back to where he's from and bury him there. Now, Bran's birds were ravens, so where they buried him there's always ravens, and so it happens, that in that very spot, they built the Tower of London. Hence the legend that there will always be ravens at the Tower of London—indeed, the legend goes that should the ravens ever leave the Tower of London, England is doomed. It will fall. It will disappear in a sheet of flame.

Now it's true, there are ravens at the Tower of London. They're chained there. The implications of this are quite enormous. It means, of all the mega-billions spent every year on defence, cruise missiles, tanks, the development of nerve gas, they slip these old guys fifteen quid a year for these chains JUST TO BE ON THE SAFE SIDE.

The point is nobody knows. Nobody knows but we don't care that we don't know.

Roger's favourite thing of all was another story from *The Mabinogion* called "Hanes Taliesin," which tells of one of the great poets of Wales, of legend, who was supposed to know everything. And how he got to know everything was he was a magician's assistant, and the magician told him to make up this broth that would give him ultimate knowledge. He's stirring it up and it spits out onto his hand and he sucks his hand to try and cool it down and, immediately he knows everything, including that the magician intends to kill him, and then it goes into this long poem where the magician chases him, and they both pass through a wild series of identities. He's a roe for a bit, and then a gazelle, a teapot, a piece of string ... and what finally struck me about it was that it was very similar to the last conversation I had with Roy when he was talking about going from being a Polish footballer to being a packet of stomach powder in rural Nigeria. And then it struck me, if these two such different people from different eras can come up with the same speech just about, then what they thought of as their own particular experience is actually one that's shared—we don't know how—and that brought home to me what I only intellectually understand most of the time: we don't know the difference between ourselves and everything else. We don't. We honestly don't. And, in a sense, I suppose, there isn't one.

So, it struck me that ... Since, however miserable and self-destructive I might think I was, I wouldn't actually push the button and send humanity hurtling to its doom ... there's no logical reason to suppose that anybody else would.

And I started to reason that my feeling that the world was going to destroy itself was because at some point in that summer around 1970 I ended up doing some really shitty things. And I'd always trusted myself totally before that ... and then I stopped.

Started feeling I was kind of a bastard. And the more I thought I was a bastard, the more I suspected that probably everybody else was, too, so I started being really rude and critical to them.

And that made me feel like a bit more of a shit, so I started to think that everyone else was a shit, and it just went on and on and on and on until it was a total nightmare, just built until I had to stop and go, Well, no. I wouldn't destroy myself, so why would the rest of the human race?

Of course the trouble with my theory is that it rests on the notion that I will not destroy myself. Well... this [*indicates the bottle of whisky*] has taught me different.

There's that crow again. Never see that crow for weeks on end and then it's around for days and days.

The truth is I've made a lot of sensible moves. I've decided not to get so excited about rock music, not to get so spiteful about rock music, not to get too into politics––it's a whole series of nots. I appear to have backed myself into a corner. And the truth is I either don't know what's going on in me or I can't figure out what's going on in anybody else. There's no reason to be a comrade of anybody's. When I go out in my mind and check up on what else is going on in the town and the people around, it's just like this massive, drugged sleep, this big dormant thing, like we can't think ...

It's funny, you know, this crow that hangs around outside my house—it niggles at me because I had this dream I was standing at the back of this castle and all of a sudden I could hear the flapping of wings behind me. It's absolutely inky blackness. I couldn't see anything but I could hear this flapping behind me and all these birds passing me, and, of course, I thought of the ravens leaving the Tower. It was a sort of frightened, joyous dream in a way.

Have to say, perfectly true, it's a very bad thing to kill yourself. It's forcing something to end, you know, cutting off the unexpected, which is something I've always objected to. I don't know whether I'll do it tonight, I don't know. But I'm doing it slowly. And I can't actually find a reason to stop.

No, that's ridiculous. You have to separate what's you and what's everyone else. Even if I was right and everyone's losing hope, what reason is that for me? Otherwise you end up like the belligerent drunk who's the way he is because the world is fucked, or the cultural critic who wants to bum everyone out to make the point that we're in despair. And while we're on the topic, I'd like to put in a bid for everyone to ignore the end of the millenium. It's just a date, like a birthday.

I suppose everyone else does this. Has to wrestle with the gods … "Oh the pain, existence, we're all doomed," and then back to work the next morning, "Hi, d'you see that thing on telly last night?" Every one of us. I mean, we always lose, but you've got to do it. Everyone … every little house. Wow. The mind boggles.

Separate yourself from everyone else … Roger and me have always had that problem … Roger and I … Roger … I. Sorry, we've always had this tendency to get beside ourselves. Beside *myself* I mean.

Anyway, thank you for the book. I have to say I wondered what it meant that you sent it. Now I realize that you and I are actually separate, so I see what the proper answer to that question is: Fuck knows.

Notes on
CONTRIBUTORS

Notes on CONTRIBUTORS

ROBIN FULFORD is a writer and educator. His other plays include *Steel Kiss*, *Gargoyle*, *Dark Song*, *Swahili Godot* and (with three others) *Sleeproom*. He is co-artistic director of Platform 9 Theatre, Toronto.

KEN GARNHUM is a writer, performer and designer. His other plays include *Building a Postmodern Birdhouse*, *How Many Saints Can Sit Around*, *Beuys Buoys Boys* and *Pants On Fire*. He has designed sets and costumes for all first productions of his works. He is a former playwright-in-residence at Tarragon Theatre and has also been associated with Theatre Plus, The Stratford Festival and The DuMaurier World Stage Festival. He studied graphic design and visual art and continues to produce drawings and objects, mainly, but not exclusively, for his performance works. His current project is a prose work entitled "Saint Impossible's Notebook." Born in Prince Edward Island, he lives in Toronto and Earnscliffe, P.E.I.

CAROLINE GILLIS is best known as an actress. She most recently appeared in *Aurelie Ma Soeur* (Centaur Theatre) and has previously appeared as Maggie in *Cat On a Hot Tin Roof* (Neptune Theatre). She has worked frequently with Daniel MacIvor, performing in his plays *Somewhere I Have Never Travelled*, *This Is a Play*, *Jump*, *Never Swim Alone*, and *See Bob Run* (Golden Sheaf Award, Best Performance, Yorkton Film Festival). She has participated as a writer-performer in the collectives *The Lorca Play* (ensemble Dora Award,

Augusta Company/Da Da Kamera) and *White Trash Blue Eyes* (Platform 9/Da Da Kamera/Buddies in Bad Times Theatre). *Caveman Rainbow* is her first play.

LINDA GRIFFITHS is a writer and performer. Her other plays include *Maggie & Pierre* (Dora Award, Outstanding New Play; Dora Award, Best Performance by a Female in a Leading Role), *O.D. On Paradise*, co-written with Patrick Brymer, (Dora Award, Outstanding New Play), *Jessica* (Dora Award, Outstanding New Play; Chalmers Award; Best Canadian Play, Quinzaine International Festival), *The Book of Jessica* (co-written with Maria Campbell, published by Coach House Press), *The Darling Family* (Governor General's Award nomination), *Brother Andre's Heart*, and *The Duchess—pieces of Wallis Simpson*, a radio play to be published by Blizzard Press. Her latest projects include the film version of *The Darling Family* and a novel entitled *Virtue or Death*.

RANDOLPH ANDREW KELM was born in 1956 on the island of Lulu—at that time a small semi-rural community in the backwaters of the Fraser River Delta. He grew up in the time of the great subdivision take-over. He studied theatre at the University of British Columbia. He pursued an acting career through his twenties, until one day he found himself twirling through an elementary school auditorium in a gold body suit, sprinkling fairy dust and unsuccessfully trying to remember badly rehearsed French. Now he lives in Toronto, writing plays and computer manuals, and occasionally performs his own material on his own terms.

JOAN MACLEOD was born in Vancouver in 1954 and studied creative writing at the University of Victoria and UBC. She moved to Toronto in 1985 and for six seasons was a playwright-in-residence at Tarragon Theatre, where she premiered *Jewel* (which she also performed); *Toronto, Mississippi; Amigo's Blue Guitar* (Governor General's Award); and *The Hope Slide* (Chalmers Award). Her plays have been produced extensively across Canada, in Britain and the United States, and have been translated in several languages. She wrote the libretto for the chamber opera *The Secret Garden* (Dora Award) and has written several scripts for radio. She was recently writer-in-residence at the University of Northumbria in England. Her latest play, *Little Sister*, will be premiered by Theatre Direct in Toronto and Green Thumb in Vancouver. She moved back to Vancouver in 1992.

JAMES O'REILLY is a survivor of Toronto's Jane-Finch Corridor and has been a garbage man, waiter, copywriter, meat-packer, sewer-cleaner, roofer, shipper and loader, daycare worker, landscaper, mover, road worker, jackhammer operator, FM disc jockey, performance artist, student, actor, singer, cook, thief, and lover. His other solo shows include *Rude Circus* and *Blood Everywhere*. *Ghetto*, his most recent stage play, was a part of the 25th Anniversary season line-up at Theatre Passe Muraille where James served as playwright-in-residence. *Work* was recently adapted for radio and broadcast on CBC-FM. He lives and works in Toronto, and urges everyone to bust a gut, shed a tear, and give your head a shake.

EDWARD RICHE writes for film, radio, and the stage. He recently wrote the screenplay for the feature film, *Secret Nation*. He lives in St. John's, Newfoundland.

JENNIFER ROSS has worked in theatre and lived in Toronto for five years. Previously she worked as a psychiatric patients' advocate in Winnipeg. Presently she is working on a play with five waitress characters entitled *Eye Liner*. She has a daughter, Emma.

JUDITH THOMPSON grew up in Kingston. She received her B.A. from Queen's University and graduated from the acting program of the National Theatre School. She has twice received the Governor General's Award for Drama, for *White Biting Dog* and for her anthology *The Other Side Of The Dark*, published by Coach House Press. Her other plays include *The Crackwalker*, *I Am Yours* (Chalmers Award; Dora Award for acting) and *Lion in the Streets* (Chalmers Award). Her plays have been produced around the world and trans-lated into several languages. Her many television plays include the acclaimed *Turning to Stone*, and *Life With Billy*, which she co-wrote. She has had many radio plays produced, including *Tornado* (Nelly Award), *Sugarcane*, and *White Sand*, which won the B'nai Brith

Award. She lives with her husband and three children in Toronto, and is on the faculty of the Drama department at the University of Guelph.

MICHEL TREMBLAY was born in Montreal in 1942. His writing includes twenty plays, three musical comedies, an opera libretto, nine novels, two collections of autobiographical stories, and seven film scripts. He has translated and adapted Aristophanes, Chekhov, Fo, Gogol, Williams and Zindel. He has received the Chalmers Award eight times, for *Forever Yours, Marie-Lou; Les Belles-Soeurs; Hosanna; Bonjour Là, Bonjour; Sainte-Carmen of the Main; Albertine, en Cinq Temps and Le Vrai Monde?;* and *La Maison Suspendue.* His plays have been produced extensively across North America and all over the world, and have been translated in many languages. John Van Burek has been translating Michel Tremblay's plays since 1972. He is the founding Artistic Director of Théatre français de Toronto, which he ran from its inception until 1991.

ALAN WILLIAMS was born in Manchester, England in 1954. After working for many years as an actor and playwright with The Manchester Youth Theatre and Hull Truck Theatre Company, he came to Canada as a resident. Since then, his other plays include *The White Dogs of Texas, The King of America,* and *Dixieland's Night of Shame* (which together make up the *King of America Trilogy*), *The Duke of Nothing* and *Welcome to the NHL.* For several years he was a member of staff at the University of Winnipeg and while living there was artistic director of The Rude Players. Recently he has appeared as an actor in both the play and the film of *The Darling Family.* A filmscript of *The Cockroach Trilogy* is in preparation.

PRODUCTION NOTES
and Credits

PRODUCTION NOTES
and Credits

ANNE MARIE'S BEDROOM was first presented at the Rhubarb! Festival in 1993, at Buddies in Bad Times Theatre, Toronto, directed by Edward Roy and performed by Ann Holloway. It was subsequently presented at Rhubarb-O-Rama! in February 1994. Performance rights, or script inquiries: Jennifer Ross, 17A Grimthorpe Road, Toronto, M6C 1G2. Thank you to Daniel Brooks, Ann Holloway, Ed Roy, Sky Gilbert, Gwen Bartleman, Buddies in Bad Times Theatre, Theatre Passe Muraille, and the Ontario Arts Council.

BLACK BRIDE was first presented at the Fringe of Toronto Festival in June 1992, directed and performed by Andrew Kelm. It was subsquently co-presented with Todd Hammond's *Fish*, at the Tarragon Theatre Extra Space, Toronto, in July 1992. Due to topical references in the script, the play is constantly changing; some of these changes are reflected in the script published here, which was used for a performance at the Rivoli, Toronto, in November 1992. Performance rights, or script inquiries: Andrew Kelm, 77 Huntley Street, #2202, Toronto, M4Y 2P3.

CAVEMAN RAINBOW was first presented at The Gathering in May 1992, at the Theatre Passe Muraille Backspace, Toronto, directed by Daniel MacIvor and performed by Caroline Gillis. It was subsequently presented in the Studio Series at Neptune Theatre, Halifax, in October 1993. CBC-TV broadcast a production in the fall of 1993, directed by Jeremy Podeswa. Performance rights, or script inquiries: The Core

Group, 3 Church Street, Suite 507, Toronto, M5E 1M2. Thank you to the Canada Council and the Ontario Arts Council.

THE COCKROACH TRILOGY was first produced by Hull Truck Theatre Company, England, directed by Mike Bradwell. "The Coackroach That Ate Cincinnati" was premiered at The Institute of Contemporary Arts, London, on Hallowe'en in 1978. "The Return of the Coackroach" and "The Coackroach Has Landed" were added to form the trilogy. It was performed at the Toronto International Festival of Theatre in 1981, and toured Canada in 1982. The script published here is a reworking which was presented at the Prairie Theatre Exchange, Winnipeg, in January 1992. Performance rights, or script inquiries: c/o Alan Williams, Tarragon Theatre, 30 Bridgman Avenue, Toronto, M5R 1X3. Thanks to the Canada Council.

LA DUCHESSE DE LANGEAIS was first presented by Les Insolents de Val d'Or, Québec, in 1969, directed by Hélène Bélanger and performed by Doris Saint-Pierre. It was subsequently presented at Théâtre de Quat-Sous, Montréal, in March 1970, directed by André Brassard and performed by Claude Gai. It was first presented in English by The Arts Club Theatre, Vancouver, in May, 1980, directed by John Van Burek and performed by Claude Gai. International productions include Rennes, France in 1989; Théâtre du Centaure, Luxembourg in 1991; and Augsburg, Germany in 1993. Performance rights, or script inquiries: Nathalie Goodwin, L'Agence Goodwin, 839 est, rue Sherbrooke, Suite 2, Montréal, H2L 1K6.

A GAME OF INCHES was first presented at Nightwood Theatre's Groundswell Festival in fall 1991. It was reworked and presented at Theatre Passe Muraille in spring 1992. It was directed by Sandra Balcovske and performed by Linda Griffiths. Performance rights, or script inquiries: Patricia Ney, Christopher Banks & Associates, Inc., 219 Dufferin Street, Suite 305, Toronto, M6K 1Y9.

JEWEL was presented, in its original version, at the Banff Centre for the Arts in Banff, Alberta, February 1985. A revised version was produced by the Tarragon Theatre, Toronto, in April 1987, directed by Andy McKim and performed by Joan MacLeod. Performance rights, or script inquiries: Patricia Ney, Christopher Banks & Associates, Inc., 219 Dufferin Street, Suite 305, Toronto, M6K 1Y9.

LOVESONG was first presented by Platform 9 at the Rhubarb! Festival in 1988, at Buddies in Bad Times Theatre, Toronto, directed by Ken McDougall and performed by Earl Pastko. It was subsequently presented by Platform 9 at the Theatre Centre, Toronto, in 1992, performed by Daniel MacIvor. Performance rights, or script inquiries: Platform 9 Theatre, 793 Euclid Avenue, Toronto, M6G 2V3. Author's note: *Lovesong* is based on the murder trial of Ralph Power.

PERFECT PIE will be broadcast by CBC Television in winter, 1994, performed by Judith Thompson. It was read by Ann Holloway at the Spring Arts Fair, Tarragon Theatre, in April 1993. Performance rights, or script inquiries: Great North Artist Management Inc., 350 Dupont Street, Toronto, M5R 1V9.

POSSIBLE MAPS was first presented at the LSPU Hall, St John's, Newfoundland, September 1991, directed by Lois Brown and performed by Charlie Tomlinson. Original maps by Gerry Porter. With thanks to Paul Pope, Elizabeth Noseworthy, the Memorial University of Newfoundland Map Library, and the Canada Council. Performance rights, or script inquiries: Suzanne DePoe, Creative Technique, 483 Euclid Avenue, Toronto, M6G 2T1. Slides available on request.

SURROUNDED BY WATER was first presented at the Tarragon Theatre Extra Space, Toronto, in January 1991, directed by Andy McKim, performed and designed by Ken Garnhum. Lighting designed by Kevin Lamotte. Stage managed by Ellen Flowers. Performance rights, or script inquiries: c/o Ken Garnhum, Tarragon Theatre, 30 Bridgman Avenue, Toronto, M5R 1X3.

WORK was first presented by Housebroken Company at the Toronto Fringe Festival 1991, directed and dramaturged by Sue Miner, performed by James O'Reilly. It was subsequently reworked and the script published here was presented by Housebroken at the Factory Theatre Studio Cafe, Toronto, in October 1991. Performance rights, or script inquiries: Playwrights Union of Canada, 54 Wolseley Street, 2nd Floor, Toronto, M5T 1A5.

Coach House Press
50 Prince Arthur Avenue, Suite 107
Toronto, Canada M5R 1B5

Editor for the Press: Jason Sherman
Design: Malcolm Brown
Cover Photograph: Floria Sigismondi